Yes!

You Are

Worthy of

Wealth!

Amethyst

ANSWERING
THE CALL

Published by CelebrityPress®, Orlando, FL

CelebrityPress® is a registered trademark.

Printed in the United States of America.

ISBN: 978-0-9912143-1-0
LCCN: 2014900535

Most CelebrityPress® titles are available at special quantity discounts for bulk purchases for sales promotions, premiums, fundraising, and educational use. Special versions or book excerpts can also be created to fit specific needs.

For more information, please write:
CelebrityPress®
520 N. Orlando Ave, #2
Winter Park, FL 32789
or call 1.877.261.4930

Visit us online at: www.CelebrityPressPublishing.com

CELEBRITY PRESS®
Winter Park, Florida

CONTENTS

CHAPTER 1

LISTEN-ACT-TRUST: YOUR JOURNEY, YOUR OFFER

BY LISA SASEVICH

You and I may have never met, but there's something I know about you. I know you have something to offer.

Now you may be well aware of this already, or you may be looking behind you thinking I'm talking to someone else, but check this out. The fact that you're holding this book, titled *Answering the Call*, tells me that you're at least curious about your life's purpose. That you've felt a tap, or maybe multiple taps. That you've begun to sense or you just intuitively know there's a unique contribution waiting to be made on this planet, and, my friend, it is yours to make.

How do I know? I know because I've spent the last 25+ years sorting it out for myself. And I know because during that process I've had the privilege of helping thousands of experts, entrepreneurs and other heart-centered people who also knew they had a unique gift—a unique blessing to offer the world—identify it, package it, price it, and yes, sell it.

You see, I'm known by many as "The Queen of Sales Conversion." By teaching people how to sell without being *salesy*, I help people make big money and a big difference doing what they love, what they were made for. Like you, I have something to offer. And let me tell you, knowing what it is you have to offer, and learning how to articulate and offer it in a way that inspires the people you're meant to serve to say "yes" and invest in themselves through you, is a powerful thing.

For me it's resulted, so far, in over $20 million dollars in sales of my own personal products and services; recognition by most of the major TV news station brands; multiple years being named to the coveted Inc. 500/5000 list of the fastest growing privately held companies in the United States; and, most important, a life and lifestyle I designed to suit me exactly. Which means I've done it all from home with my now seven- and ten-year-olds in tow, and traveled the world at my discretion for pleasure and sometimes business, too.

I call this lifestyle, Living Sassy. And I'm excited to share with you exactly how you can get started creating your version of a life and business you love, with your own personal flair!

WHAT IT MEANS TO LIVE SASSY

Sassy is an adjective. Its definitions include "exhibiting boldness, possessing vigor and imparting spirit." I also like that "sassy" can mean "distinctively smart and stylish" and of course, it happens to be a take-off on my last name, Sasevich. No wonder "Sassy" is the nickname for my flagship year-long training program, formally known as the Sales, Authenticity & Success Mastermind. I've designed this program for heart-centered experts and entrepreneurs who are answering the call in their lives and want to follow our formula for making big money—and a big difference—doing what they love.

It's a bold adventure to be out in the world doing what you were made for. After all, if it were easy, everyone would be doing it. But it doesn't have to be that hard if you follow someone who has gone before you and developed a proven process.

American mythologist Joseph Campbell once said, "The cave you fear to enter holds the treasure you seek." Sounds mystical, magical and a little bit scary, doesn't it? Of course, "treasure" means different things to different people. For many on my Sassy campus, it represents the ability to design a life you love while doing your work in the world and being paid handsomely for it. But no matter what your version of treasure is, something bigger than you is calling you toward it, and most likely that call was preceded by a myriad of life experiences—both fun and not-so-fun—that have perfectly qualified you for the adventure that awaits you.

After discovering I had something to offer—that I could teach people how to make irresistible sales offers so they could make the difference they wanted to make in an even bigger way—I started to wonder what had led me to create the programs I'd developed. I already believed that we were all made to bring a unique gift to the world. But why did I manifest my gift the way I did? And what were the events in my life that supported its unfolding? This is when I discovered an amazing template called "The Hero's Journey," created by Joseph Campbell.

YOUR HERO'S JOURNEY

Campbell theorized that across all human cultures, a hero's journey fits the same distinct pattern. Every adventure story from Gulliver to Harry Potter follows a cycle: the hero progresses from *status quo* through obstacles that eventually force him (or her) to seek assistance. When help arrives, if the hero accepts it, he is transported to another world where he answers the call of even greater challenges and, ultimately, the biggest ordeal he has ever faced. After the hero overcomes these seemingly insurmountable challenges and fears, he continues with his own life. But he is no longer satisfied with the old *status quo* because now he has known the treasure found through adventure. And I would add that this revelation only came to be because he said "yes" to the challenge.

Sound familiar?

As you look around your life and business with curiosity about your own hero's journey, you will likely begin to see connections and themes. To help you see how the challenges of your hero's journey have shaped you, I'll share a few tidbits I've learned recently from looking at my own. Think of my story as an overlay to yours. What is the "why" behind what you do? What people and events have impacted and influenced you? When was the turning point that inspired you to step into the adventure and go for it, despite the risks and challenges? Or maybe your turning point still lies ahead!

As I looked back to find the "why" of my own life, I discovered a few themes that emerged from experiences that shaped me and explain the way I've designed my life and my business world today. Reviewing what I've created since my turning point, I see that:

- I work to create a bonded and passionate community wherever I go.
- Freedom and abundance are always priorities for me.
- I always gravitate toward creating conversations and interactions that expand what is possible.

Here's how I came to notice these themes in my own hero's journey. See if you can use my insights to glimpse ways your experiences have shaped who you are and what matters most to you now. This is one access point to discovering what you have to offer.

My first insight had to do with my mom. I've found, from over 25 years of personal development work, that many of the experiences that shape us originate with one or both of our parents. My mom, a wonderful woman, was married four times. We also moved frequently, so my brother and I had a lot of people coming in and out of our lives. It felt very unstable, and we never really experienced the feeling of being part of a bigger family unit or community.

So it's no accident that as an adult I've strived to create a bonded and passionate community wherever I go. One of the most beautiful communities I've created thus far is my yearlong business and personal-development mastermind program, filled with amazing, positive, and forward-thinking people. Many of our members stay in the program for years and in my life well beyond that. We enjoy a feeling of family. As a change agent and mentor, leading this community is one of the ways I bring stability and belonging to other people as they navigate the entrepreneurial path, which can be very lonely and overwhelming.

What have you created in your personal life or business that may have originated from an early childhood need or desire?

As I continued tracing my hero's journey, I next took a look at my fierce commitment to abundance and freedom to see where it evolved from. I remembered an episode from my childhood when my mother became overwhelmed by all the requests, whining and arguing my brother and I aimed at her. One night she literally locked herself in the hallway bathroom of our little house. I thought she would come right out again, but instead she had a total meltdown. We could hear her sobbing behind the door for what seemed like hours. She kept saying we didn't understand how difficult it was for her and that we didn't appreciate anything. I guess she had reached her limit with the pressures of being a single mom, and that night she just cracked.

I'll never forget how scary that experience was. It ignited a determination in me. I decided then and there I would never let myself become trapped that way. So it's no surprise that I went on to become very successful in business at a level that ensured my financial freedom.

Today I work very hard to bless other people with the ability to create this kind of freedom for themselves. In fact, I love being an example of what's possible for entrepreneurs, women in business, working mommies and experts. Being ranked #169 on the 2012 Inc. 500 list of the fastest growing privately held companies in the United States was such a proud moment for me because of what it represented and showed as possible for other work-from-home experts around the world— especially those with young children!

See if you can use this part of my story to identify a significant moment that shaped who you are and what you do today, or maybe what you're hungry to do today! What is the torch you carry? How do you consistently strive to bless yourself and others, whether they ask for your help or not?

Answering these questions will likely illuminate significant moments that shaped and influenced your current priorities and values. Also be on the lookout for your turning point—the one moment that really set you into motion. Here's what I saw when I went looking for my own.

Although she didn't have much money, my mother was very much a philanthropist. She had a gift for making deals and an ability to attract and inspire people far beyond the capacity required for her job as a corporate forms manager. And when she worked on things she felt passionate about, she made miracles happen. From her tiny office cubicle, she sold stuffed animals, watches and other gadgets she'd persuaded companies to donate, and then she gave the money to charities she supported. In fact, people used to say my mother should have owned her own company, because they recognized her passion for helping people and making a difference. But she never moved beyond that cubicle.

My tipping point came when I was 19 years old and my mom, then only 48, was diagnosed with lung cancer. In less than a year, she took her last breath in my arms. At her memorial service, people hoping to console me commented on how great my mother was and how sad it was that she'd died so young before she had a chance to achieve her full potential. That's when it really hit me.

Life is not a dress rehearsal. This is not a practice round.
You don't get a second chance.
Why not achieve your full potential today, so that tomorrow
you don't have to live, or die, with regret?

My mother felt trapped; she felt scared. So she never took the lid off the box to see what her full potential might be and what difference she could really make if she took the leap. I never wanted anyone to say that about me, or worse, to live my life always speculating about what I might have been. I call it a "coulda, woulda, shoulda" life. No thank you. My mom's death was my turning point. After that, I became open to accepting help, the stage of the hero's journey that Joseph Campbell calls "supernatural aid."

Shortly after my mom's passing, a coworker invited me to attend a personal development seminar. I said "yes." The speaker fascinated me. She said it was possible to say "yes" to your life and create the life you want. I know it sounds simple, but after experiencing my mom's death, that concept made a huge impression on me. I accepted that moment as my invitation to start playing full out in my life. To listen for the call over and over, and step forward with a "yes" as often as possible. And to inspire others to do the same.

Today, I am a person who works to motivate you to say "yes" to yourself. I offer training to show you how to inspire others — your potential clients — to say "yes" to themselves, too. I even believe that as experts, it's a disservice on our part not to give people what they need in order to say "yes" to themselves and to the transformation we provide and they desire.

Following this path, I've had the pleasure, while working from my home, of helping heart-centered entrepreneurs in 134 countries. I'm a mom of two young children who were only toddlers when I started my business five years ago. Thanks to technology, I touch people all over the world without needing to be on a plane 200 days a year like older models in my industry dictated. It has been and continues to be a priority for me to maintain a lifestyle I love while doing my work in the world, and it's my honor to show others how to do the same.

Looking at my hero's journey revealed the "why" behind what I do today. I saw that my life experiences, although at times difficult or painful, helped me discover what I had to offer the world. Your unique life experiences change the very fiber of your being; they leave a mark on your soul and drive your future desires. Those challenges you overcome during your journey become quiet encouragers on your path that keep you from returning to *status quo,* and help you encourage others to embark on their own journeys.

Along with looking in the rear view mirror to make sense of who you are and what you have to offer today, you can take a few simple steps to make sure you're taking advantage of opportunities in the present moment. I call this little formula "Listen – Act – Trust." As an ongoing practice, it will help you see and trust the path that's unfolding for you right now, whether or not you're ready to explore your past journey. Here's how it works.

STEP 1: LISTEN

Many times we sense a little intuition, an inkling about how we should move forward. "I should call that person." "I should buy that gift." "I should contribute to that foundation." "I should take a nap." But often we don't act on these flashes. Instead, we second-guess ourselves and ignore that little tap. Where does it come from? It depends on your beliefs. God, Source, your intuition, your Higher Self—you decide. What's important is that you learn to pay attention and act on it, because when you do, even if it doesn't make total sense at the time, magical things happen.

Part of Living Sassy is opening your level of awareness and paying attention to little taps. The key is to act on them quickly and then to trust the action you took. This is important, because otherwise you can waste a lot of time second-guessing yourself. But if you take the route of trusting the action you took and then stay aware, you'll either discover directly or from another source what that inspiration was all about. When I look back at the magical times in my life and what led to them,

I realize it's been when I had a small thought or inspiration and acted on it even though it didn't make total sense. More often than not, that little tap turned into something transformational for me or someone else.

STEP 2: ACT

There will be times in your life when you feel a tap—and because you still have free will—you may decide not to honor it. But I can tell you, and I've heard Oprah quoted as saying something similar, be careful about not listening to those taps, because next time you might get a 2x4 instead. If there's something Spirit really wants from you or for you, and you're not willing to listen to little hints about it, don't be surprised if you get slapped right on the forehead. You may have heard this phenomenon described as "First God throws pebbles, then He throws stones, then comes the boulder . . ." So I invite you to think about an area of your life where you felt a small tickle and didn't pay attention, and it took a 2x4 to really get to you.

For example, a few months ago I began sensing a tap telling me it was time to up-level my work in some way. I tried to shuck it off because I really love what I do and the way I help people, and I wasn't really interested in upsetting my perfect apple cart. But I should have known that if I ignored them, the taps would only become more intense. Without going into all the gory details, let's just say things that used to be easy started getting harder and harder for what seemed like no apparent reason.

When I noticed this trend, I decided right away not to wait for the 2x4. Instead, I got to work, beginning by asking Source what my next level of service to the world would look like: "Please God, show me what I'm not seeing." I'm still in the process, but at this writing I've come to see that my true gift, beyond what I do as "The Queen of Sales Conversion," is to lift people up, show them a new perspective, and open their worlds.

Not long ago, I conjured up the courage to share this insight in an e-newsletter, and within hours I received confirmation from my tribe that, sure enough, that's what they're already experiencing! This recent Facebook post by one of my Sassy Mastermind Members is an example of how quickly the universe delivers when you listen to the taps and take action.

"I'm having one of those Sassy moments. You know those moments where you notice what you're doing and suddenly realize that your current life is unrecognizable from your pre-Sassy life? I'm sitting in Malibu, on an 86-degree sunny day in January, overlooking the ocean, talking to my wealth manager, while my team members are taking care of the business.

"When I started my business, my greatest aspiration was to replace my salary and try to help people not have to suffer the way I did. I think the most important thing that's happened to me in Sassy is that my sense of WHAT IS POSSIBLE keeps getting bigger. So yes, Lisa Sasevich, while you are "The Queen of Sales Conversion," I do believe your true gift is lifting people up, showing us a new perspective and opening our world! Thank you for all you do!"

I'm so glad I finally responded to those taps as they got louder and louder—before a 2x4 came along!

STEP 3: TRUST

After you've listened and taken action, you might feel somewhat vulnerable. That's the time when other people may judge what you did. I remember when I made the choice to register for a mastermind program that cost $100,000 for a year of coaching. My accountant, my friends and others in my life all thought I was crazy. I had an infant and a toddler at home, a husband in medical residency, and I'd barely made that much money ever in a whole year! I learned from that experience that there are two things to do after you have trusted the tap and acted: Stand firm and stay open.

First, stand firm. Trust that you took that action because of the tap you got. It wasn't random, and while no one else may have felt it, and no one else was in on that unique experience that led to your action, you were—and that's all that matters.

Second, stay open. You need to stay open because after you listen and take action, you may receive an additional bit of information, an additional tap guiding you about the next thing to do.

I thank God that I did stay open even after investing $100,000 in myself to transform my business, because other mentors continued to show up along the way. It was hard for me to believe that I needed to pay anyone else after that kind of investment, but I did.

Because I stayed open, I listened and took action over and over according to what felt right to me, and in that next year, my business skyrocketed from $130,000 in sales to over $2 million. Now I'm always on the lookout for new opportunities to learn, and always listening for the next tap to up-level personally and professionally. The key to taking advantage of these moments when I've listened to the tap and said "yes" to myself has been trusting that action. And that can be the hardest part.

ANSWERING THE CALL

One of my favorite quotes is from author Maxwell Maltz: "A step in the wrong direction is better than staying on the spot all our life. Once you're moving forward you can course correct as you go. Your automatic guidance system cannot guide you when you're standing still."

It can be difficult if not impossible to move the wheels of a car when it's not rolling, but the minute it's underway, the power steering kicks in, and suddenly it's easy to navigate. It's the same with your life. That's why continually moving forward is part of Living Sassy.

If you keep moving forward even when your plan isn't completely clear, even if you can only move toward what you think your plan is, what your direction appears to be from that tap you received, then more information and inspiration will likely come to you. A pond without a spring flowing through it can stagnate. So can people who don't keep moving forward. But when you consistently take what I call "inspired action," you become like a river that's constantly flowing.

So yes, my fellow agent-of-change, it's true. You have something to offer. And whether you begin to see it clearly by looking at the milestones that have shaped your life or start answering your call by adding a little "Listen – Act – Trust" momentum to your life, I'm here to tell you, as a living example, that it's worth it.

Will it feel uncomfortable at times? For sure. But getting comfortable being uncomfortable is part of the Living Sassy path. What if life begins where your comfort zone ends?

About Lisa

Recently honored as one of America's Top Women Mentoring Leaders by *WoW Magazine*, recipient of the coveted eWomen Network Foundation Champion award for her generous fundraising, and proud owner of the No. 169 rank on the prestigious Inc. 500 list of America's Fastest Growing Private Companies of 2012, **Lisa Sasevich "The Queen of Sales Conversion"** teaches experts who are making a difference how to get their message out and enjoy massive results, **without being salesy.**

Recognized sales expert by *Success Magazine*, Lisa delivers **high-impact sales-closing strategies** for turbo-charging entrepreneurs and small business owners to great profits.

According to best-selling author Brian Tracy, *"Lisa Sasevich is one of the greatest discoveries in America today!"*

Kym and Sandra Yancey of e-Women Network say that, *"Without question she is brilliant at teaching others how to leverage their unique gifts and qualities and convert them into a financial windfall. She is one authentic, heart-centered expert that delivers in spades!"*

Robert Allen, author of multiple New York Times Best-Sellers says, *"She added a zero to my income today just by watching her. Lisa Sasevich. Watch that name and whatever you do, be part of what she's doing. You're going to love it."*

After 25 years of winning Top Sales Awards and training senior executives at companies like Pfizer and Hewlett-Packard, she left corporate America and put her skills to the test as an entrepreneur.

And in just a few short years, **Lisa created a multi-million dollar home-based business** with two toddlers in tow. Lisa really is the undisputed expert on how to make BIG money doing what you love!

To experience life on Planet Sassy for yourself visit:

www.Sassy21DayChallenge.com. Get started today with a complimentary 21-day sample of our hot new business model for those who are answering the call in their lives.

You can also join me at www.LisaSasevich.com for updates on current trainings and live events. I hope to see you around our Sassy campus soon!

CHAPTER 2

FOLLOW THE LIGHT POSTS OF SUCCESS

BY CHRISTA O'LEARY

As a Hay House author, marriage and family therapist, interior designer and green living expert, I'm often asked to share my insights on building a business, becoming an expert in my field and navigating the publishing world. I believe all successful people have similar characteristics that steer them along their path, catapulting them to the next level. These traits and attitudes make the difference between realizing their goals and dreams and falling short. I'm sharing five insights common among successful entrepreneurs who are answering the call to embark on the most fulfilling path of their lives.

As I've traveled my own life's path, it didn't always make sense to me as it meandered in irrelevant directions, but I came to realize it was filled with light posts that illuminated the way. Light posts are synchronistic events that ultimately lead us along our course, guiding and revealing an infinite potential of possibilities. At pivotal moments these light posts help us create the life and business of our dreams. If we are tuned into these guideposts, they can light the way. I look back along my journey and see a string of beautiful glowing lampposts and I realize they helped me navigate at crossroads, listen to the whispers of inspired insight, be open to possibilities and take inspired action. All of these factors allowed me to create three successful businesses and a dream life that continues to unfold.

The first time a light post began to twinkle and draw me into the world of entrepreneurship, I almost ignored the whisper. It was a rainy, gray, cold New England day when even the vibrant fall foliage seemed dreary. I was supposed to go golfing with a new friend, but as a fair weather golfer, it wasn't my kind of day. Yet something inside nudged me to move from my warm, cozy bed in that early morning hour.

When my friend and I made it to the country club, the caddies grabbed our bags and we immediately headed inside to find beverages to warm our fingers. As we made our way out to the golf carts, our clubs had inadvertently been placed in different carts. The two of us as newfound friends, were disappointed; we were excited to play together and get to know one another. But the caddies did manage to place us in the same foursome, so we decided to keep things as they were, staying with our respective partners to avoid being rude.

I jumped in the cart beside a lovely older woman with silver hair, funky glasses and a dynamic demeanor. She was the successful business owner of an interior-furnishings boutique in one of the nearby bustling communities. She asked me to drive, which was a small price to pay for what I later would realize was a wealth of knowledge. As we bounced along the cart path, I curiously asked questions about her business: "What was it like being a business owner?" And "How best to start a business?" Then "How do you know when it's the right business for you?"

For nearly five hours her enthusiastic words, seasoned perspective and strong opinions spun the wheels inside my head. Looking back, I see the golf cart modification as divine interference. It was a light post that twinkled and moved me along my path on that steely, rain-soaked New England day. The gift of this conversation inspired me to think outside my comfort zone, allowed me to imagine infinite possibilities, investigate how to make them happen and motivate me to take action. I was so thankful the whisper of my soul moved me out of my bed in the wee hours of that cold dawn.

Many successful entrepreneurs hear a tiny voice inside their heads that hints at something that will move them along their path to success. The majority of people ignore this call. Most rationalize it as a fanciful thought that could never be brought to fruition. **The mark of a**

successful entrepreneur is to hear the whisper and pay attention to the message. A switch has been turned on and the light post is able to illuminate the path ahead. It is our willingness to listen to the call and move through the illusion of self-doubt that will allow us to cast light on our shadows and reveal clear passageways to fulfilling our ultimate purpose and destiny.

As entrepreneurs, it is a common experience to feel inadequate or incompetent upon hearing the whisper or beginning a new venture. The mind might give us a plethora of reasons why we can't or shouldn't. The mind-game reasons can range from ideas such as: you don't have enough credentials or degrees to stand on, or you haven't had enough experience to begin your enterprise. Well, I am here to say you are not alone. Go ahead and take that first step! It is in the first baby steps that one is able to create enough momentum to stride past the nattering negatives of the doubting mind. Push through and persevere! Everyone, even those who are now considered experts, had to start somewhere.

I remember feeling like a fraud every time I began to work with clients and help them design the home or the life of their dreams. It wasn't until the finished product was revealed and they were gushing with enthusiasm that I finally felt I actually knew what I was doing. The feedback loop playing in my head kept telling me I needed one more degree or credential to be worthy of walking into their homes or their lives. At this point, I have diplomas and certificates from years of schooling, seminars and programs that could hang on every wall of my home and cover a good portion of a large castle. My light post switched to a vibrant glow when I finally came to the realization that I could **ignore those self-defeating thoughts** that told me I shouldn't, couldn't or that I needed one more degree to do the work I loved. This removed an obstacle from my path and allowed me to skip along to my own heartfelt beat.

Being **open to the infinite expression of possibilities** is fundamental in achieving success. The question to ask ourselves at every turn is, "How can I?" This opens up a direct line of communication to a higher 'knowing' that will answer your call and give you needed insight and answers. The on-switch will appear and another light post will light your path. When I made the shift and began viewing every problem as a challenge that could and would reveal a solution, the world opened up and my mind was able to see possible creative answers in all situations.

An illustration of this phenomenon comes from what could have been a costly mistake. I ordered a very expensive fabric for a window treatment to be installed in a high-end client's home. Being meticulous with details, I asked the person at the design center numerous times which way the stripe ran on the bolt of fabric, horizontal or vertical. When my workroom received the fabric, they called me in a panic to let me know that the stripe was the opposite of what we'd expected. I raced over and inspected what everyone construed as a huge and expensive problem. I took a few deep breaths and asked myself, *"How can I make this okay?"*

I ended up changing the design of the window treatment and used the horizontal pattern to our benefit. The treatment came out fabulous; I actually liked the new design better than the original—and the client was thrilled. To this day I have a sign in my office that states in big bold letters: "How Can I?" We put up barriers that block success when we look at a situation as a problem that can't be solved instead of a complexity that requires a new perspective.

Build a foundation based on *"How can I?"* instead of *"I can't."* The buildings blocks of success come from the questions themselves. These questions need to be formulated into answers that will fortify the foundation, build the structure and design the business and life of your dreams.

I have always been one to **take calculated risks**. The ability to make a quick assessment is an important characteristic of a successful entrepreneur. We must be able to evaluate the risks and jump in before the monkey mind of self-doubt takes over and sabotages the opportunity. That being said, it is always important to assess a situation and apply due diligence before jumping in.

A couple of years ago, we ventured to a ski mountain that was new to our family. Invigorated with anticipation, our twelve-year-old ventured out alone on the first ski run of the day. He didn't want to wait for the rest of the family because in his enthusiastic state we were moving much too slowly. As he began his descent down the mountain, he spied an enticing jump that called to him. He decided to throw caution to the wind and headed straight for that snow mound. On the way to the hospital, he explained he knew he was in trouble when he crested the jump, hurtled into the air and gaped at the slope thirty feet below.

Through tears of gratitude (thankful we were dealing with a broken extremity and not a broken neck) I tried to explain how important it is to take calculated risks. It's okay to make the jump when you've assessed the situation, have an idea of what's on the other side and have determined whether or not you can handle the impact if something goes wrong. This is true in business and in life as well. Pushing yourself beyond your comfort zone is essential to achieving success. However, strategically assessing a situation or opportunity will help you calculate and determine the risks and rewards of the jump. By sidestepping defeat and strategizing advantageous positions, we triumph in our endeavors.

To accelerate towards our goals, whether personal or professional, a laser-focused approach is essential to achievement. I put blinders on and go for it! All too often entrepreneurs have amazing ideas that are never brought out into the world. For one reason or another their ideas never generate the needed momentum to propel them forward to realize success. When the light posts of inspiration begin to twinkle, the right questions are asked and the encouraging answers become evident. That's the time to evaluate the risks, and it is then that **the successful entrepreneur takes inspired action**.

During that golf cart ride I was given all the necessary information to move ahead to create the first of three businesses that would flourish. The silvery-headed woman with the eccentric glasses and spritely attitude literally gave me the step-by-step building blocks necessary to hang out a shingle and say I was open for business. There were lots of reasons why I shouldn't have begun this new adventure, but instead of listening to the sabotaging voices within or from others, I fastidiously moved through the steps I was given with my eye on the end goal: I wanted to have a successful business. Taking action separates those who live in an unrealized dream state from those who successfully build the life of their dreams.

Entrepreneurship is about heeding the call. When we hear the whisper, our soul sings and opens the door to expansive possibilities by shedding light on our promising path. It is critical to be receptive to these opportunities and the brilliant potential that can unfold. Evaluate the risks and rewards and don't hold back when your heart senses the luminescent glow of a light post. When the dark shadows on your path are lit by an inner radiance and your personal light posts begin to lead the way, that is the time to take inspired action and to fulfill the potential for your extraordinary life.

About Christa

Christa O'Leary, MA, MFT, is an Interior Designer, Marriage & Family Therapist and Green Living Expert. She teaches people how to "Design Inspired Living" and has been featured on CBS, NBC and Dr. Laura. As a motivational speaker, up-and-coming Hay House Radio Show Host and Hay House Author, Christa offers people concrete solutions to living their most fulfilling lives by creating inspired, healthy, vibrant homes that alternately enliven, nourish and soothe body, mind and spirit.

Christa has created three successful businesses within the past 10 years while raising a family of four active children. Her first business, *Home in Harmony Designs*, is an internationally-recognized design firm catering to the discerning tastes of clients from around the globe. The acclaimed Kravet Fabric house has featured her designs alongside some of the industry's most renowned tastemakers, Calvin Klein & Candace Olson. Her designs have also been seen on CBS, NBC, in numerous national print publications as well as international design industry publications.

Because of her affection for the well-made and one-of-a-kind details in older homes, she opened Pillar Properties with her husband, restoring treasured homes to their original character while enhancing surrounding communities.

Christa's most recent endeavor is founder and CEO of *Home in Harmony Lifestyle*. Just as calm well-ordered environmentally conscious spaces influence our emotions and physical wellbeing, so does anchoring inner peace and our own authentic light affect our home lives, our success and our influence on the world. Christa's background as a therapist enables her to incorporate the foundational pillars needed for her clients to live vibrant, fulfilling and abundant lives.

At *Home in Harmony* headquarters, she continuously creates needed programs that enhance our wellbeing, including: Inspired Home, Healthy Body, Calm Mind and Radiating Inner Light.

And as the published author of *Home in Harmony Lifestyle* and print and TV veteran, Christa knows the ropes to attracting media attention. Her third company also designs programs to help entrepreneurs realize their dreams of creating well-branded companies with book-worthy content. Christa engineers the trainings they need to become media savvy entrepreneurs, including the art of the successful book proposal, as well as the polished speaking and on-camera assurance that results in increased sales and satisfaction.

CHAPTER 3

CIRCUS OF FREAKS

BY SANDI CORYELL

As a Leadership and Mental Edge Speaker, Strategist and Business Consultant, I'm often asked the best way to engage teams, build strong leaders, and strengthen businesses down to their very core – so that they can effectively build a magnetic brand in competitive marketplaces, attract and retain 'kickass talent' that drives ideas and first-to-market innovation, and ultimately builds income and profitability year over year.

Three decades of leading award-winning teams in the relentlessly competitive and highly-demanding entertainment advertising world as President of DDBEntertainment created the backbone of my response. During that time, while earning the nickname "The Don" for my street-style leadership methods that partnered highly distinctive individual talent with a "no man left behind" team mentality, I zeroed in on what it takes to have the confidence, know how, and guts to separate yourself from the pack and deliver consistent and dynamic results.

One instance in particular crystallizes the response to those questions I get most often.

It had been three weeks of long hours, outrageous client deadlines, and a seemingly endless mountain of revisions to hard-worked plans. My team was about to crack, so nothing seemed more appropriate than blowing off a little steam with margaritas and sizzling fajitas. And off we all tromped to the local El Cholo restaurant. Car after car of bleary-eyed, overwrought, advertising people hellbent on having a little fun.

Not surprisingly, the mood of our group flanking the huge wooden tables inside the cantina was raucous. Given the sideways glances we were getting from diners at other tables, perhaps we had actually left raucous behind and were headed straight for wall-rattling obnoxious.

Normally, my inclination would have been to corral the group into a more moderate celebration, but there was no denying they had earned this. A ramekin or two of flan delivered to neighboring tables courtesy of our team would hopefully allay bad feelings.

- As basket after basket of chips and guacamole were devoured, the team bonded over stories of their misadventures of the past few weeks.

- How clients would call from the comfort of their homes late at night, remembering directions they "forgot" to pass on.

- How the printers would crash at critical moments due to the sheer volume of reports cranking through them.

- How late night raids on the company's stash of Red Bull had been the only antidote to escalating sleep deprivation.

And ultimately,

- How, through it all, they had delivered killer work to the client.

The chest-pumping pride in what they had accomplished as a team was starting to come out in the stories they were telling. And then, through the din of the self-congratulations, I heard it.

We're Sandi's" Circus of Freaks," someone shouted above the other voices.

Instantly, I was taken aback.

Did they think of themselves as Freaks? Did they think I thought of them as Freaks? Was that bad?

After a few moments listening to a chorus of tone deaf advertising people humming calliope music at the top of their lungs, I realized just how great it actually was.

The name not only stuck with our group for years to come, but also became a rallying cry as to what was to become our brand, our mission, and our success.

The spirit of the name signified how to build a successful organization. Any organization.

It is about how to unleash what is so distinctively unique about each individual player on the team – so much so that they naturally excel. It is also about how to intentionally combine the best mix of those individual advantages together to create an exquisite "circus" that people pay to work with.

And the spirit of that name is what I now use to support people in bringing about their own advantage. It's what brings about engagement, innovation, and a team of leaders who create excellence.

It's also what ultimately leads to year over year profitability.

There are <u>four key elements</u> in building your own advantage:

1. *Relish the "craziest" part of people.*

2. *Create "stoops."*

3. *Twist the normal.*

4. *Create the tent pole.*

1. RELISH THE "CRAZY"

Everyone has what I call "their Deviant Advantage" and it's simply where you deviate the most from the people around you.

There's an internal motivation driving everyone and it's that motivation that influences how you make decisions, how you see the world, how you behave, and how you react to the behaviors of others.

Oftentimes, it's also what people push down and hide because deviating from average is often thought of as strange or "not right," particularly in organizations.

That advantage, though, is where the magic lies.

Not only allowing, but also ferociously encouraging people to be who

37

they are naturally is a freedom that builds internal motivation, passion, and confidence. Knowing that what you uniquely bring to the table is important and really stepping up and owning that advantage, gives you the mental edge to make strong decisions, bring new ideas to the forefront, and lead others to their own success.

To get to this advantage, it's important to look beyond skills and training and get as close to the root of what really drives someone. Not reward vs. pain motivation, but that same motivation that drove you to do things as a kid. It's what gave you an advantage on the playground....before you knew you had to do things a certain way. It's what gave you confidence.

For my clients, I provide a shortcut to understanding those advantages. By using a model with ten archetype roles ranging from *The Enforcer* on one end to *The Communicator* on the other, you can get a good idea as to where you and others naturally deviate.

For example, a natural Enforcer tends to be protective, they may "come out fighting" looking for weaknesses that need to be shored up to keep the team safe, or they might push a little too hard to keep things in line. An Enforcer naturally steps in to a "take charge" role.

A Communicator, on the other hand, sees her role as the one to "get the party started", always ready to buoy people's spirits when things get tough. She is comfortable talking to anyone and will jump in and keep the lines of communication going in the group.

When you put those two types of "crazys" together, you have what is the start of a 'kickass' partnership that brings different points of view as well as balance to the team.

If you stop for a moment and think about how you, how your partners, or even how members of your family tend to naturally react to situations, you have an idea as to what their natural advantage is. It also gives you a great starting point for how to influence them, how to partner with the right person at the right time to come up with ideas you wouldn't naturally think of on your own, and how to create a team with the best combination of people.

That's what you want to tap into for your own success as well as for that of your team. Think about where the natural strengths lie on your team.

- Do you have too many of the same type of advantages?
- What type of role is naturally missing from your team?
- Who do you need to partner with to get the best results in different situations?
- Pinpoint who is most naturally comfortable in different roles and let them "own" the space.

2. CREATE "STOOPS"

One of the greatest assets you can create in your organization is unbridled fearlessness. I don't think most leaders would argue with this. The evidence, though, shows an uncanny lack of fearlessness in business today.

It's not unusual to hear whispers of what people think should be done to make things better, yet the whispers rarely turn in to bold action plans that really lead to positive change. Whether it's because people are scared to speak up, don't know the best way to bring an issue up to those in charge, or struggle with breaking protocol by walking into the office of their own boss' boss, a lack of fearlessness stymies many organizations despite mission statements to the contrary.

Successful organizations overcome this dichotomy by creating "stoops," or random gathering places throughout the office space where people are encouraged to gather naturally. The best ones are like the gathering spots in old neighborhoods where the stoop in front of the house serves as a spot to sit and relax, first for one person, and then another, and then another, and.....

The more casual and unstructured the gathering spots the better. Fling poofs on the floor; add a television set, a pool table, a basketball hoop. Anything that says relax.

And, no matter what your "rank" in the organization, top to bottom, be sure to spend time there. The conversations that start in these unstructured safe zones invariably lead to topics that typically stay in the shadows. As a leader, when you tune in to the nuances of the conversations that just crop up over an afternoon bull session, your mere presence will sanction the openness to hear what's really going on, new ideas, and struggles that you might not otherwise be privy to. Ultimately, the comfort with speaking up bleeds over into formal conversations.

Fearlessness doesn't happen overnight. But it does happen if you consistently share in "stoop sitting."

- Are you fearless?
- Is your team fearless?
- Do they know that failure is a part of fearlessness?
- Do they know that failure is often what leads to innovation?

3. TWIST THE NORMAL

You've been there. You get an email that there will be a brainstorming session at 3PM. You're told to come up with some great ideas that can be discussed. You get to the conference room at 3:10 and immediately start scanning for what snacks are there to eat. You listen to the same three or four people throw out some ideas while everyone else scrolls through their smart phones praying for a client message that will grant them escape.

Brainstorming sessions *almost never* produce crushingly fantastic ideas if all they are is a break in an otherwise "business-as-usual" day.

Brainstorming should be happening, should be acknowledged, and should be rewarded many times throughout the day, banishing ordinary and looking for the twists on how to do things differently.

In line with valuing the genius in how things deviate from average, I am a proponent of rewards for "Random Acts of Deviance." The idea is to be on the lookout for anyone doing anything differently that creates a better solution, no matter how big or small. When you spot it, you grab a bullhorn, rally your team behind you, and march parade to that person and reward them on the spot for boldly twisting an old idea into something new.

I have seen teams flip a switch from sleep walking through projects to devil's advocating and pushing each other to come up with one idea wilder than the other when efforts to twist things are rewarded immediately, publically, and with gusto.

To get to the big bold ideas, you have to reward frequently the small but daring ideas first.

- Do you have a process to spot random acts of deviance?
- Do you know who consistently makes processes or ideas better?
- Do they know that you know?

4. CREATE THE TENT POLE

No circus can perform to peak performance unless people know that they are all performing under the same Big Top, one that is firmly help up by a solid tent pole forming the backbone right up the middle.

In your organization, the culture you create is that tent pole. It's what keeps chaos at bay. It's what eliminates crazy for crazy sake and instead turns it into magic. It's also what lets performers all of types take the stage at different times as well as together.

The Circus of Freaks was a tent pole. People instantly understood that the culture of the organization was a combination of strong individuality coupled with an expected spirit of teamwork.

Intentionally designing and branding your culture requires a clear understanding by all involved of the specifics of your joint mission. It requires a clear and oft repeated rallying cry that is distinctive enough to repel as many people as it attracts. And it requires frequent celebration of who you are as individuals and as a team.

- Do you know the five or six traits that support your mission and pull your people together?
- Do you have a memorable rallying cry?
- Do you have habits, celebrations, and policies that support the tent?
- Do people instantly identify your culture with your team and think it's either absolutely fantastic or absolutely bonkers?

Statistics tell us that over 70% of workers today would just as easily go to work for the business down the street as stay where they are right now. Some organizations write unending manifestos declaring their *culture du jour* and imploring talent to adopt it. Others administer survey after survey to gauge the level of employee engagement and satisfaction. Still more pay exorbitant salaries to people they recruit from elsewhere to salve the gaping wounds ripped open by a revolving door of people looking for a "boss that sees their value."

All of this crushes your ability to flourish year over year.

Results from working the 4 Key Elements outlined above deliver quite the opposite story. In using these strategies, unwanted attrition is often kept below 10%, profitability in the robust double digits inks the spreadsheet year over year, and passionate employees allowed to be themselves in a fearless environment generate first-to-market strategies that keep client retention at all time highs. The key is in intentionally developing all four elements and then living and celebrating them loudly and unabashedly day-after-day.

About Sandi

Sandi Coryell is a Leadership and Mental Edge Speaker, Author, Strategist, and Trainer.

For more than 25 years, Sandi spent her days dedicated to persuading you to spend a good chunk of your free time at the movies or theme parks she was marketing. Working with some of the biggest brands in the competitive entertainment industry, Sandi honed her skills at communicating and influencing behaviors in a way that was sharp and distinctive, gaining a unique insight into what it takes to connect with people and convert them into raving fans.

Recognizing a pattern to this success, Sandi developed a proven methodology, The Deviant Advantage, knowing that others could learn how to leverage their own potent combination of connective communication, innovative solutions, and the power of influence with the right training. Combining her deep business experience with extensive research, this blueprint provides the roadmap for leaders who want to leverage this training to accelerate their own success or that of their company.

As a Leadership and Mental Edge Speaker, Author, Strategist, and Trainer, Sandi is now dedicated to working with people to unleash their ability to do just that. Her book *Own Your Advantage* is due in First Quarter 2014.

A graduate of the University of Southern California, Sandi also holds a Master of Science degree in Management with an emphasis in Organizational Behavior from the University of Texas at Dallas.

CHAPTER 4

FROM TRASH
TO TREASURE

BY BONI OIAN

Answering the call is much like being in the state of knowing you have to do something but you don't know what or why. When that call came to me I felt that I had an unquenchable thirst for understanding everything all at once. Ever since I was little I had to know how things worked, what the process was. Not everyone around me thought this was a good thing. The more people discouraged me, the more it felt urgent I understand.

It all started with this basic question for me:

Why are some people just happy, and everything seems to go their way while others of us, especially me, seem to struggle at every turn?

For as long as I can remember I felt driven to find out how people's thought process worked. I tried to ignore the impulse and desire then finally gave up and started taking every class I could find.

I read as many books as I could and while I was glazing pottery in my husband's business, I listened to books on tape. There really was an overwhelming 'we are running out of time' feel to my appetite to learn. Even one of the instructors in a relationship class would chuckle and ask, "What do you know that the rest of us don't?"

I didn't know then but I got my answer while teaching a week-long retreat in the Smokey Mountains. We were on the last day of the 6-day Akashic Record class when the group of 18 people realized we had been in a past life together and had things to tell each other that never got said from that lifetime.

My role and commitment from that lifetime was to bring everyone together and have a healing of the souls. We had to say things to each other in this lifetime that we couldn't say in that time. We had to apologize for things we did and didn't do. Some people had to ask for forgiveness and other people needed to forgive.

We have never been all together since in the same room, but no one would ever forget the experience. Some of the people present totally changed their lives afterwards while others changed their names. For me, it just reassured me that there was a much higher purpose for me being pushed so hard to learn so much so fast.

So what have I learned after 30 plus years of delving into the process we use to allow ourselves to be happier?

First, you really have to <u>know</u> that you deserve happiness. I have had clients that left million dollar homes, their families, and their high paying jobs just because they still were not happy. They believed they would 'find' happiness if and when they had all these things. It wasn't true. They were still unhappy. They didn't know happiness was a choice they needed to make. Knowing they deserved to be happy and they are worthy of happiness was a new concept to them.

Understanding how the mind system works might be easier to explain by using the example of the computer. After all, the computer was developed to replicate the brain and mind system.

So there are different levels of programs that make us work. The default system - Theta frequency, the operating system - Alpha frequency, and (after 7 years of age) the data input system - Beta frequency. Luckily we have an extra default system, Source, the Divine or God. We came in to this life with this system installed and it overrides everything else – when we let it.

This is where I found the struggle for me was taking place. I thought I was here to override Source so I could get things done. Once I learned how the system worked and that Source was actually on my side, life started to become fun.

The other thing I learned was that we were reprogrammable at the Theta and Alpha Levels. That also made life much easier. There are actually three parts to the reprograming process. One, you have to be at that original level the program was set in place in order to reprogram it, two, you have to know what you want, and three, you have to talk in that particular level's language.

Then I started having fun with the systems, you know - playing. I started watching for red flags such as: uncomfortable feelings or relationships, and things showing up in my life that I didn't want.

Noticing these signs then clearing the old program and replacing that program with new ones became a fascinating hobby of mine. Luckily, I had friends and family by this time that enjoyed my enthusiasm about this hobby. These wonderful, trusting people let me introduce them to my newfound techniques so I could see if it worked for them also.

The more people I introduced to these techniques, the more I narrowed down the techniques to the ones that were most effective, worked on everyone, and lasted until reprogrammed again. Also I learned by combining and refining techniques I could make the transformation faster, easier and more user-friendly, thus putting the tool in everyone's hands with a minimum of instructions.

My life has just been a joy since. I'm not saying I don't still find things to reprogram, believe me I do. The difference is that I know how to notice what is happening and how to change it. The best part, to me, is I now get to share this understanding many other people directly and indirectly.

I have gone from reprograming myself to teaching others how to reprogram themselves to training people how to instruct others. With each new step up, I also have to go deeper and wider so I have a solid foundation. Since I love what I do, I really see and feel this process as playing.

Even though it is very sincere and profound work, my original intent was to be happy, know I deserve happiness and know that I am worthy of happiness. This is what I have gotten. Sharing with others has become an additional bonus.

I am not going to leave you thinking it has all been easy – simple yes, but not easy. My husband says if I had a nickel every time I quit we could have retired years ago. When I hit my wall and I think 'it's too hard' and 'why am I doing this anyway' something unexpected and wonderful happens to me.

For instance a client or student will call that I haven't heard from in years, and will tell me how their life has changed. They trace the change back to the session or the class with me. They usually start with 'you won't believe what happened.' Of course I believe it, but I know they didn't believe it before it happened. They couldn't believe that all that happiness was just waiting for them.

Now that I am teaching instructors, yes, there is some of the same whining I used to do, but more and more there is the 'you won't believe what happened' – only on a much larger scale. This makes me really grateful that I haven't given up and that I answered the call even though I really didn't know what I was being asked to do or why.

Trust never came easy for me, so when I hear myself telling the new instructors 'just trust the process' I still chuckle to myself and know what I thought when I was told that – yea, that might be easy for you.

Now I do trust, and no matter how crazy it might sound I do it anyway. Once when I was building my studio on our property, I needed an electrician and I couldn't even get an electrician to return my calls. I consciously connected to Source and I heard go to lunch now. I knew I was to go to a particular Chinese restaurant in town. I went and when getting out of my car, I saw an electrician's van in the parking lot. Coming out of the restaurant were the two electricians. Before lunch I had my contract for the work I needed.

Sometimes I still have to remind myself to ask for divine guidance and trust the answers I receive, but every time I do, life gets a little easier and I get a little happier. I haven't found my pleasure tolerance yet, but I am still reaching for it.

Now that I have talked around this process and have even given you wonderful reasons to try it, maybe you would like to see the process yourself.

Originally, I called the process 'Taking out the Trash' because that was what it felt like to me and it has a 0 to 10 guide to step you through the process.

Step 0 – A normal or typical day.
Your day progresses like any other normal, ordinary day. The breakfast choices are the same as always: bagel, cereal, toast, or bacon and eggs. You dress in your normal fashion, and the day proceeds in a normal way with you arriving at work via the same route, in the same morning traffic, and in the same vehicle. You greet the same people, drink out of the same mug, and talk on the same phone.

Step 1 – You think about something new you could have in your life.
We start the process by thinking about something new you are choosing to create in your life. It can be anything. Daydream a little or think about something you have wanted for a long time but were afraid to ask for it.

I have had two clients that were afraid to go for the job in their company that they really wanted. Both felt they didn't have the degree for it. They started on this step with that job position as a daydream. And yes, by following the guide through to the end, they not only got the positions, but they got a huge raise. One even received an assistant.

Step 2 – You notice that others have things or relationships you would like in your life.
At this point you could start questioning your own validity, value, or self-worth by wondering why that didn't happen to me. We, of course, are not going to go down that rabbit hole. We are just going to go on to the next step.

Step 3 – Hurt or frustration surfaces by someone or something that makes you mad.
Someone does something and you feel hurt by his or her actions. You may not realize you are hurting. Instead you may notice you are being critical of someone, or that you are judging someone harshly. These are red flags to notice.

Step 4 – You tell others so they can align with your point of view, or whine, moan, bitch, and blame other people for where you are in your life.
If you do not recognize this as an opportunity, your resulting actions are a replay of unwanted behavior patterns. Some of the unwanted behavior

patterns could be whining, avoiding places where things could happen to you, retreating to a comfort zone, attempting to take control of your environment, looking for self-verification, or blaming your whole life on someone else.

Step 5 – You or someone else breaks your pattern.
At some point, you or someone else lets you know it is time to get off the stage or brings it to your attention that your behavior patterns are destructive.

There are two ways to achieve this: (1) Get slapped without love or (2) Get slapped with love.

Step 6 – Ask questions of yourself.
Remember that now is your opportunity to ask questions to locate that unconscious block or the program that is blocking you from having what you want in your life.

Step 7 – Realize it is about you.
The hardest part to swallow is when you realize the feeling of agony, avoidance, dismay, etc. has to do with you. This is what you have been avoiding by experiencing or acting out in Step 4 – which by the way, is an optional step.

Step 8 – It's time to choose.
You can choose to hold on to the delusion that you are a victim of the situation as long as that belief serves you.

Or you can choose not to stay invisible about who you really are, which is the creator of the situation.

Step 9 – Time to be grateful.
Starting with yourself, list and thank everyone involved in the situation you are analyzing. Make sure you list all of those wonderful people that at a moment's notice jumped into your life to help you play out the scene. Also, add to the list everyone you remember who played a part in your play, going as far back in your life as you can remember.

Step 10 – Receive the gift of joy.
Relax and breathe. Take five deep breaths slowly breathing in and out while acknowledging yourself for completing Steps 0 – 9. Allow yourself to be filled with joy.

About Boni

Boni Oian is a *Dreams Come Alive* Strategist.

Helping people uncover their potential has always been her dream. This includes assisting people in knowing they deserve and are worthy of having everything in life they want. Being happy before and after they receive that dream life sometimes is the challenge.

She is the Author and Instructor of *Claim Your Life – Transform Your Unwanted Subconscious Beliefs into an Exhilarating Source of Power.* She also trains teachers to instruct her **Claim Your Life** process worldwide.

She is certified by the International Medical and Dental Hypnotherapist Association and she's certified as a Catalyst Coach by the Ace Success Center.

Boni's certifications as an Akashic Record Teacher and Consultant are from Akashic Records Consultants International and Akashic Knowing School of Wisdom.

She has been published and/or featured in many publications including *Enjoy Whole Health, Sassy, Focus on Women,* as well as business magazines and has her own radio program.

Boni started on this path in 1980 with Silva Mind Control and the Natale Institute Relationship workshops. Since then Boni has branched out into Shamanic, Reiki, and other energy related work in order to establish faster ways to help make permanent changes for people.

Her belief is that: <u>the secret of happiness is freedom and the secret of freedom is the courage to change.</u>

She believes true freedom widens your path. Your path is where you can walk, the people you can meet and the experiences you can have with comfort. When you first start down your path, it is very narrow because the comfort of your experiences is based on the first seven years of your life. This is where you learned what is acceptable in the world around you, what is allowed and what is proper.

By clearing the conclusions you came to as a child and the disempowering conditioning you received at this time in your life, your path widens to allow more choices, therefore you get to decide what is right for you. The beliefs that people gave you about what is right, proper or acceptable may have worked for them, but may not be what is working for you now in creating the life you want.

It's much like clearing the minefields at the edges of your path. The minefields are the hurt, frustration and anger that result in stepping in a new direction as you make your way through life. With the path cleared of these unpleasant feelings erupting from time to time, you have many more chances of choosing with each step you take. Really getting clear of these eruptions allows you to get clarity about what you want your life to look like without guilt, nagging thoughts and feelings of regret.

Please accept her blessings to all of you who have the courage and strength to change consciously because "the only constant in the universe is change."

You can connect with Boni Oian at:
www.ClaimYourLifewithBoni.com
www.AllEncompassingRetreats.com
www.AkashicRecordsTraining.com
BoniOian@gvtc.com
Office: 830.537.4523

CHAPTER 5

FINDING THE "MONEY SPOT" OF YOUR EXPERTPRENEUR™ BUSINESS

BY SHERYL WOLOWYK

Are you an Expertpreneur™? You are an Expertpreneur™ if you are a consultant, coach, speaker, seminar leader, author or other expert... who leads, advises and inspires others from a position of established knowledge, experience and credibility. In other words, you know your field like nobody's business.

I coined the word Expertpreneur™ to describe the experts who I work with in my business, **Expert Elevation**. If you are an expert in your field, and you work hard to make a positive difference in other people's lives, you are the reason I developed the Expertpreneur™ Roadmap. Most of the clients I work with are making money from their expert knowledge. However, their current business strategy is self-limiting. They only make money when they are in front of others (or on the phone) sharing their expertise.

My goal is to assist them, and you, to find your *money spot* — that perfect convergence of your knowledge, strengths and passions with the right clients at the right time. Many of my clients have a deep expertise in their field, but they are just beginning to understand the wealth of opportunities available to further monetize their expertise. Together, we refine their business processes so the Expertpreneur™ can work *on* their business, not just *in* their business. They earn a lot more money while fulfilling their dream of making a difference in the lives of others. That's where my own story began and it might not be so different from your own.

It took me a while to answer the call to my **Expert Elevation** business. My story is partly one of resistance and staying stuck... How I resisted doing what I do now, because I already was a partner in a consulting firm and enjoying financial success. But something was missing. Working in a partnership for big brand clients, everything felt like it boiled down to budgets and bureaucracy and I felt that limited the difference I could make in people's lives. At the same time, I was interested in the rise of video marketing and attended a 3-day conference to find out how to use it to reach more people. After speaking on stage to a large group of entrepreneurs (who were perhaps a lot like yourself), I felt great! I was energized, and felt a deep connection with the audience, something I was lacking in my current work. Feedback was positive from the audience and the hosts of the event asked if I had considered professional speaking and coaching as a career. Although I found it appealing, I made excuses why I couldn't pursue this.

I knew in my heart that I wanted to share my business expertise with entrepreneurs who were excited about their businesses, and wanted to do anything they could to grow their businesses into vehicles which would provide them the enjoyment, fulfillment, income and lifestyle they desired. But I was still hesitant to make the jump.

My turning point came when several life experiences over a four-day period reminded me that time waits for no one. In one weekend, my son lost his guinea pig, my daughter lost her best friend's mom, my aunt had a stroke, and an uncle had a heart attack. It made me question what I was waiting for. If not today, when? That weekend reminded me how short life is and it was the impetus for me to answer the call to my true purpose and start my business, **Expert Elevation**.

Today I bring to my clients business expertise that can make an immediate difference.

Business owners tend to make the same critical mistake, regardless of the business they are in. They believe the way to make more money is to expand and reach a larger audience, thinking everyone can benefit from what they have to offer. Reaching a larger audience is fantastic, but it is more important to reach the *right* audience. Too many expert business owners make the costly mistake of chasing success by trying to be all things to all people. But as I like to say, your riches are in the niches.

Entrepreneurs, like you, can find their *money spot*, that magical place where the Venn diagram of your knowledge, skills, and experience intersect with a viable market niche, by clearly identifying the ideal client for their product or service. The right clients are attracted to you because you either help them achieve their hopes, dreams and aspirations, or you help them eliminate their fears, frustrations, and problems. In my programs, I teach Expertpreneurs™ like you to develop a clear picture of your ideal client, for whom your products and services will fill their specific need. When you have a deep understanding of who your ideal client is and what motivates them to buy your unique expertise, you are well on your way to finding your money spot. Your business will be focused specifically on the people that are ready and willing to pay for your help.

Some Expertpreneurs™ also struggle because they try to sell by identifying potential clients one at a time, chasing after them and desperately trying to get them to buy. This approach is usually ineffective and isn't an enjoyable way of selling. What you really need to do is to use proven marketing techniques to gather your tribe of ideal clients and build a relationship. Help them to come to you, and to get to know, like and trust you. Use your understanding of their hopes and frustrations to provide them with valuable information so they will become loyal clients and fans, giving you excellent testimonials and referrals.

My **Expert Elevation** strategy for becoming an Expertpreneur™ and finding your *money spot* is made up of the Five P's: Platform, Position, Package, Promote and Profit. When you have mastered the Five P's, you will be on the road to maximizing your profitability as an expert in your field. Here's how you can master the Five P's…

1. **Platform**. Your platform is every channel you utilize to reach your ideal client. Becoming a successful Expertpreneur™ requires an integrated, multiple-channel marketing platform. This might include activities like speaking engagements, blogging and posting videos, to name just a few. It doesn't matter so much which marketing channels you use as long as you choose ones that are effective for you to reach

your ideal client. The goal is to leverage different marketing channels to get your message out, and to expand your reach.

You might be a knowledgeable coach or consultant, but if your ideal client never finds out about you, then you can't make a difference in their life. Your platform will be effective in growing your business when you have established your niche, then deliver your expertise and value via channels that will reach your intended audience. Reaching your ideal client will do you no good, however, if your tribe cannot distinguish you from others in your field who offer a similar product or service. You must position yourself as unique in some way for the tribe to take notice and choose you over other options.

2. **Position.** What is your unique advantage? Know that you must be clear about this. As you expand your reach, and people begin to find out about you because of your marketing platforms, they will ask, "Why you?" They want to know why they should choose you over all of the other "expert" options available. Additionally, you want your position to be strong enough that not only would they select you over all the other options, they will select you over the option of doing nothing at all.

Once you establish your reach with your marketing platform, you have to explain why your clients should choose you, and not the competition. Establishing authority puts other business owners without authority positioning at a disadvantage. Position creates your signature solution, your unique advantage, and must be specific enough that no one will mistake you for someone else. For example, you might be unique because your approach includes exploring the client's background all the way back to their childhood to find their passion and creativity, and helping them to incorporate that into their business. That unique approach makes you different and you need to communicate that to attract clients. It's your job to offer them a unique solution that only you provide.

Your "signature solution" is your unique way of combining products and services as a specialist to support the features and benefits you provide. It might be helpful for you to think of positioning in terms of businesses that have done it exceptionally well.

Consider the success of Cirque du Soleil. Everyone has heard of the circus; that's old hat. But, whoever thought to combine a circus with a story and music? They completely changed the game and eliminated their competition by creating their own niche. So, looking in your industry, consider how you can do it differently.

Here's another example: Domino's Pizza revolutionized their business and the industry with their '30-minutes-or-it's-free' deal. Pizza is pizza is pizza, but pizza at your door in a half-hour or it's free changed the game. They didn't need to make pizza better or different, they only had to promise quick delivery to differentiate themselves.

Getting your message out to your market by publishing will also differentiate you and your business by establishing your credentials as an expert in the field. Public speaking also positions your expertise and increases your visibility. However, if you are nervous about speaking on stage you can always share your knowledge and position your expertise by creating videos and posting them on YouTube or other video sharing sites.

One final element of positioning is to be genuine. Don't hesitate to tell your own story in a way which people can empathetically relate to. When you meet people, they will naturally want to know the driving force behind your business. Your story might be a rags-to-riches story, or a story that excites people about how you overcame significant obstacles to get to the success you enjoy today. Your story is important; it can be golden to your positioning because it builds credibility and relatability with potential clients.

I use my turning point story to describe my own, personal "ah-ha" moment. I summarized it earlier and you can hear the full story on my **Expert Elevation** website. Personally, I develop stronger relationships with the people I do business with when I know their story and share a bit of my own.

3. **Package**. Package is your branding – from the look and feel of your business cards to the personal image you present to the world. You are the product. Your packaging affects people's perception of your brand. As an Expertpreneur™, little things, such as how you dress or the persona you create will affect your brand. Package yourself intentionally, then, package your products and services to reflect the

quality and personality of your brand. For example if your brand is a high end, luxurious brand, then your products and services and the way you price and bundle them should reflect this. What you package in your offering, how you price and how you present your products and services all affect your brand and ultimately the type of customers you attract.

The combinations you create also help to differentiate you from the competition. Can you be a highly responsive brand whereby you create membership sites and share new information on-demand? Can you offer certifications for acquiring the knowledge you teach, creating a credentialing system and positioning your expert status? What about establishing a mastermind group or offering V.I.P. days for high end clients? Think of ways you can package your products and services and add revenue streams to your business by adding value for your clients.

4. Promote. Your promotion broadcasts why clients should come to you as an Expertpreneur™. At first they may not be ready to purchase from you. However, when your ideal client gets to know, like and trust you, then you are in a strong position to ask for the sale. It's about giving value first and timing your offer correctly.

At first meeting, your niche market will need to get to know you. They want to relate to you. Sharing your personal story can be beneficial at this juncture. Your personal story sets you apart from others and is the "something" they may remember long after they have met you. Remembering you at a later date will prompt your list to open the email you send or read the next *free-mium* piece you give them. *Free-miums* trade a bit of knowledge for the client's contact information. When you have their email address, you can continue to send more free information and build the relationship.

Promotion begins with marketing to establish you in front of your ideal clients, and nurture the relationship with them. You start with *free-miums* such as free e-newsletters, white papers, tweets or Facebook posts to build a following for your unique message. After establishing your credibility with your target audience, you can begin to capitalize on the relationship by positioning an offer for your product or service.

5. Profit. Profit comes from building multiple revenue streams by creating a "prosperity pyramid™ ." In order to create a lucrative business you need to understand various ways to monetize your knowledge. You can create free and low-priced products and services at the bottom of the pyramid, with higher-priced, more customized solutions at the top.

For example, you might currently coach one client for $150 per hour, but suppose you group ten clients together at $150 per hour per client, or $1500. Now you get a greater return for that hour of work. And your clients benefit from learning from you and from sharing with each other. You could also share your expertise by offering mastermind group sessions for three weekends and earn $10,000 per participant. Another option is to schedule one-on-one appointments with top clients for $5,000 V.I.P. days.

Additionally, for most experts, they only earn money when they are sharing their knowledge in person. The hours you can spend in front of people are limited. And that limits the number of clients you can help. If you create and package an information product or coaching program once, and then offer it on the Internet, you can sell it over and over, and literally help clients while you sleep. Imagine how that would expand your bottom line and your impact.

While the Five P's of becoming an Expertpreneur™ will be invaluable to establishing yourself as an expert and help you find your *money spot*, they work best when applied to the right business model from the beginning.

If you select a business model outside your expertise, you will always be dealing with a learning curve and likely not be successful in your business. And you won't be operating from your *money spot*. If you are passionate about something and exceptionally good at it, but there isn't a market for it or you have not done a great job of establishing your unique value proposition, your business will suffer. To build a lucrative business, find your *money spot.* Locate that juncture where your expertise, strengths, passion and the right market intersect, and you will be able to create the ultimate business venture - the Expertpreneur™ business of your dreams.

About Sheryl

"Make It Easy, Simple and Lucrative. That is My Motto."

The unexpected death of the class guinea pig at her son's school was just one of three wake-up calls Sheryl Wolowyk received in quick succession to cause her to exit a lucrative yet unfulfilling corporate career to blaze a trail as a successful, fulfilled entrepreneur.

Since 1996, Sheryl Wolowyk – a successful serial entrepreneur – has created four multi-million dollar expert businesses serving clients in English-speaking nations around the globe. Each success – one right after the other – was created by following a simple, yet powerful operating style and philosophy. It is all about ESL. Make it Easy, Simple, and Lucrative™.

Today, Sheryl deploys the strength of her talent, experience and voice to inspire and guide aspiring experts to follow her lead to build lucrative businesses and influential brands all their own. She guides them to create lasting and fulfilling legacies that leave a profound and favorable mark on the world.

Sheryl walks her own expert advice by amplifying her voice and message across the globe through a fast-growing radio and video platform. She is Executive Producer and host of the *ExpertPreneur™ Radio Show,* airing on the Amazing Women of Power Radio Network, serving 3.5 million listeners worldwide. Sheryl is also creator, editor, and publisher of *ExpertPreneur™ Magazine,* selling on the Apple newsstand since 2013 in 155 countries.

Action-focused aspiring experts rave about their success attracting clients, growing their revenues, and charging their worth as a direct result of the lessons they learn at Sheryl's invitation. Clients engage in the ways that are the "best fit" for their learning styles, need for direct access and personal attention, and urgency to welcome results. To learn how you can work with Sheryl, go to: www.expertelevation.com.

CHAPTER 6

ANSWERING THE CALL
TO FREEDOM

BY ANGELA G. SOLOMON, ESQ.

Have you ever felt like you were making a living, but not doing what you were born to do? Do you feel that there is a bigger purpose for your life but you aren't yet sure what it is? Are you sure you deserve better but just feel stuck?

If you answered yes to any of those questions, I know how you feel. I felt the same way too, until I made a powerful discovery that put me on the path to freedom through fulfilling my life's purpose.

My story is fairly traditional. I got married in my 20's, raised my children in my 30's, and then I turned 40 and began to wonder what I was going to be when I grew up. It wasn't that I hadn't had a professional career or two. Out of college, I was recruited to work at a major corporation as a financial analyst, which I did for three years until I decided to attend law school. After graduation, I worked as an Associate Attorney at a law firm practicing business and corporate law where I helped small business and corporate clients with everything from setting up corporations, to filing trademark applications and drafting and negotiating contracts. I also helped my husband build a successful marketing business. All of this while being a mom to three busy boys. Whew! A lot, I know. But there was still something missing. Something unfulfilled inside of my soul.

In January of 2011, the beginning of my 40th year, I think I had a mini mid-life crisis. I realized I had given so much of myself to help my husband and to raise my children, but I had not given enough of myself to me and my own goals and dreams. Women are often nurturers and helpers resulting in us finding ourselves at the bottom of our own list, tending to the needs of everyone else before our own.

Sure, it looked like I had the perfect life - husband, children, law degree and a successful business. But I felt that my purpose was to help more than my own little family. I wanted to do more. Be more. And I'm not ashamed to say that I wanted to HAVE MORE! My mother taught me to be an independent woman, and I still had that burning desire to build my own empire, even though I had helped my husband be very successful in his business for many, many years. But I wanted my own success - engineered and created by my own self. I knew there had to be other women like me who put their own goals and dreams on hold - or worse, maybe had given up on them all together - to be wives and mothers to those we love more than anything else in world.

I struggled with guilt even making the decision to take more time for myself to pursue my goals and dreams again. I also felt ashamed for wanting more because by all accounts my life was good. People would say I had enough - why should I be greedy and want an even better life? People would think I was being selfish or being a bad mother spending less time with my children to work toward my own dreams. But deep inside I knew I wanted to affect more people and share the life and business lessons I had learned with more women to help them experience freedom in their lives. I felt I had a deeper calling to share with the world. And it was my duty to answer the call.

After a two-year process of self-discovery and soul-searching that seemed like a lifetime, I was finally able to connect with my true calling. After months of frustration, false starts, failed business ideas, I figured out what I was born to do. And what a blessing it is to be able to stop searching and get down to the business of living your purpose! I want every woman to have this information so they, too, can have more freedom and happiness in their lives. The satisfaction I feel for being able to create my own thing and help others do the same is like Wow! I wake up everyday knowing that I am helping people exhale and relax into their own success and that feeling is priceless.

The information I am going to share with you is perfect for you if you've ever wanted to discover your true purpose, if you've ever felt like you weren't living up to your full potential, if you've always wanted to have your own business, or if you've ever felt like you could be more, do more, and have more but you just didn't know what to do or how to do it.

Let's be real. The days of working 40 years for the same company and retiring with a gold watch and pension are long gone. We all need a Plan B. There is no job security - companies layoff, furlough, and downsize without warning. Freedom is knowing how to generate income that is not dependent on anyone else – boss, spouse, or government. There is nothing like the feeling of accomplishment you get from doing something with your own efforts that makes your heart sing and makes you money, too. You deserve the freedom to splurge and treat yourself to nice things, live a life filled with happiness, have work that feels like play, and enjoy time with those you love, doing what you love.

So let's get to it. Here's how to discover exactly how to use skills and talents you already have to create a profitable business that you love because it aligns with your true calling, passion and purpose.

I call it my **Freedom Formula**.

The formula has 5 parts that all begin with the letter P:

♦ PASSION

♦ PROBLEM

♦ PEOPLE

♦ PLACE

♦ PLAN

I. Passion:
The first P of my Freedom Formula is Passion. The dictionary defines passion as "any powerful or compelling emotion or feeling, such as love or hate." We live on the LOVE side of the passion spectrum because our goal is to create a life we absolutely LOVE and be passionate about living each day to the fullest. Everyone is passionate about something, the challenge is identifying what it is and building a business that magnifies it. When I work with clients who want to discover their passion, I always start with this question: WHY? Why are you inspired

to take this path? What do you believe? How do you hope to make a difference in someone's life other than your own?

Answering the question WHY is important because your WHY will fuel your passion. Passion is important because it is what will keep you going when things get tough. Will things get tough on your journey to building a business you love to create a life of freedom? Absolutely. All sorts of Fear, Doubt, Haters, Betrayers, Guilt and Shame will show up. The reason WHY I hear most often is "To make money." Surprisingly, to make money is not a big enough WHY. Your WHY should be tied to something bigger than yourself because it is too easy to talk ourselves out of progress and too easy to let ourselves off the hook when we don't meet our own expectations. It's too easy to let ourselves down and be ok with it. The person in the mirror is not your ideal accountability partner. You'll say, "I can do it tomorrow." Or, "I can do it next time." Or, "I'll try." I call that self-sabotaging voice in our heads "Negative Nelly." Negative Nelly is a dream stealer. She's toxic. Every time we say we are going to do something and don't do it or don't finish, it diminishes our self-esteem and confidence. Each time, it whittles away at our belief in ourselves and makes it more and more difficult to fulfill our dreams and goals.

After you identify your passion, you will have to take a good, in-depth look at your skills, talents, strengths and abilities. A good way to find out what you are good at is to think about what people are always asking you to do. Or, you can send an email to 5-10 people asking them what they think your best qualities and strengths are. I also find that creating a survey is a great way to get this information from family and friends. There are websites that allow you to create surveys easily at no cost. I work closely with my clients using a method I call the STEPP Analysis which is a series of questions specially crafted to determine your skill set that will be most useful to partner with your passion to create the perfect business for you. Your passion + your skill set = your Gold Mine Gift. Once you identify your gold mine gift, you're on your way to freedom. This step is huge!

II. Problem:
The next P is Problem. What problem will you solve? The best business ideas are ones that solve a problem people are already willing to pay to solve. The Internet is such an awesome tool because it allows us to do

some very basic and necessary market research at marginal cost.

You'll need to tie your gold mine gift to one of the "Big 6." The Big 6 are six proven categories in which people commonly have problems AND for which they are consistently paying for solutions. These are health, wealth, success, looking better, feeling better, and relationships. People want help being healthier, wealthier, more successful, more attractive, more vibrant and with the plethora of online dating sites I think it's fair to say that people want to be in love. There is a gold mine within each of these 6 categories. I'm sure you'll be able to find yours there.

The remaining 3 P's - People, Place, Plan - are equally as important.

III. People:
For People, you must identify your ideal customers. You have to connect with your ideal customer's thoughts, dreams, desires and fears to create an offering they would love to have that meets a need for which there is already a high demand for a solution. This is a key process that can either guarantee the success of your business, or if you miss the mark, can cause even the best business idea to fall flat.

IV. Place:
The next P is Place. Every business today needs an Internet presence. You should create an attractive website and grab social media virtual real estate for your business on Twitter and Facebook before someone else does.

V. Plan:
The last P of the **Freedom Formula** is Plan. Using the 4 P's we already covered, you now have a solid head start on creating the essential elements you need for a complete marketing plan to officially launch your business. This is also the time to begin to handle the legal aspects of your business by filing business and intellectual property registrations and making sure you are using proper contracts with service providers and customers.

Freedom is calling to those who are willing to answer. I find that the biggest barrier to freedom is fear. Fear of what other people will say and think about you. Here's a newsflash: people are going to talk about you anyway. We only have one life to live and life is short. Where would you be today if you weren't worried about what people would say?

Not everyone is fortunate enough to find their path to freedom in their lifetime. It is my hope that you find yours.

Freedom means flexibility – to choose your work, when you work, where you work, how much money you make, and how you spend it. Having choices means no more feeling stuck knowing you deserve better and not knowing what to do to get it. Everyone deserves to experience this kind of freedom in their lives, but, sadly, not everyone is brave enough to claim it for themselves. I would never say that finding your freedom is easy. But I would *always* say that finding your freedom is worth it.

About Angela

Known as the "Trusted Attorney and Business Advisor", Angela G. Solomon helps women breakthrough barriers to reach their full potential. Her passion is helping women create and protect profitable businesses that allow them to generate income no matter what life brings their way.

A business owner herself for over fifteen years, Angela and her husband have been featured in *Success From Home* magazine and in *Washington Life* magazine.

Angela graduated from the University of Michigan – Ann Arbor with a Bachelor of Business Administration. After working in corporate America for three years, she attended the George Washington University National Law Center, where she earned her Juris Doctor. Angela is a licensed attorney in the State of Maryland, practicing primarily in the areas of business and corporate law.

Angela enjoys reading fiction novels, traveling, and spending time with her family.

You can connect with Angela at:
www.AngelaGSolomon.com
www.twitter.com/AngelaGSolomon
www.facebook.com/AngelaGSolomon

CHAPTER 7

A REDBIRD TALE

BY CATHY SAINATO

Far away in the rainforest of Batanta Island in West Papua New Guinea, lived a family called the Redbirds. The Fathers name is Gabriel, Mom is Jenella, and three children, son Redric, and two daughters Pieretta and Grace. The Redbird family loved living in Batanta Island because of the great community they created there. Gabriel and Jenella Redbird were leaders of the rainforest and all were welcomed in their house. Their children were each unique in their own way. Redric was the responsible one. He watched over his little sisters with pride, and always made sure they were protected. Pieretta, the middle Redbird, loved being active and had a mind that was alert and very wise. And of course, little Grace was artistically graceful, dancing around the rainforest from branch to branch with ease and beauty.

Everyday after Redric and his sisters were done with their chores, they went out and played with their friends. They loved to play games like tag and hide-and-go-seek! They'd play for hours until the sun went down and their mother would call them back to their cozy home. Aaron, a rainbow lorikeet, and Violet, a beautiful parakeet were their best friends. Their feathers were brilliant shades of deep purple and blue. Each day they ate lunch together, mostly eating delicious tropical fruits and berries off the trees, and sometimes even insects!

Redric always watched over his sisters. You see, the Redbirds are a very unique bird of the rainforest, they are very beautiful and they also had a secret. Redric has a mark on his wing that shines like a diamond on a new ring when he is flying. When Redric was born, his parents noticed a gem on his wing. They brought him to the doctor to see what this mysterious gem was and he told them this... "A long time ago a queen and king ruled the rainforest and they each were born with a gem on their wing. This gem held great magical powers and allowed them to perform miracles. With this gem they cured other birds of the forest of illness and made wishes come true. The King and Queen were the only ones with this power and they never had any children to pass along the power to. Because of this, they made a powerful wish: one redbird in the rainforest would be blessed with this diamond gem and whomever this bird was would perform miracles and be the ruler of the rainforest, as long as they used their power for the greater good of the rainforest. Once the word got out about the gem, hunters immediately went after the birds to try and capture the gem! They searched for days through every inch of the rainforest, rain or shine to find the bird with the gem, to no avail.

Meanwhile, Redric knew he was special and that he had special powers. He found this out by accident while playing with his friends and sisters. One day, while playing tag, his sister Pieretta's wing got tangled in a tree branch and she could not get out. Pieretta screamed, "Help! I'm scared! Please save me!" As Grace, Violet and Aaron tried to untangle Pieretta, she became more panicked by the second. Redric then flew over her and tried to remove the branch to untangle her when suddenly a light flashed down from his wing and onto the branch! In a flash, Pieretta was free and the branches all turned into ashes.

Redric's sisters and friends could not believe what they saw! All the Redbirds talked about Redric's heroism and magic powers all the way home.

When they got home that evening, Pieretta and Grace couldn't wait to tell their Mom and Dad what happened and how Redric saved Pieretta from being tangled in the tree. They were shaking with anticipation and excitement wondering if their parents would even believe them. When Mom and Dad Redbird heard this unbelievable story, they then realized that their son Redric had the magical powers that the King and Queen had granted to the Redbirds. They were concerned about hunters finding out about Redric's powers. They knew they had to keep Redric as safe as possible from the hunters. His parents warned Redric about his powers, to use them wisely and the need to be safe and not to get captured.

The next week while playing with their friends high up on the trees, they looked down and noticed two strange men looking around. Redric knows that there are hunters that look for beautiful birds but was afraid they might see the shine from the gem under his wing. Redric called for his sisters Pieretta and Grace and started to fly home when a hunter noticed a bright light coming from Redric's wing. The hunter started running towards the direction of Redric and his sisters and started shooting a type of gun called a tranquilizer. This gun will not kill them but put them to sleep temporarily. Redric protected his sisters by opening his wings as far as he could and suddenly he felt a sting on his back. He looked up and saw that his sisters were still flying. He didn't remember anything else until he woke up and there he saw the two men he saw at the rainforest.

Redric looked up at the two hunters staring down at him. They were studying the gem on his wing. "Where are my sisters?" Redric thought. Pieretta and Grace were nowhere in sight. He worried if they were safe and at home. This was all he could think about and these thoughts kept running through his mind. He noticed his surroundings and knew he was not in the rainforest anymore. He was in a bright colored room and there was a cage standing next to him. One of the hunters tied Redric so he could not spread his wings to fly and put him in the cage and locked the door.

Redric could not move and couldn't help himself because he was tied and he had no power when his wings were not spread! Pieretta and Grace rushed home to tell their parents what happened to Redric. They immediately went out to try to find tracks and clues that could lead them to Redric. The news of Redric missing spread to the neighbors and community very quickly. Everyone gathered and made groups to start looking for Redric. Redric's parents and sisters were the first group, Violet and Aaron were the second group. There was a total of six groups that took off flying North, South, East and West in search of Redric. Each group looked for clues all over Batanta Island.

By the end of the day all were exhausted from searching for Redric. The Sun was starting to go down. Redric's Mom, Dad and sisters were starting to lose hope when suddenly they looked down and saw a small house in the middle of the rainforest! This house did not look familiar to any of them, so they decided to fly down to get a better look. Redric's Father Gabriel perched on a window on the top floor. Jenella perched right next to him.

Pieretta and Grace flew around the house to the front and looked into the first floor window. The room was dark and they could not see inside. They flew around the back of the house and thought that nothing was there when they heard a cry coming from inside! It sounded like Redric! Redric's Father had an idea, he noticed a chimney on the top of the house and advised Pieretta and Grace to stay with their Mother Jenella. He told them to fly to the front of the house and perch near the front. He told them he would fly down the chimney to get a better look.

When Redric's Father flew down the chimney he landed in a small room that was dark and cold. He started quietly calling out Redric's name as he slowly flew into the next room, "Redric, Redric are you in here?" Suddenly Redric heard his Dad calling him! "I am here Dad, in a cage! Please help me!" Redric's Dad flew towards the voice that was coming from another room. The Moon was out and he could see a little light shining threw a window. Then he saw something on a table and when he flew to it, it was a cage and there was Redric! His Father was so happy to see Redric, he told him not to worry that he will get him out. He flew over to the front door and was able to turn the lock with his beak and the door opened! Redric's Mom Jenella and Sisters flew in and right to the cage! Gabriel, Redric's Father quickly started to work on the lock on the door of the cage. They were all trying so hard to get the cage door open and to get Redric out! Pieretta and Grace started searching the room for a key, Redric's Mom stayed with Redric while his Father was working on the lock! They knew they had little time before the hunters returned to the house! Redric's Father had a great idea! He asked Grace to pull one of his feathers! Grace looked at her Dad surprised that he asked her to do this! Her Father told her he would try and pick the lock with the end of his feather and try to get the lock open!

Grace flew over to her Dad and pulled very hard on one of his feathers and she couldn't pull it out! Grace then called Pieretta over and asked for help! Together on the count of three they pulled so hard that they both rolled onto the floor with the feather! They gave their Dad his feather and he put the pointed end into the lock and jiggled it a few times...

after a few minutes the lock opened! As Redric's Mom was untying Redric, they heard voices outside! They quickly gathered and flew up the chimney and out to safety!

When they got home they all hugged! Redric's Mom and Dad contacted the neighbors and all who helped in searching for Redric to let them know he was home safe!

When Redric went to bed that night, he was thinking about what happened and knowing that he had special powers only when his wings were spread! He knew that the hunters were aware of this and that is why they tied his wings down. When Redric's Mom and Dad came into his room to say goodnight, Redric asked them why he was born with this special power, and finally his parents explained to him about the spell that the Queen and King gave the Redbirds because they did not have children of their own, and how special he was to have this gem on his wing. They also told him that soon he would be the King of the Redbirds! Redric finally smiled for the first time since he was captured and was happy that his Mom and Dad told him the reason he had this gem on his wing and was so special! Redric was also excited knowing that he would be King of the rainforest in the Batanta Island!

Redric kissed his Mom and Dad goodnight along with his sisters Pieretta and Grace. After they left the room, he snuggled in his warm bed and thought how lucky he was to have such a wonderful family that loved each other so much!

About Cathy

Cathy Sainato was born and raised in Albany, New York. A lifelong resident, she and her husband are the proud owners of family-owned "Sainato's Market" for over three decades where they created a family-style deli as well as long-lasting community relationships. Cathy also worked for New York State as a secretary and a Compliance Representative before retiring in 2009. Her love for cooking and baking has been instilled in her family as well as in her business, making delicious food for the Albany Tri-City area residents for years.

As a musician and artist, Cathy was inspired by her three granddaughters to write a children's book. The stories that she made up to put them to sleep at night became a requested favorite every time they stayed over, and thus a book was born. Beyond being a storyteller, Cathy is a proud mother of two children and her three granddaughters are the loves of her life. Cathy is an avid and creative gardener, and in her spare time you can find her in the garden with her husband Luigi where they still reside in Albany.

CHAPTER 8

PELVIS WELLNESS — ANSWERING THE CALL

BY LORI ZELTWANGER, PT

SEX! That's what you were thinking when you saw the title, right? That's pretty much the response when I ask people what they think of when I refer to Pelvis Wellness. And that, precisely, is my point! While the health and wellness of our pelvis definitely affects our sex life, there is so much more to the topic.

As a physical therapist specializing in Myofascial Release, which bridges western medicine with holistic care, I feel called to be a voice to educate people about the availability and benefits of Pelvis Wellness treatment and how this needs to be a part of standard medical care.

Pelvis Wellness is a topic so obscured from our consciousness we can't even understand the term. Now, more than ever, it is important to go into the subject of connecting our energetic presence with our physical tissue. More important than intellectually understanding Pelvis Wellness is to allow ourselves the time and space to actually experience what this is all about; to experience what it feels like to be present in your own pelvis.

This is something that cannot be read about in a book. This is something that needs to be felt and experienced. It is necessary to live fully! This is a process of connecting with the creative, powerful survival energy that belongs there. This process will uncover your specific 'pelvis-print' essence (similar to an energetic finger print), helping you feel at home in your body and allowing you to express your purpose this lifetime.

Most people, when referring to their own pelvis, think of it in terms of connecting to another, for example, with their partner for sexual intimacy, and for most women, with their children for childbirth.

What if we brought our energy into our pelvis for our OWN self? What would that be like? How would we live our lives? How would we connect with our partners?

The lack of presence in your pelvis can manifest as physical and emotional struggles of various kinds and intensities, and may cause problems anywhere in your body and life. Many traumas and wounds occur in this area and get stuck in your tissues.

Pelvis Wellness balances the pelvis and reconnects our energy field with our physical tissues through awareness exercises. Myofascial Release treatment is the physical handle used to release trauma and restore the tissue back to its fluid and flexible matrix. This brings about effective results efficiently when nothing else seems to resolve symptoms.

The pelvis needs therapeutic treatment externally, and also internally, because it is made up of tissue just like all other areas of your body. But we all "save" our pelvis for private activity and rarely think of getting it treated to add to our generalized health and well-being. We may get regular exams, but this is not treatment. In what way are we therapeutically addressing this physical tissue to allow healing to occur? From my clinical experience, this is a very neglected area and creates needless suffering when unaddressed.

For me, Pelvis Wellness treatment saved my career and gave me my life back. I was in two car accidents six months apart and was experiencing an excruciating, nagging ache in my shoulder blade – which was making it hard for me to use my shoulder and making my work as a physical therapist very difficult. The only thing that actually resolved this pain was treatment to my pelvic floor tissue, internally. It seemed crazy to me then, but I now understand that during those car accidents my survival was threatened, and my pelvic floor tissue went into spasm. Treatment to my shoulder blade area alone was not addressing the core problem in my pelvis (which had become bound up during the crash) and therefore my symptoms were unable to resolve.

How is this possible? The **myofascial system** is the connective tissue in our body weaving all of the cells of our body together. Its job is to connect, support and protect all of the cells that lie underneath it. It can suddenly or gradually tighten down on us, forming restrictions in a way in which we are very unaware. This creates all kinds of little problems that eventually add up to loss of mobility and distress in the body where we are unable to relax and enjoy our life. And these restrictions do not show up on any standard medical testing done today, so there is no validation for our problems, when in fact, they are very physical in nature and fairly easy to address.

A myofascial release therapist looks at the relationship of your whole body and notices where your body is pulled out of alignment from these restrictions. A variety of sustained pressure and stretch is then placed into these restrictions, waiting for a minimum of 90-120 seconds and often up to 3-5 minutes or more, following the release of the tissue as it unravels and melts under their hands. The therapist also supports the body as it needs to move to release the trauma which became locked in the tissues and guide the reconnection of the energy field back into the cells in which it belongs. The therapist is trained to listen to the wisdom of the body, guiding it as it unravels itself and reconnects to it's wellness blueprint.

When we experience trauma of any kind, our bodies go into shock. A part of us either gets buried in our tissue or disconnects from our body. Our body is doing this to protect itself. But if this process is never reversed, then our vital life force, meant to flow through every cell in our body, becomes locked up or locked out, leaving us less able to respond to life in the way in which we were designed to respond. We feel panicked or shut down.

This means our body uses a lot of our energy to keep us from feeling the trauma that we just went through, so this energy is no longer available to help our body heal and function. We become unaware of what is happening in our body, as we are no longer in a connected, feeling state but are operating in a partially disconnected state. Pain and problems begin to develop and we can't figure out what we did to cause them. We feel disconnected from ourselves, others and life itself.

For example, do you have a C-section, episiotomy or abdominal scar of some kind? Did you ever think a scar of this kind could be causing you problems even if your surgery were many years ago or if the problem was some other place far from the scar itself? Back pain, digestive issues, headaches, and a myriad of other issues, many of which don't show up in standard medical testing, could be caused by these scars.

This scar tissue has a way of spider-webbing (accumulating and reaching) anywhere throughout your whole body, creating restrictions which cause painful friction in your joints, impinging nerves, binding muscles, crushing blood vessels, suppressing vital organs and creating twists and turns throughout your body in unique and individualized patterns.

Heidi was suffering from debilitating migraines and would bury herself in bed for a few days every month. Medication helped reduce symptoms by 50%, but this still left her unable to work or care for her children during these times. She also experienced symptoms of urinary incontinence since delivery of her last child. Only from scar release treatment directly on her episiotomy scar, which occurred during delivery of her second child 6 years prior, was she freed from her headache and incontinence symptoms. These two seemingly unrelated conditions were coming from the same restricted source, where she felt no symptoms at all. This scar had reached up through her body via the fascial system, placing a strong pull on her bladder and all the way up to her head.

Have you fallen on your tailbone or experienced whiplash in a car accident, and are now suffering from symptoms that cannot be explained? Even if no surgical scar exists, you most likely have internal scars called fascial restrictions and adhesions. This is due to the body tissue adhering itself inside in an attempt to protect you from traumas and invasions. The body has an incredibly intelligent way of defending itself against both real and perceived trauma.

It could be that the trauma may not have broken any bones but your body hardened up in an attempt to protect you from the trauma. Your body may remain in a protected state, unaware that the trauma is in the past, because your body did not get the chance to fully process the experience and release itself.

The naturally occurring healing process may have been interrupted due to numbing medications, lack of emotional safety and support, misunderstood belief systems that became embedded during the trauma and continue to create miscommunications in the nervous system, or accumulated holding in the body from previous problems which confuse and complicate the healing process. Remember, your body holds an intelligence and wisdom differently from your brain and this needs to be respected and addressed. Approaching healing only from the place of mental understanding will not clear the trauma. It must be dealt with in the body itself.

As in Selena's story, she was suffering from back pain and headaches that were so debilitating she dropped out of high school and spent nearly five years of her life in bed. Everyone was treating her head and back symptoms and no one was addressing the cause of her problem; the trauma locked in her tailbone from a fall. This fall was complicated by emotional stress from a move to a new location and a new school. Only when she began to receive Myofascial Release treatment internally to her tailbone did her problems begin to resolve. She was able to reclaim her life because finally the actual cause of her problem, which was different than where she was feeling symptoms, was addressed.

The pelvic floor tissue is a supportive sling of muscle and fascial tissue at the base of our pelvis. It attaches to all of the bones of our pelvis and hips.

Often we begin to unconsciously tighten in our pelvic floor tissue in an attempt to find stability within a body that has been twisted and shaken from trauma. This puts a twist with compressive pressures on the spine and hips, which begins to affect our nervous system and our ability to move and rest properly. Once we are unable to rest properly, the body really struggles to heal itself. We find ourselves in an unconscious survival mode.

The energy field of the pelvis relates to all our issues surrounding survival. This might be life or death in the physical form but it could also be the life or death of a relationship, job or our finances. These emotional life stressors cause our fascial tissue to bind itself together as it attempts to protect and stabilize us internally during challenging times because emotions are actually physical molecules, as discovered by the scientist Candace Pert.

These emotions often are poorly addressed and do not get resolved. This creates the same holding and spider-webbing effect in our tissue as the physical trauma created. This can lead to all kinds of unexplained symptoms, including chronic fatigue, fibromyalgia, anxiety and depression, and so many other conditions that you are being told is all in your head, when in reality, is all in your physical tissues.

According to recent research, the body sends out well over 5,000 times more signals to the brain than the brain to the body. If we really understand this science, we will spend a lot more time listening and paying attention to the signals, sensations, feelings, images, emotions, and movements (or lack there of) which are occurring in our whole body, recognizing that it truly is alive with its own intelligence. The body sends messages in the form of sensations, and even pain, as a way to guide our healing process – not to torture us or make us miserable.

Pain is not the enemy. It is part of our internal guidance system desperately attempting to deliver a message to us in the only way it knows to get our attention.

I invite you to take this moment and tune in to the messages in your own body with the following simple exercise. Place both hands on your pelvis. Feel underneath and in between your hands. Now imagine there is a little 'you' sitting right inside your pelvis. What is it like for him/her to be there? Simply notice what captures your attention and feel whatever is present there.

For example, I tuned into my pelvis and noticed I couldn't feel into this area at all but instead noticed a feeling of pressure in my head and heart. As I gave it time, I became aware of a lightness and a lack of breath there. As I felt this, I spontaneously took a deep breath. As I exhaled I noticed a tightness, a holding and an ache in my shoulders and between my shoulder blades. I began to feel a bit of a panicked sensation. The little girl was not sure it's ok for her to be there. The thought arose: "Wow, that's interesting. If she doesn't belong there, where does she belong or who does belong there???"

It's not enough to think about the process. We must go into the experience: we must feel the sensations and emotions which arise.

As I sat with these feelings, I felt a calming as I felt what was there and recognized I needed further support with unraveling my own web. Often times we can't let go or listen without enough safety, appropriate pressure and support. The acknowledgement to reach out and receive support was an important next step for me leading to my Pelvis Wellness.

This simple Pelvis Wellness exercise only takes a few minutes and is meant to be done over and over again, giving you the experience of truly embodying your presence. We are beings in a body in constant change, and giving repetitive attention to this area can allow greater wellness in your life. (There is a guided, expanded version of this on the website PelvisWellness.com.)

What occurred during my myofascial release treatment was a release of memory from my tissue of feeling numbed out to my own birth from the anesthesia my mother was given during the delivery process, which was standard care in those days. It seems like a significant amount of my own energetic awareness wasn't able to fully connect with my body at my birth.

Now I am answering this call and finding my way back home to the body I was given to inhabit during my life on earth. I feel my purpose is to expand the awareness of how necessary it is for all of us to make stronger connections to our whole body including the whole pelvis region in very therapeutic ways.

The center of our being lies in and around our pelvis, so being in our pelvis and keeping our energetic essence in alignment with our physical tissue will contribute to living a more centered, connected life – one in which we are less likely to be reactive – bringing more peace, vitality and love into our existence.

Pelvis Wellness work allows you to put into practice what you have been hearing and reading about for years about being present, and in so doing, live a life more connected to yourself and your calling.

I invite you to say yes to yourself, take responsibility for your own health and well-being and answer the call of your own body mind's Pelvis Wellness.

About Lori

Lori Zeltwanger, PT is a licensed physical therapist and owner of Advanced Release Therapy in Sedona, AZ, specializing in pain release and Pelvis Wellness treatments and retreats.

Lori has mastered the ability to assess and listen to your body's needs during each treatment. She gently and gracefully facilitates the letting go of physical, emotional and energetic restrictions that you no longer need and nurtures the emergence of your potential, helping you to release your pain on many levels, giving you your life back.

Lori attended Purdue and Indiana Universities and completed manual therapy studies in the Netherlands. She has participated in extensive continuing education training. She has been a leader in Myofascial Release for over 20 years, training therapists internationally and treating thousands of patients in chronic pain and is considered to be one of the leading myofascial release therapists in the world facilitating healthy change in many lives. She masterfully applies her therapeutic art facilitating thousands of individuals on their path to pain release and greater well-being through her divinely designed Pelvis Wellness Retreats and individualized Myofascial Intensive Pain Release treatment programs.

In her Z-way training programs, Lori is Creating Masters of Myofascial Release, guiding therapists to develop competence and confidence in their own skills. Her teachings honor the John F. Barnes' principles to myofascial release while flowing from a feminine perspective in combination with principles from the Learning Love Institute as applied to hands on healing. She offers training programs in a whole different way to refine therapist's skill levels by focusing on their individual strengths, helping them discover their own unique essence and take care of themselves while they work so they can have long lasting careers. Z-way Trainings are not about doing it her way but instead she helps the therapist find their own way to enhance results and be the best they can be. She conducts her live training programs in seminar settings around the USA and in a clinical setting in Sedona, AZ called the CSI program.

Lori helped to establish Therapy on The Rocks and was the Director of the Western Myofascial Release Treatment Center for 8 years, and Consultant and Instructor of the John F. Barnes' Myofascial Release Seminars for 14 years, co-creating and instructing the Myofascial Healing Seminars. She has created and taught internationally a range of seminars, which has instructed thousands of professional therapists on their path to becoming compassionate and empowered practitioners in their fields of expertise.

Lori taught the myofascial release program at the Northern Arizona Massage Therapy Institute in Sedona, and the Live Without Pain program at Los Abrigados Resort and Spa.

She is the author of the books, *Pelvis Wellness* and *Creating Masters of Myofascial Release* and producer of online training programs for the therapist and the patient.

AdvancedReleaseTherapy.com
PelvisWellness.com

CHAPTER 9

PREPARE TO BE HEARD BY MILLIONS!

BY AMETHYST WYLDFYRE

I'm Amethyst Wyldfyre and I've enjoyed a life of magic, money, miracles and the blessing of being Heard by Millions for the last decade since I "Answered the Call" from my Spirit to leap in to a bigger life than I ever could have imagined for myself.

I used to be a real estate developer and was in a partnership with an older man who was more of a "father figure" to me than a real partner. He "held the purse strings" in the relationship and even though I was a partner on paper I never felt like I had any capacity to have control over my financial destiny. Not only did I feel held hostage in the business financially, but I also spent 18 years under the onslaught of almost daily sexual innuendo and inappropriate advances which I kept my mouth shut about because I was too frightened to rock the boat and get cut off. Even though I never succumbed to his advances I didn't have a lot of self-confidence, nor did I have the courage to leave.

At home, I was married to a man who made less money than I did and contributed significantly less in commitment, energy, and support to the marriage. I was more of a mother to him than a spouse. When I became a mother myself it became exhausting and unsustainable to be mothering a full-grown man too. Eventually it became clear that something needed to shift. By the end of 2002, I finalized my divorce from my first husband

and realized pretty quickly thereafter that I needed to "divorce" my business partner too. I was a single mom – I had the mortgage to pay and a small boy to raise and all the "liquid cash" went to my ex in the divorce (around $100,000).

Simultaneously I was having my own spiritual awakening. I was "RECEIVING THE CALL" from Spirit to do something more with my life. My divorce was final in October 2002 and by December, I knew I needed to get out of my business relationship or I was quite literally going to die. I felt that to the core of my being.

Was I freaked out about walking away from a guaranteed $50,000 a year income? ABSOLUTELY.

Was I questioning how the heck I was going to pay the mortgage and support my son without a paycheck? UM…. YEAH!!

Was I faced with a ton of resistance from my family (especially my mom) who thought I had to be LOSING MY MIND to leave behind a predictable income? OH, DON'T YOU KNOW IT!

Was I wondering if I was indeed crazy to believe that "Spirit" was actually speaking to me? YES INDEEDY!

Well here I am 11 years later, still being guided by Spirit. For two years I cultivated my connection with Source, discovering parts of myself that I never knew existed. My author, performer, artist and healer all came on line to be expressed. I've written five books of my own and been a contributing author in seven Amazon.com bestselling books including two that went to the top internationally. I created an award winning Crystal Singing Bowl Healing CD. I've been juried as an artist, photographer and jeweler. I owned an art gallery and healing art center for two years. I produced a street festival two years in a row that brought over 6500 people to the heart of my city. As a speaker with almost 400 "virtual" and live engagements on the books, I have directly participated in the healing of millions of people around the world and I hosted my own radio show for over a year that reached a global audience.

I answered the call of Spirit and have prospered. I, my family and my world have prospered because I have been able to see and take action and boldly step forward into my destiny.

Since 2009 I have been serving a global clientele of leading visionary entrepreneurs with my virtual speaking business and I generated over $750,000.00 in revenues in only four years in my PAJAMAS, working from home and raising my son as a single mom.

Here's what I know about Answering the Call…..

The call is a stirring that is coming from your own heart, your soul, your core essence. It is the you that you are becoming beckoning you forward. It's the hand of your destiny, of your future self, reaching back through time to the present moment to bring you out of your shell and into the embodiment of your dreaming.

The call is the prayers of the people who have the problem that you personally were uniquely designed to solve. Those prayers are going out into the universe all the time – and they set up a force field that is signaling you, signaling your heart, sending the call.

You have probably been praying for a solution to your own challenges and problems. Right now you are receiving the answer because Spirit answers your prayers through people: writers, authors, speakers, coaches, trainers, who deliver messages of hope, inspiration and transformation. Spirit answers your prayers through books, audios, videos, movies, TV shows, live events, and of course, through "signs" like a hawk flying overhead or a fox crossing your path or a coin at your feet.

The call requires that you become a messenger, someone who is here with a message of hope, empowerment, triumph over tragedy, inspiration, uplift or transformation. You don't need to be "airy faerie" to be a messenger and your message doesn't necessarily have to have a "spiritual tone" to it either, although in my case that has been true. I believe that all truly impactful messages are coming from a spiritual place and your connection to your own personal source of inspiration, hope, encouragement and faith is the solid ground upon which you need to stand to be able to bring a message to millions of people.

Answering the call requires that you step into a leadership role. Answering the call requires that you are willing to share your message, be heard by millions, serve with abandon, attract and lead others, and prosper too. Lisa Sasevich, one of the featured authors of this book, was a client of mine. Here's what she said about that experience:

"True Leadership stems from the willingness to ask for help and that's what I did myself a little more than a year ago when I reached out after hearing from Source to see if Amethyst Wyldfyre could assist me. Let me tell you, it was one of the most powerful decisions that I have made on my journey! Working with Amethyst was a "soul opening" experience - one that opened me up to step into my leadership role in a more powerful and free way. Being firmly grounded in my power was key to being able to DOUBLE My seven Figure Business last year! If you are ready to leap FEARLESSLY into your highest level of service and profit handsomely from following your Spiritual Path, then I recommend you speak with Amethyst right away!"

What does it take to Be Heard By Millions? When you first Answer the Call you might be confused and unclear! The call is undeniable but you aren't exactly sure how you are going to respond and deliver. How will you get your message out, your work, your unique gifts and to whom? How will you make money doing this? These are all very important and valid questions.

Here are the seven steps that I've discovered that have become my Crystal Bridge to Clarity Solution™ to help you leave behind the fog of confusion and discover your crystal clear message so that you can answer the call of the people who are praying for the solution you came here to deliver and cash in on your calling too!

C – Clear your Connection to Your Source of Inspiration – This is the most important step. When you have consciously chosen to clear your fear and open the channels to your Creator (God, Goddess, Universe, Source, Spirit) you will begin the journey to greater clarity, confidence and courage in sharing your message with millions, because you'll be aware of the fact that the message is meant to come through you. Your only real job is to keep that channel clear and that connection strong!

R – Review Your Journey – Your stories of origin are powerful tools for transmitting your message and blessing. They are also a major component in connecting with your audience. The more willing you are to glean the lessons and gifts from your journey and share them with the world, the more powerfully you'll be able to touch hearts AND open wallets!

Y – Your Heart's Yearning – Get in touch with your own heart and how it yearns to express all the goodness, love and light you were uniquely born to deliver. People respond to emotional connection much more readily than they do to intellectual lecturing and tactics. You might not remember all the nuts and bolts of what I'm teaching in this writing later, but you will remember the parts of my story that you resonate with and can connect to emotionally. I need to be in touch with my heart in order to touch yours!

S – Skillsets to Serve – Throughout your journey you have acquired a very specific skillset as a result of all the choices you made about employment and education. These skills and talents are meant to serve you as a messenger. Re-acquainting yourself with all that you know and have experienced that's been of tangible value in the marketplace will enhance your ability to have a clear and powerful message. Your skillsets also provide credibility allowing your message to be received well by your audience.

T – Transformation that you Offer - When you pull it all together – the review of your life, your heart's yearning, the skillsets to serve – you discover that not only are you here to deliver your message to millions, but as a result of answering the call and sharing your message you are also offering transformation to the people who choose to receive from you. Take the time to collect and share the testimonials of the people who have been transformed as a result of your work and then share those too – just like I did with Lisa's words above.

A – Align with Your Audience – Here's where it gets good! Your audience has actually been praying for you – they are the folks who sent out "The Call" that you are now answering! You want to be meeting them where they are at – are they online, at live events, in corporations? Do they belong to associations? Align with where they are so you can connect them to the bridge you offer that's the shortcut to where they want to go!

L – Let's Talk About Money. Getting your message out to millions absolutely requires that you are willing, ready and able to generate money – and lots of it! Be in 'right relationship' with money and have the right mindset and training to sell yourself and your services. Getting the money relationship right is often a big challenge for "heart centered" entrepreneurs and visionaries and was something that I had to overcome too – I just wanted to share my message and assumed that people would line up to pay me. I discovered instead that I had some serious resistance to receiving and valuing myself (remember that old business partner???) that needed to be cleared before I could really connect my calling to my cash flow in a positive and profitable way.

When Answering the Call we all need help and guidance. We were put here to support each other – clients can even become mentors, just like what happened with Lisa and I. Remember to say YES to yourself when it comes time to get support.

Invest in yourself and Prepare to Be Heard By Millions because you really are worth it!

About Amethyst

Amethyst Wyldfyre, The Empowered Messenger Master Mentor is an internationally-known spiritual leader and transformation artist who specializes in helping visionary entrepreneurs who want to expand their reach to serve and be heard by millions of people around the world.

Amethyst is:

- A multiple award-winning life-long serial entrepreneur.

- An author of five books and contributing author in 7 bestselling books including 2 international best sellers.

- A speaker on hundreds of virtual stages around the globe as well as a live speaker and enthusiastic emcee.

- An owner of a multi six-figure business built in less than three years – mostly in her pajamas!

- A blogger with articles featured in the *Huffington Post* and *Inspire Me Today.*

- A media personality with appearances on TV, Radio and in print, including CNBC in the Bay Area and the *Boston Globe.*

Amethyst's client list includes NY Times Best-Selling Authors, Hay House Radio Show hosts, and an array of international thought leaders in a variety of fields including personal growth, executive recruiting, sales and marketing, health and wellness, finance, government and adult education.

Her signature program *Be Heard By Millions Virtual Speaking Business Builders Bootcamp™* is designed to serve the empowerment of global messengers of change. She also has a full suite of homestudy courses available for the online learner. Amethyst believes that when people everywhere (and especially women!) feel clear speaking their truth, confident asking for money and prepared internally and practically to be seen and heard, then the world will naturally change for the better.

Prior to her journey into the realm of personal and professional empowerment, Amethyst was active in Real Estate Development and Community Management Consulting and worked as a consultant with the US Agency for International Development, the World Bank, the Department of Housing and Urban Development and several Fortune 500 builder/developers. Active in her community – Amethyst has served in many volunteer leadership positions and been an avid supporter of the arts for years.

Discover more about being an Empowered Messenger, Answering the Call and how Amethyst can serve you on the path to the top of your own "Messenger Mountain" by visiting her site at:

http://www.theempoweredmessenger.com/CALLGifts
Or by phone at: 603-557-9633.

CHAPTER 10

THE SOCIAL MEDIA PHOENIX — SOARING FROM ASHES TO BLAZING SUCCESS

BY ERIN TILLOTSON

Sent! The last corporate correspondence I'll ever send, my letter of resignation, done. Never looking back. As I head home to my beautiful newborn baby girl it sets in, this part time business has to kick it up a notch. You know those things I do on nights and weekends that I love, my true mission? Yep that one! It's time to focus.

Now this single mom has a lot on the line. I have just quit my job, cold turkey, no turning back. Not a ton of money in the bank account or rich relatives to save the day. To add a second layer of urgency only three months prior I was diagnosed with cervical cancer. No denial, no hiding it anymore, something had to be done and quickly. Finally, and most importantly we have my new baby girl, the center of my world, my pride and joy...this has to work!

Just the thought of another J-O-B makes me sick to my stomach, plus I made a terrible employee anyways. My fast-paced nature, my get-it-done-now mentality coupled with my very stubborn drive for the highest success possible didn't sit well in corporate America. After beating deadline after deadline... to only be rewarded with more work on my desk. No light at the end of the tunnel, just more work, or at least that's how my brain interpreted it. I needed more, my creative brain had been collecting cobwebs and I was just downright bored.

> Now that's all behind me! Freedom, motherhood,
> entrepreneurship and creativity – here I come!

I had the commitment to make it happen, to make this business thrive. I also had some pretty big complications trying to stand in my way. I asked myself, "How can I build this part time business of mine quickly so I can support my daughter and myself? And spend all the time I need and want with her while dealing with this cancer crap?" Suddenly the pressure kicks in. The realization hits me. Here's what I knew: I have to have a sustainable business and I must sustain a flexible schedule.

The solution didn't come to me overnight, it actually took me about six months to nail down what would actually work for me. I found myself pondering, "How can I attract new prospects on an ongoing basis when I'm personally not available?" This was the hurdle, and I stumbled over it time and time again.

I tried local networking groups, nice folks and, of course, had a fabulous time. Despite my gifts of being social online, I was not the best face to face. Now I'm awesome at what I do, but let's face it, I'm a computer geek. My shy, introverted personality isn't my best marketing tool. I tried cold calling, yes I know – awful. But hey, I came from corporate, had to give it shot.

I put money, and a good amount of money, into traditional advertising. You know: newspapers, TV ads, all those things I personally ignore on a daily basis. *What was I thinking?* If I don't pay attention to those things, …the in person networking, the cold calling, the TV ads, then neither will my ideal clients. There it was, my light bulb moment.

I grabbed a notebook, yes they're scattered all over my home for these special moments. I begin to scribble questions furiously so I don't forget. What do my ideal clients pay attention to? Where are they talking online? What organizations are they a member of? What books, magazines and blogs do they read regularly? What are my clients' other professional interests? I'm sure you can see where this is going. I wrote for about an hour, just getting it all on paper and out of my head.

After this open journaling session, I started to use the knowledge wrapped up in my head on my blog. They inspired posts for my social networks and content collaboration with other experts. The dots started to connect. By providing helpful content on all the various networks, I was creating a beacon for my business. I started to look for hot, trending topics and created content around them as well. When entrepreneurs would search the web for these trending topics, guess who came up in the search? Yours truly! Wow, that's powerful. Things started happening.

The next phase came at a vital time in my health saga. I needed to be away at doctors appointments and save energy for those precious play dates with my daughter. More time in a day, that sounded like a good fit. How can I make that happen? I added scheduled posts, content I could work on when I had time, and drip feed them to my network while I wasn't personally available. The most amazing thing started to happen.

While I was away, out of office, away from my computer, nowhere near a phone…my business was collecting laser-targeted leads. Filling my company with folks that trusted my expertise, and who came to me when they needed help with social media marketing and they thought of me when someone needed a referral. My lead nurturing system would walk entrepreneurs along a specific path, guiding them through each step and showing them the way to social success. My calendar started to book itself thanks to the amazing power of technology and automation.

As things started to grow, I craved consistency and templates. I began to document the various campaigns I tested. What post schedule worked best? What activities drive the biggest awareness to an event? What questions attract the most engagement? As I began to document these activities, my plug-and-play processes were born.

So based on what I've learned, tested and put into action time and time again, here are the five steps to achieving real, tangible social media success for your company:

1) First step, your *awesome free goodie*. This is something special you offer your prospects in exchange for their primary contact information. This is the piece that invites your visitors to come one step closer to working with you, to join your company's mailing list in some fashion. Here are a few examples of gifts that work very well:

- A video series; these can be delivered over time so you keep delivering support right to their inbox.

- A live training call; they join you live for a training on a scheduled date and time.

- A free report; this can be a guide, easy steps to get something done or maybe mistakes to avoid.

No matter the gift you give, make it your best content. If you give away something powerful that adds value to their life, then the interest in working with your company starts to build.

2) Your follow up is the second step. You must guide your newest prospects along a clear path with your pre-designed sequence, often referred to as autoresponders. This includes the delivery of your free goodie and following up to ensure they consume the information. Successful nurture campaigns end with an irresistible offer they can't get anywhere else. How can you provide deeper support? The final step, the call to action, needs to match the work they've just done. Think through your offers and find the perfect fit.

3) Third step is vital, without this piece you will *not* experience social media success. The top two reasons social media posts drive traffic is variety and consistency. You want to spread the love, with your content and build your list, with irresistible invitations. With all the hustle and bustle going on inside social media there are key posts that convert much higher than others. You must create a schedule to stay consistent and plan ahead. Remember every posts matters. One bad, or not thought out post, can result in a decreased reach for your company that you can't get back.

Your schedule can include a variety of these time-tested posts that convert:

- Image posts can vary from quotes, to teaching points, infographics, screenshots and even stats. Image posts generate two times more engagement, so don't leave them out.

- Ask questions, get to know your audience better, have fun, ask their opinion on a trending topic and get their input on an upcoming project. Keep them short and seek one-word answers to get a ton of engagement. Getting your audience involved in the outcome will lead to more sales when it's finalized.

- Invitation posts, these by far are the most critical. They take the most time to strategically plan and must be written correctly or will repeal your audience. Keep in mind you want to come from the mindset of inviting them to something great. You also don't want to over promote. There's a common rule of thumb to keep in mind as use as guideline:

80/10/10

Content/Personal/Promotion

4) Measuring for success, step four. If you don't know what's working and what's not you have zero room for improvement for bigger, faster growth. Let's talk about a few of the key metrics you need to know to remain successful:

- What conversions are you looking for?
- Are you looking to boost your online authority with a large social network?
- Is your company looking to really build your prospect list?
- What sales are you looking to come from your social efforts?
- Are you looking for more traffic?
- Place tangible results behind these goals, what specific numbers do you want to see?

There are a million ways to track conversions. There a few ways you can easily start tracking now, let's get started there. Web traffic, you can install Google Analytics on your website and see where your traffic is coming from and how you're improving each month. To track your social network growth you can use a tool like SproutSocial. You're looking for how much your network grows on a monthly basis. If you see a big boost in your numbers dig into your actions from that month so you can duplicate the success. To track lead and sales conversations, set up an affiliate account that will be used exclusively for social media posts. This will allow you to see how many clicks, opt-ins and sales come from your social media work. Watch these numbers every month to track your return on investment (ROI).

5) The final step, your ongoing goodies. This is one of the most powerful ways to stay top of mind with your prospects and clients. Too often I see businesses hit the ground running and pull in an amazing amount of new leads, and then the energy drops. The key to long-term success with the leads generated from social media is: stay in touch with them. Keep sharing helpful information, which now this doesn't equal a ton of work for you. It's as easy as sending an ezine regularly. You can throw in some live training calls, where of course you can offer an upsell. As you write new blog posts or create new resources, share them with your email subscribers. You want to keep the connection going, so when the time is right for them, you're right there and ready.

No matter what comes up in life your business can succeed. Your marketing can continue to attract new prospects – even in the midst of crazy life challenges...they love to pop up and test our commitment. This marketing avenue gives you the time you need, crave and desire outside the office!

About Erin

Growing up in a family of entrepreneurs and blanketed with technology, to Erin Tillotson, social media is her natural language.

Erin's vision is simple: to craft an extraordinary social media experience so powerful your company becomes completely irresistible to your clients and prospects!

An experienced professional, Erin began her marketing career in 2006 working with speakers, authors and experts, providing them with a unique method of online marketing.

Known as The Social Media Phoenix, Erin challenges the common misconception that companies should hold back the problems and obstacles they have overcome on the way to success. Those problems are the raw beauty a business MUST show the world. Not only are they the elements that have made the company successful, they are often the very things that clients and prospects need to hear to lift them into action. Erin's buzz-building business strategies all gravitate around her two core beliefs; *competition is non-existent* and *driving a deeper connection with online prospects is key.* These two elements are vital ingredients in this new digital age.

Recognizing that online marketing is ever changing, Erin dedicates herself to staying abreast of the latest and best technology and systems for online marketing success. Holding dozens of certifications in social media, online events and online marketing she has the rare ability to create personalized marketing experiences for her clients and their customers. These are proven strategies that can be used again and again to replicate success year after year.

Erin supports local business groups, online summits and national business associations as a speaker and teacher of social media marketing. She provides marketing strategies that attract targeted prospects for businesses that build online authority and increase revenue.

Her clientele ranges from small businesses and solopreneurs to Inc. 500 companies. In addition, Erin has been recognized as one of America's PremierExperts™ and has been quoted in SEO-News, NBC's affiliate KSL, and Writers Talk. She co-authored *Facebook for Business* and was featured in *Virtual Entrepreneurship.* Erin lives and works in Tennessee's beautiful Upper Cumberland Plateau.

You can connect with Erin at:
ErinTillotson.com
www.twitter.com/ErinTillotson
www.facebook.com/Erin.Tillotson

CHAPTER 11

HOW TO BE MESMERIZING ON VIDEO — HOW TO DO IT AND WHY IT MATTERS

BY DIA NORTH, VIDEO PRODUCER

I've always been a performer. At the age of 3 my mother enrolled me at the Tony Marchetti School of Dance, and by age 5, I was on-stage with Anna Maria Alberghetti in five sold-out performances of the popular opera **Madame Butterfly**. I played *Trouble*, the blond 3-year-old child of the two lead characters. Although *Trouble* is a non-singing, non-speaking role, there's a significant amount of acting required. I loved it.

But does that mean I'm a natural performer in all media? Quite the contrary.

In fact, being onstage in front of thousands of people is not great preparation for being on the world stage, because today that stage is video, and video is unlike any other performance.

Learning how to mesmerize an audience on video is an essential skill in the 21st century. The most effective and least expensive way to sell anything – including your business's products, services, or ideas – is for

YOU to be known as a celebrity. And that means more than just being "good" on video. You must learn how to create visual magic.

As luck would have it, being great on video is actually quite simple: Learn a set of specific skills and practice them, so that you can use them naturally in front of the camera.

This chapter is about what separates the very best from everyone else, and how you too can be mesmerizing on video.

WHY YOU MUST LOOK GREAT ON VIDEO

As a video producer, I have produced almost 1,000 professional online videos for Fortune 500 clients including Chevron, Autodesk, Sheraton Hotels, and superstars in medical research, clean technology, nonprofits and The Arts. I have filmed literally thousands of interviews and I know the qualities and skills that make people appear to be much more attractive and authoritative on-screen.

What is that "it" quality that sets those special people apart? They are not always the best looking, yet they have that "special something" that makes viewers take notice and stay engaged long enough to hear, and act on, the message.

Knowing how to do this is the most important thing you can do to bolster your career, grow your business, and increase revenue.

Through online acting YOU are the personality – the "face and voice" of your business. You make technical information more interesting, and bring products and ideas to life! Nothing could be more important in this age of celebrity influence. The future of your business literally depends upon learning these skills.

TERRIFIED

People are fascinated by my job as a professional video producer. They say they know they should be doing video – that they HAVE to make a video for their website – but they don't know how to get started. Or worse, they're afraid of how they will appear on video.

I understand.

When I was in corporate life before attending film school, I ran a successful seminar program for my employer, Xerox Corporation. I was a confident public speaker, so I jumped at the chance to be interviewed on television. I wrote the script and practiced for days, bought a special outfit for the event and showed up more than an hour early for the video shoot, relaxing and joking with the crew before the interview.

Finally, we were ready to begin and the director asked for "quiet on the set." Perfect silence descended on the room. I took a deep breath and stared at that unblinking hunk of metal – its huge lens an unforgiving eye whose sole purpose was to capture all my flaws – close up! I froze, and then did the only logical thing.

I fainted.

VIDEO IS UNIQUE

As I learned that day, appearing on video is unlike any other presentation you will ever give, and because it is unique, it has its own special rules and skill set.

When you give a live presentation, your audience is engaged in the moment, feeding off the excitement of the crowd as well as your speech. And they have a choice about where to look – at PowerPoint slides, anywhere else on stage, at other audience members, or more likely their cell phone!

In addition, you are physically far from the audience – sometimes many hundreds of feet – so things like intention and subtle gestures aren't as visible. Not true with video where you are likely to be seen from the waist up (or closer) and your performance is just 12-24 inches from the viewer's eyes. In other words, there are no distractions.

THE CAMERA LIES

Another difference is created by the video camera itself. It sees much differently than the human eye. For one thing, our 3-dimensional world is compressed into 2 dimensions, and colors change under artificial lighting and may clash with other colors or skin tones.

Make-up colors must match the skin and be well blended because the camera will pick up irregularities. Close patterns on clothing can appear as optical illusions.

Once you understand how the camera "sees," you can use this natural camera distortion to your advantage.

HOW TO DIRECT THEIR GAZE
AND HOLD THEIR ATTENTION

In film school I learned to "see like a camera, and hear like a microphone." This secret gives me information to direct the viewer's gaze and hold their attention.

Professional filmmakers tell viewers what to pay attention to by what we include inside the video frame, and how we make it appear.

SMILE! YOU'RE ON CANDID CAMERA

A warm, genuine smile is the single most important thing you can do for yourself and your viewer. Smiling (even faking it) will make you feel more confident, but you do not want to fake a smile in a video presentation because your viewers will subconsciously be turned off. Evolution has trained us to spot a fake smile so that we can determine friend from foe, and truth from deceit.

HOW TO CREATE A REAL SMILE

We're programmed to know a real smile from a fake, and we use those instincts when we're asked to trust someone – like a person asking for our business in a video.

The difference between real and fake smiles is about eyes and timing. Real smiles cause us to crinkle up our eyes, and the length of the smile is not fixed in time. Eyes don't "smile" with fake smiles, and we can hold them for as long as we need to.

The secret to creating a winning on-camera smile is to find something to genuinely smile about. These tips will help:

- Sleep well the night before being filmed and get centered in your body with a walk or bit of exercise before going on-camera.

- Be genuinely happy and excited about what you are presenting. (If you are not excited, your audience certainly won't be!)

- Just before the record button is pressed, think about someone or something that you care about that makes you happy. Imagine a picture of them and dedicate your presentation to them.

- Then take a huge deep breath and start to smile slowly on exhale. Smiling helps to naturally lift your face for a more youthful appearance, and the deep breath helps relax and balance your shoulders, and reduce tension in your face and jawline.

EYE CONTACT

Humans have relied for thousands of years on looking into someone's eyes to understand how the other person is feeling and whether or not they are telling the truth. The cold staring eye of the video camera lens can be unsettling. Unlike a real person, it doesn't blink, smile, or give you encouraging feedback.

Actors and TV presenters are trained to deal with this, but most people unfamiliar with video come across very differently on camera than they do in person.

HOW TO WIN EYE-TO-EYE COMBAT
WITH THE VIDEO CAMERA

I often hear from clients who are new to it that they don't like how they appear on video. They say they feel "awkward" or like they're "talking to themselves." I get it. It can feel artificial talking to a machine that has a cold, staring eye.

The first thing to know is that it's natural to feel uneasy because being filmed is not the same as having a person-to-person conversation or even presenting in front of a live audience. You can learn to feel comfortable, and that's important because when you present to a camera framed in a medium to close-up shot, the viewer can see every nuance in your eyes and facial expressions.

I discovered a mindset that solves this problem: Imagine the camera as a person (or a beloved pet) who simply adores you. There is nothing you can do wrong in their eyes, no matter how many times you stumble over words or make mistakes.

The camera is the best listener you've ever had – patient and riveted on your every word. It also doesn't interrupt, and never gets bored or makes you wrong. In fact, the camera is your friend whose only job is to capture your thoughts, words, and actions <u>unconditionally</u>.

"HOW" TRUMPS "WHAT"

How you say it (and how you look saying it) is often more important than what you say on video. Empathize with your audience to create natural rapport with them. Imagine how they will feel about the message you are presenting. Get emotionally involved in your subject matter and "feel" the words so that your facial expressions match your message.

Smile with your whole face – especially your eyes – and "soften" your gaze as if you were looking at a dear friend. Look directly into the center of the camera lens and imagine you are looking into your friend's eyes.

SPEAK WITH YOUR HANDS

The camera will exaggerate any movement you perform in a close frame. Keep your head relatively still and relaxed, and your gestures "specific" to highlight your key points and avoid unnecessary movement.

For example if you are making a call-to-action you could gesture towards the camera, or while telling a story about your own experience, lightly touch just below your neck. Make sure you don't bump your lavaliere microphone!

Bonus: Studies show that if you use hand gestures while rehearsing, you're more likely to remember the message as well.

INFLUENTIAL BODY LANGUAGE

To persuade people to get excited and quickly take action:

- Be animated, upbeat and eager in your video presentation
- Lean forward
- Speak a little faster than usual

Plan gestures and emotions ahead of time, and rehearse words and actions together to feel more natural while you are presenting to camera.

DO YOU NEED MAKEUP? YES!

Both men and women need grooming to correct distortions caused by the camera lens and lighting.

Men must be immaculately groomed with a good haircut, shave, and facial hair trimming. Consider having eyebrows professionally shaped. Shine accentuates imperfections, so lightly apply translucent powder or gel "mattifier" to shiny spots on your face and head. Use a natural, not glossy, clear lip balm.

For women, exfoliate and moisturize your face and use a foundation that matches your skin. Since the camera and lights wash out features, pay special attention to making up your eyes with eyeliner and mascara.

What you wear has a big impact on how you will be perceived by your audience, so dress a little better than your best client. And since the camera makes people look bigger than they really are, women look best in tailored shirts and jackets with collars, rather than sleeveless outfits, very short skirts, or low necklines.

VIDEO ISN'T "NORMAL"

Looking "natural" on video doesn't mean acting "normal." If you think about "relaxing," you may talk slower, lean back in your chair, and be low-energy – all things that do not communicate well on video. Instead, think about being "alert" to psychologically prepare yourself to genuinely "show up" in the video. Here are some easy ways to counteract camera distortion:

1. Make hand gestures higher than normal – at chest level.

2. Hold props within the camera frame between chest and face height. (Make sure we can see your face!)

3. Match the pace of your favorite TV commercials. Long pauses or slow speaking can frustrate your viewer.

4. Learn to communicate with your eyes, because the camera captures every nuance, twitch, and eye sparkle. You can do this by feeling comfortable about what you're going to say and putting your "heart" into the message.

5. Keep your head and chin level.

6. Hold a mental image of being "alert" rather than "relaxed."

7. Use gestures sparingly and "on-purpose" to avoid the appearance of fidgeting.

8. Don't touch your face or move your hands in your lap.

9. When seated, avoid swiveling or rocking in your chair.

10. When standing, don't rock side-to-side or shift body weight.

LEARN YOUR LINES

The biggest cause of fear and looking like a "deer in the headlights" is not knowing your content well. Make sure this doesn't happen by writing a script that sounds like you and communicates what you want to say, and then practice gestures and intonation along with the words.

How to know if you've practiced enough? When you can start from any point in the script and not get lost, you're ready.

WARM UP

Prior to the interview, warm up your vocal chords by humming or having a light conversation with your video producer, a crewmember, or friend. Warm up your face and jaw muscles by intentionally yawning or fake smiling as wide as you can. Warm up your eyes by opening them very wide, then squeezing them shut a few times. Gentle neck rolls and shoulder shrugs dissolve tension.

HAVE FUN!

Have fun in front of the camera. It will help you look natural and free of tension. Chances are great that if you're having fun, so will your viewer.

DO-IT-YOURSELF VIDEO

The tips in this chapter will help whether you are being interviewed for online or broadcast television, or appearing in a video about your company's products or services.

You can also star in your own do-it-yourself videos for distribution on your website, social media or YouTube channel. DIY video enables you to make many more videos cost-effectively than if you had to hire a video production team or videographer each time. It also gives you control and access to video production when you are ready to do it.

One of the easiest types of video to produce is a Video Blog (also called VLOGs). Video Blogs are short videos that explain your product, service, or idea one "bite" at a time – to introduce viewers to your company or brand, and of course to YOU.

Video Blogs can establish you as an expert in your field, and provide valuable information (for free) to your prospective audience. Your goal is to have them asking for more!

You can be making DIY (do-it-yourself) video at a quality level well above the normal YouTube movie in just a few weeks with my **DIY Video Secrets** online training system.

About Dia

Dia is the creator of *DIY Video Secrets*, the popular do-it-yourself video system that teaches savvy entrepreneurs how to make professional-looking videos for websites and social media. DIY Video Secrets is a simple and pragmatic way for the do-it-yourselfer to learn how to make a video with essential skills like camera selection and settings, scriptwriting, and editing. With DIY Video Secrets, savvy entrepreneurs learn how to make great-looking business videos in no time, including YouTube videos and video blogs, while looking great on-camera.

Dia's video production company, Dia North Productions, has produced nearly 1,000 online videos for Fortune 500 companies including Chevron, Sheraton Hotels, Autodesk, and nonprofits for medical research, clean technology, and The Arts.

The Smart Spot (Conari Press, 2003), Dia's book about intuitive business decision-making, won an IPPY award, and her video, "Dream," was featured at the Apple Digital Film Review in San Francisco.

Dia's story of business success is featured in *Great from the Start,* John B. Montgomery's book about conscious business leadership in Silicon Valley. Her entrepreneurial success is the subject of a case study in the textbook *Women in Business: Shattering the Glass Ceiling* by Hope Gale.

Dia is on the Education Team for BNI by the Bay in Northern California, and is a member of the American Association of University Women. She is a supporter of the historic Smith Rafael Theatre Preservation and a long-standing member of the California Film Institute. She has been a guest on *Pacific Venture Club,* a Chamber of Commerce Internet television program.

Contact Dia: Dia@DIYVideoSecrets.com.

Learn more about *DIY Video Secrets: Do-It-Yourself Video for Savvy Entrepreneurs* at www.DIYVideoSecrets.com.

View an online portfolio of corporate and nonprofit videos produced by Dia North Productions at: www.DiaNorth.com.

CHAPTER 12

TETHERED TO PAIN

BY ESTHER HATFIELD MILLER

I loved tetherball as a kid. I was short, could jump mightily and lost nearly every game of tetherball in Catholic grade school. I could never beat those tall, lanky, blonde-haired girls but I sure kept on "trying." I was this verbose, stout, black-haired "Jewtina" (Jewish Latin girl) who had chutzpah, the kind of chutzpah that kept me toggling from compliance to innovation that would drive the Catholic nuns bonkers. I had to find out what those other Catholic schoolgirls knew about winning a game of tetherball.

As I watched those giant, skinny, white girls, palming their way to a victory in tetherball, I noticed that sometimes they'd change up their hand procedure. One ball revolution meant their hand position was palm sideways. If they wanted the tetherball to go faster, their palm was nowhere to be seen, it was a closed fisted pounce to the yellow tetherball. If they wanted the tetherball to be out of reach of their undersized opponents (namely me), they used the cocked hand palm version of hitting the tetherball using only the palm area closest to their wrist.

I really wanted to be hailed the winner of morning, lunchtime and afternoon recess tetherball. Most of my Catholic school friends would watch the ball, swirling wildly to reach the top of that 7 foot galvanized steel pole. Not me, I kept my slanted dark brown eyes focused on the tricky hands of my opponent. I figured out, early on, that if I was ever going to win, I needed to be a keen observer of those schoolgirls and learn their **S**trategies, **T**actics & **P**rocesses, the "S T P" (what entrepreneur and brain researcher John Assaraf calls it), to win!

Some 49 years later, I too wanted another big win, but a win in my healing from Clergy Sexual Abuse. But I didn't know how! All the victims I knew were expert in victimhood so I'd never seen a victim of Sexual Abuse survive, let alone thrive. Just like the ball that was tethered to the pole, I was tethered to pain.

By definition 'the free online dictionary' cites a tether as "to fasten or restrict with." So the tether anchors something that's moveable to a fixed point or fixed device. So what's wrong with tethering? We tether astronauts, dogs, balloons and sometimes children. It's for their own safety, right? Wrong, in my case. The frozen, unmovable, untransformed thing that I'd become, <u>kept me tethered to pain</u>; tethered in silence. My daily memory of sexual abuse was the fixed device to keep me tethered to the pain, long after the perpetrator was gone. Having survived the traumatic effects of ritual abuse, coupled with physical acts of sexual abuse as a minor, my life was a train wreck. I was a hot mess, a crazed drama-queen. I was the proverbial emotional volcano, ready to spew the residual pain and agony of soul contaminating my being. I needed a change, a transformation, a new way of life because physical death was knocking at my door, as evidenced by swirling suicidal thoughts.

Early on in grade school, I knew that I had a different way of looking at things. That was confirmed by the Catholic nuns who'd expend their religious superiority making me try to conform, to try and see things just the way they wanted me to see things. By second grade, I had this instinct, this intuition, and this *je ne sais quoi*, about seeing things differently to make new discoveries. OMG, even today I see letters of my name in Tether; if one substitutes the T for an S there I am. Esther= tether, gulp!

The ability to see things differently, or as Emily Dickinson suggests "Dwell in Possibility," was a platform that catapulted me to *Answer the Call*, the transformational Call. If, that's a big "IF," I could see what it looked like to be healing, to be transformed from marinating in the pool of pain that I had grown accustomed to, perhaps, I could have an abundant life, a healed life. If, another big "IF," I could have another "win" in healing, then I could teach others what they didn't know.

I don't mean abundant as in money. I had already sued the Catholic Church, received an abundance of cash, so abundance of healing was what I was seeking, not more cash. Heck, all the cash did was afford me more visits to the therapy couch and LOADS of Twinkies for breakfast.

A foundational Jewish trait that I inherited from my ancestors' DNA was that of questioning authority. So in arguing and wrestling with G-d, like any good Jew does, I began to make inquiry, to question. Why me? Why not me? What do I need to do to begin the transformation process? What will I do after I transform? G-d and I were still wrestling, it didn't stop, I didn't stop…I still wanted a transformational "win." But I needed a proven, tested system to follow. Where was the system, the steps, the processes to follow? I knew about emoting, I had a PhD – an advanced degree – in suffering, so I didn't want more of that!

I needed a swift but steady return, an about face. There were only two about faces that I already learned from. One was in Reseda High School Drill Team. I was precise, unwavering and expert in compliance (remember I'd been taught by nuns) when our fierce adult leader, Ms. Dickerson yelled, as an army drill sergeant does, to 'pivot and about face.' The other more recent about face that I had a "win" with, was a "teshuvah" or return to Judaism (which felt more akin to a conversion). It meant intensive studying, an immersion in sacred Hebraic text, traditional religious practices and a two year course with an Orthodox Rabbi. Grueling and fascinating all wrapped-up in one course!.

The wins & lessons gained with Reseda High School Drill Team were the exact things I replicated in my healing. Practice doesn't mean perfection; it means progression. You see, when auditioning to be a member of one of Los Angeles Unified School Districts' elitist Drill Teams, I just went with the flow. I didn't question, I just executed. I didn't need to reinvent the wheel; all that was required of me was to follow the "wins" the well-respected Drill Team already had. I was able to stand on the Drill Team's giant shoulders; you know, those drill teams and cheerleader goddesses that seemingly transform a young girl's hopes and dreams.

So in looking around to figure out the path to healing in order to transform my life, to *answer the transformation call*, I took precise, calculated steps. I learned about these four topics from experts in these fields:

A. Mindset and the brain

B. Mental Rehearsal and the body

C. Trauma Triggers and the soul

D. Silence and Secrecy

I didn't have a clue where to start, but I had great research skills that were fine-tuned when doing my graduate work at University of Southern California. Dr. Wes Burr and Dr. David Hartl contributed to my understanding of how I could transform. I can still hear their voice in Public Administration group project assignments, "Esther, start with what you already know; don't reinvent the wheel." I'd sit there, with that deer-in-the-headlights look, asking myself, what do I already know? I was a jack-of-all trades and definitely a master of none.

I knew stuff; I knew the City of Huntington Beach library hours, the code to my gym locker of 35 years past, the placement of every rubber band in my home. I even can still see the high school chemistry formulas (only if I close my eyes) that I'd write on an index card and tape to my bathroom mirror, that I was forced to share with my two younger sisters.

Soon after reading the first two chapters of Napoleon Hill's book, *Think and Grow Rich*, I started to pull on that thread of inquiry. I knew I was onto something; I didn't even have to finish the entire book. I began seeing a pattern of resolve, a pattern of desire, the same "stick-to-itiveness" drill team pattern of falling down 6, get up 7, falling down 7, get up 8. I had that same thing happening inside of me as Hills' book references of industrial tycoons such as Andrew Carnegie, John D. Rockefeller, Cornelius Vanderbilt, JP Morgan, Thomas Edison, John Jacob Astor and Henry Ford did. They had desire. I too had desire. It wasn't for abundance of wealth though; it was for abundance of healing!

I come from a lineage of inventors. My adoptive grandfather, whom I didn't know, Doc Hatfield, invented and later cheaply sold the patent for his electric blanket. I'd spend some nights or weekends watching my dad tinkering in our attached garage. I'd see him tool and die, even modify his own creations/inventions of tools. When a specific hand tool didn't work just the way he needed it to, he'd bring out the sawzall, the vice grips or the blow torch. He'd hammer away, pound, bend and twist said contraption just until it worked in the most beneficial manner. He wasn't afraid to modify. I was terrified to modify, after all, the Catholic nuns made sure that modifications to anything in life was a mortal AND venal sin!

My DESIRE for transformation overrode anything else. I had money, I had children, I had a paid-for sports car, I had the last of the 4 husbands, I had gorgeous shoes, I had grandchildren (God's generosity of a "do-over") but I didn't have healing from Clergy Sexual Abuse. My full-time job was me. I became a selfie. SELF-ish, SELF-focused, SELF-contained, SELF-relevant. These were attributes needed for me to craft the first step in achieving a healing transformation. I began to eliminate toxic friendships, and cease doing media events that kept me regurgitating my abuse story. I was like a dog that returns to its vomit. I stopped and took notice of me. I learned the power of saying "no." I learned the power of silence. Silence and secrecy are two different things. I stopped talk therapy and sought out a life coach. TED talker, Sophie Chiche, was my life coach angel. I learned from Sophie to use authentic words, instead of lazy words like "AWESOME," "AMAZING" AND "COOL." So I began using words such as "BENEFICIAL," "INSIGHTFUL" AND "USEFUL." These were words that were connected to how I was truly feeling. Words began to match the emerging transforming new version of me. I learned about the brain, emotions and studied experts in marketing, psychology, spirituality – even sales techniques. I had assessed if those types of gurus could sway followers to make a purchase, donate money or time, I could sway, trick or even lie to my own brain to make a shift. To make the biggest transformation in my life required chutzpah; the very thing that was already in my DNA... "Win!"

I learned to stand tall & erect in my truth . After all, that's all I had... my truth – my truth of being a victim of a crime. This was a crime against my body, my mind and especially my soul. Gut wrenching at best, that was difficult to do. I trained my mind, body and soul since those were the areas that were "all jacked-up," to stand up, to be in the stillness of life. I was learning about the power of the silence. I learned how secrecy keeps us victims toxic and sick. I needed to transform from victim, to survivor, and emerge as a thriving being, and I did!

HERE'S THE DEVELOPMENT OF MY HEALING FORMULA:

Healing = start with **Notice** stuff + have fine-tuned **Desire** + be **awake** then **aware**, then get to a **choice to make a decision** and take inspired

action + **learn** from other gurus, experts, giants + **sift and stand** on the giants shoulders + develop **S, T, P** like the military.

That's it. That's all. I began to piece together my healing formula. I learned that if I could have 21 days (3 weeks) of continued success with something like quitting smoking, I could have a new habit. Since I wasn't a smoker; I could learn the **S**trategies, **T**actics & **P**rocesses of habit busting, then apply these to acquire a new habit of healing. I kept racking my brain with how to do this. Then, listening to experts and how they use their genius, the shift happened. I sifted their expert information via products/programs that I purchased, lectures I attended, studying their expertise through my own life's sifting bowl. Out came the stuff I could learn to "untether from my pain" so I could transform.

My favorite singer, Barbra Streisand, sings a Sondheim song, "Putting It Together." Well, I was actually living the lyrics:

"Bit by bit,

Putting it together

Piece by piece,

Only way to make a work of art.

Every moment makes a contribution

Every little detail plays a part.

Having just a vision's no solution,

Everything depends on execution:

Putting it together -

That's what counts!"

Bit by bit, I put it together. I was making a work of art called healing and transformation. Every little detail from the experts, the gurus, the giants, I applied. It's all in me, the vision transformation from victim to survivor to emerge as a thriving being actually happened. That's what counts!

I've ANSWERED THE TRANSFORMATIONAL CALL. Using humor, whimsy and insight, I now mentor Sexual Abuse victims to move from CHAOS to CALM. In this 5-step SELF-HEALING system, they learn how to transform their lives to live a powerful, calm and drama-free life, so they too can no longer be tethered to pain!

I have a new appreciation for tethering; after all, it's a means of connecting one thing to another.

I remain tethered to the gurus, experts & masters who have shared their genius with me. I'm now fastened to healing; healing from the pain that once kept me a victim. Let's stay connected and fasten our healing tetherballs together!

Welcome in and stay connected…www.abusehealed.com.

About Esther

A survivor of clergy sexual abuse, Esther Hatfield Miller, transformed from victim to survivor and emerged as a thriving being, uses her uniquely crafted 5-step heal yourself system in moving from chaos to calm. Esther now teaches others how to do "whoopass healing" on their trauma from Sexual Abuse, Child Neglect, Domestic Violence and Victimization, and to live a powerful, calm and drama-free life!

Educated at the University of Southern California, New Mexico State University, Texas Tech and California State University at Northridge, Esther tweaked and implemented university level strategies, tactics and processes to begin to heal. Esther's personal journey has been featured in media and press events to include: *New York Times, The Wall Street Journal, USA Today, Los Angeles Times, Orange County Register, Huffington Post,* ABC television, Fox News, Univision and Fusion TV direct cable shows, blog talk radio, Clear Channel's KFI radio and many more.

Esther has been actively speaking with media outlets – speaking on behalf of those victims that still haven't found their voice. She has been involved in speakers series at colleges and universities lecturing about the crime of Clergy Sexual Abuse and the process of "grooming." Her continued goal is to raise awareness to prevent future sexual abuse and focus on restorative justice for all victims.

Esther continues advocacy work to stomp out child sexual abuse and to abolish Statutes of Limitations when it comes to crimes committed against humanity. Her multilingual and multicultural advantage allows her to speak to groups both large and small, to encourage others how to "dwell in possibility," and how to heal this crime against the mind, body and soul.

Esther is a grandmother of three, mother of two adult-daughters and wife of one. You can find Esther briskly walking the dog beach in Huntington Beach, California along with her hubby, Bruce and sometimes even with her maltipoo grand-dog, Harry Connick, Jr.!

Stay connected with Esther at:
Esther@whoopasshealing.com
www.twitter.com/EstherMiller1
www.facebook.com/EstherHatfieldMiller

CHAPTER 13

NICE TO FINALLY MEET ME —SELF LEADERSHIP, YOUR GREATEST RESOURCE FOR SUCCESS

BY JOSIE TYTUS, CPC
SUCCESS ALIGNMENT
VISION COACH & MENTOR

Respond to every call that excites your spirit.
~ Rumi

I didn't know whether to hold my breath, exhale, swear, scream or pass out. I go silent. Standing in the middle of my living room, he breaks the news. My husband, the man I chose to spend my life with, announced, 'our marriage was over.' This was the guy who promised we would build a life together, who made me feel safe, who made sure that our family had comforts, who assured me there would be a happily ever after.

All I could remember about what happened next was having this very strong vision of me standing on a very tiny piece of earth that was just big enough to hold me. Everything else fell away. I felt so disoriented and so very alone. No matter what direction I turned, there was only darkness. In that moment, my world and everything that was familiar to me was gone.

Just five months earlier we were on a cruise ship celebrating our twentieth wedding anniversary. What followed were several very difficult and painful years of trying to sort my life out and a chance to meet myself for the first time.

It was during that time, I discovered three of the most profound guiding principles which allowed me to springboard into an extraordinary life.

You've been around long enough to know a little about how the world works. You've likely been through a lot too. You're working hard, you're trying to achieve more, and you're doing your best. Yet, it still doesn't seem like enough. Your breakup could have been a lost job, a car accident, feeling unappreciated or simply feeling unfulfilled.

The three principles I'm going to share with you will help to clear a path to accelerate your success in unimagined ways. Once implemented, life feels good, life flows with ease and nothing, no matter how unexpected, can knock you down. Once I figured these out, I was able to become the entrepreneur I had always dreamed of being.

As you apply these principles, you too can find your voice, gain the confidence and freedom of doing work that energizes you. You will have access to unlimited wealth while making a difference in someone's life. You will be led by a compelling Vision for a life that pulls you forward.

Most people want the dream, but most people won't claim it. Most people *think* they can't, because they are trapped in a runaway life that won't stop — until it does. The paradox is that they box themselves into a 'limited potential' life, then wonder why they're not happy.

Our world is moving at an unprecedented rate. If you don't get that, you're already behind. It's not going to wait for you to catch up.

Today, a regular person can have a global impact. Careers are no longer a lifetime commitment. Education alone no longer guarantees a good income. Family and relationships are no longer just defined as a married man and woman. Communication is instant. We develop friendships with people we've never met. We have more information than we know what to do with. Never before have we had so many options.

We are in a Reinvention Evolution.

Whenever there is this kind of turbulence, there is conflict, chaos and confusion. We're navigating our way into new territory that has yet to be discovered. What we're finding is that the roles we used to play are no longer serving us for the purpose we were trained for. And that can be scary.

It can also be amazing, even if it doesn't seem like it at the time. So how do we navigate our way?

When my marriage ended, I was a stay-at-home mom that had been out of the workforce for five years. I didn't have a 'career' to fall back on. I had to decide how I was going to survive. There came a defining moment when I knew this was my chance to step into *my* life.

I had to do something, anything, to shift my energy. I took courses, joined groups, explored options, read ferociously and talked to experts. It was a lot of hard work and it was a struggle. There were times I just wanted to throw in the towel, sell my house, find a job and settle into the rest of my life quietly without expectations.

But the very thought of that made me feel dead inside. I persevered until all the work I was doing led me to my heart's desire. What sprang up from there was the creation of the 3C FUSION SUCCESS FORMULA™.

CLARITY + CONSCIOUSNESS + CONFIDENCE = SuCCCEss

CLARITY

For as long as I can remember, I struggled with trying to figure out what I was meant to do. I felt that if I could figure that out, everything else would fall into place. The problem was that I could never figure it out. I did all the personality tests, I excavated my skill sets, but the answer kept eluding me.

What I wasn't doing, was taking the time to really figure out what *I* was *meant* to do. I was busy calculating success based on what other people were doing and how society defines success. No one had ever asked me what mattered most to me. The reality was, I was afraid to ask myself.

Since I didn't have the answers, I adopted someone else's version of how to do life.

If you aren't getting the results you want or are feeling unsettled, it's time to have a meeting with yourself. Getting really clear about what you want is the first critical component to having the success you desire. You need to know who you are, what you value and what you want. From that, *create a Vision* that reflects those aspects of you.

Here are 9 powerful questions that can fuel your life with CLARITY:

- What am I doing with my life?
- What do I really want?
- What is most important to me?
- What is going to restore the joy in my life?
- What's stopping me from having that?
- What can I do about it?
- What can I put in place to make it easier, to make it happen, to never again feel the struggle?
- When is it going to be the right time to get going?
- How committed am I?

If your answer to the last question is anything less than 100%, go back and start over or else you will be doomed to repeat life the way it has been. You might as well sign a waiver indicating that you relinquish all potential for a grander life and resign to a life that's some version of what you already have.

Your breakthrough is going to happen the moment you decide to have a bigger, grander VISION for your life, even if you can't see it yet.

CONSCIOUSNESS

Research has shown that we use only 5-7% of our brain's capacity. That's our conscious mind. It's the part we use to have control over our lives. However, we operate from the subconscious mind, the part of our mind that holds our beliefs. Our beliefs are what we adapt as truth, when in fact, the real truth is within us. It's always been there. Getting to the truth is the real work we have to do in order to find the kind of success we talk about having.

Have you ever had the experience where you put on a specific outfit so that you could feel a particular way? Only on this day, it's a little tighter than it used to be. After deliberating, you decide to hold your breath a little more and wear the outfit anyway. Your mind has convinced you that wearing it today is going to get you what you want.

That lasts until you walk out the door. All day long, you're struggling with the feeling of being uncomfortable and hoping that no one notices. You're still hoping that they see the version that was in your mind when you put the outfit on. It doesn't work that way. You can't hide your discomfort, especially from yourself. Now, you can't wait to get home where no one can see you, to strip it off.

This is what we do with our personalities, only the process lasts years. We spend the first part of our development putting on the personality outfit and get by with it for a time. At some point, the personality and what it accomplishes, or not, gets really uncomfortable. This is true whether you have gained financial success or not as you can see in the chart below.

Thoughts / Feelings	Without Financial Wealth	With Financial Wealth
Work hard but do not have what you want	✔	✔
Confused about why things haven't turn out differently	✔	✔
No control over circumstances	✔	✔
Going through the motions day by day	✔	✔
Don't feel appreciated	✔	✔
No one gets (understands) you	✔	✔
Feel isolated	✔	✔
Feel lonely	✔	✔
Feel different than everyone else	✔	✔
Don't recognize yourself	✔	✔
Don't even like yourself	✔	✔
Secretly concerned, maybe there's something wrong with you	✔	✔
Ashamed, you don't have it all figured out by now	✔	✔
Have results, with fulfillment		
Limited results, unfulfilled	✔	
Massive results, unfulfilled		✔

While you may be driven by money to achieve success, it's clear that money does not measure success if you include quality of life in your definition.

To gain that quality of life, to have the wealth you desire and to feel fulfilled by what you do, requires an unlayering of the outfit, the personality, to get to the really good stuff. It's an awakening process that requires peeling away those layers until you get back to the True Self, which is your True Nature. This part of you already knows your unique gifts, talents, passions and purpose. It doesn't just come to you, you must pursue it. When you get there, you'll find comfort, it feels good, and it fits right.

Your purpose is not something that your mind makes up. It's not something that can be dictated or picked for you or demanded of you, as it is when you pursue things you believe make you valuable. Your purpose is already in you.

CONFIDENCE

When you get to the place of knowing who you are and what your unique gifts are, you no longer operate from a place of angst. When you begin to awaken to your own potential, you no longer have competition. When you feed and nurture the gifts you have come to recognize, you are no longer subject to the piercings of critics. When you finally put your footprint in the sand, life opens up to you.

Life from this perspective is rich and juicy and delicious. You begin to soften and strengthen at the same time. You no longer need the approval of others to acknowledge and validate you. You swing the door wide open and put out the welcome mat to receive those that are now finding their way to you.

Your risks are purposeful and unabashed. You live without regret. Problems become an advanced step to pulling you forward, not pushing you down. Failure no longer takes you out of the game, but helps you to write the rules.

It would be hard to argue that Steve Jobs, founder of Apple, has not changed the way we communicate, do business and use technology, even if you don't use Apple products. He left his mark on the world with innovation and technology.

But in my estimation, the real impact, the real gift he left the world was not just the brilliance he exhibited in his masterful creations, but he left us with the gift of seeing what's possible when you believe in yourself, when you recognize and listen to your True Nature, when you uncover and trust your True Purpose – despite what others around you would have you believe. It's an invitation for you to become aware of that something unique in you that is waiting to be expressed. That to me is his legacy as he so beautifully expressed in his commencement address to the 2005 graduating class at Stanford University when he said,

"Your time is limited, so don't waste it living someone else's life. Don't be trapped by dogma – which is living with the results of other people's thinking. Don't let the noise of others opinions drown out your own inner voice. And, most importantly, have the courage to follow your heart and intuition. They somehow already know what you truly want to become. Everything else is secondary."

Identifying, allowing and using the possibilities that are uniquely yours is a sure recipe for CONFIDENCE. No one can give that to you. You have to decide to want it.

CLARITY is of the spirit. It is something you have.

CONSCIOUSNESS is of the mind. It is who you are being.

CONFIDENCE is of the body. It is what you do.

Fusing these three principles together is the very foundation of success.

Having this new understanding, I came to see my life in a whole new light. The reason I was surrounded by the dark was because I wasn't present in my own life. Once the things I identified with were gone, there was nothing left. I later came to see the darkness as space in my life; a space to allow myself to show up. The darkness turned into my drawing board.

And the patch of dirt that I stood on, well, I recognized it as my connection to Source letting me know that I am always supported. I was standing on solid ground.

Success has nothing to do with how your friends, family, boss, colleagues or society measure you by. It has everything to do with who you uniquely are.

Now that you understand the core elements for leading a successful life, keep this in mind along the way.

Take regularly scheduled time to reflect, explore, dream, create, question, learn, discover, and synthesize what you know about your Self.

Speak out loud what is most important to you.

Use your passions as a gauge to know if you're on track.

The first thing you can do to gain positive momentum toward your success is to sit down and come up with four to five things that you can do differently right now. Schedule them and commit to getting them done.

Answering the call is about paying attention to what your life is requiring of you. The successes, the riches, the rewards, the joy and all the happiness you seek are found here. Those who answer the call are awake enough to hear it, are wise enough to recognize it and courageous enough to accept the invitation. The rest will be revealed to you as you pursue it.

It starts with one step, followed by another. Your life is calling.

About Josie

Josie Tytus is a Success Alignment Vision Coach and Mentor.

She is the founder of 3C FUSION where leaders and high achievers go to optimize meaning, passion, success and results in their life. Using the concepts of 3C FUSION SUCCESS COACHING™ as the foundational work, Josie has developed programs and processes to accelerate desired results for the achievement of meaningful success with absolute joy.

Josie's background includes working with top-level executives to the entrepreneur. Her training started at the age of 3 as she witnessed her own family business flourish. Along her career path, she has been able to create jobs that never existed and land management positions in industries she had no previous experience in. But what she did consistently is access jobs to fit her lifestyle and swiftly move into positions of leadership.

Her experience encompasses roles as a Product Category Buyer of a National Catalogue chain, Conference Sales Manager for Corporate Events at a prestigious resort, a Retail Manager of a Flagship store, Expanding the Family Business, Advertising Manager of a Business Periodical, and her biggest role bar none – being a mom.

The really tough work began when her twenty-year marriage ended abruptly. Turning fifty, not having a job or a clue as to what to do next, set her on the voyage of her life to discover what she was truly all about. What she discovered would change the trajectory of her life forever.

She uncovered the path and the systems that would take her out of Conflict, Chaos and Confusion into a life of Clarity, Consciousness and Confidence. That's how 3C FUSION emerged. Now, she guides those who want to live the fulfilled life that welcomes the fullest expression of who they are through Self Leadership.

Josie is a Certified Professional Coach (CPC) trained at the Institute of Professional Excellence in Coaching (iPEC), an NLP Master Practitioner (Neurolinguistic Programming), Energy Leadership Index Master Practitioner (ELI-MP), and Licensed Passion Test Facilitator™.

Josie's mission is to awaken your Vision to what's possible, identify and ignite your passions, and design a powerful life that takes you to your optimal level of meaningful success.

She publishes *Footprints In The Sand™* Success Newsletter filled with articles, strategies, tips and tools to inspire you to create a life that you love while being your complete Self.

You can learn more about Josie Tytus and 3C FUSION at: www.3Cfusion.com.

Walk with purpose ...

The real work of our lives is to become aware. And awakened. To answer the call.

~ Oprah Winfrey

CHAPTER 14

EVER NOTICE HOW OFTEN YOU WORRY ABOUT THE FUTURE AND YOUR PLACE IN IT? — HOW TO JOYOUSLY RE-FRAME AND ARRIVE HEALTHY, WEALTHY AND WISE THROUGH HINTS™

BY JEAN GADDY WILSON

Systematically working on "what's coming" is some of the most important work on the planet. Systematically working on "what's coming" absolutely is YOUR most important work on YOUR planet!

To make a difference, to make money, to lead a company to prosperity, to be an entrepreneur — to even matter in the future — all depends upon your figuring out possible futures today. Then, you can take actions so that you, your clients and your business grow with the flow.

If anyone counts on leadership from you, this is your call – creating a road to the future, not fixing a road to the past.

For more than 25 years, I have worked with leaders, entrepreneurs and intra-preneurs that work in organizations to "pick up the road" and move it. Why is that important? When leaders systematically imagine possible futures, they can change the possibilities for so many humans.

Here's an example. Nelson Mandela's memorial service attended by world leaders is now, the very day I write this. Future-thinking work persuaded South African white leaders to abandon Apartheid. To change the world for the better took so many actions. Future-planning, individual leadership by Mandela and other leaders, expressions of world concerns and freedom songs undid that racist system. Yet, it was the systematically forecasting where Apartheid was probably going to take the country that helped policy makers envision what could happen in the future – if they did NOT change.

Here's a story you'll recognize when individuals are undone as the future arrives. Two days before the Mandela service as I was having my photo taken, my photographer asked me what I did. "I help people and companies create their place in the future," I said. Wistfully, she said, "I wish I would have had your help five years ago when I was creating this business. The bottom dropped out. Everybody now has a camera, a smartphone, a printer and friends. They don't need me."

I wished she could have talked to me five years ago, too. Every single person benefits deeply from future-planning.

I don't do a lot of looking back. But, when I do, I see how I keep answering the call to help people and organizations take action to get up to speed so they will matter in the future.

When I was 22, I directed 60 journalism students in a newspaper's Women's Section to look beyond food, fashion and frivolousness. My stories kept bumping off the usual coverage that was supposed to hit the front page. The secret to my stories pushing other content off the front page? It just looked strange to me that the news did not equally cover women and their impact on the world. So, we did something new.

When I was 25, my shocking chartreuse mailers inviting students to enroll in a formerly sedate college spoke "student-language," won awards and—incidentally—jumped an increase in enrollment helping turn that college's future to gold. Success key? I kept looking at what students yearned for in their education. The neon-colored brochures fostered change in faculty and set new expectations.

At 26, and seven days after delivering my first daughter, a Chicago executive insisted he come to Missouri to recruit me. (Yikes! 7 days.) It looked to him as if my "take" on colleges was new. I simply then flew around to a dozen or so Midwestern colleges seeing things differently and producing results in both student admissions and raising money. Whether in colleges, consulting, banking, teaching, my "different" insights seemed to sync up with customers' aspirations, change organizations and benefit both.

I, like you, helped all those organizations make so much money! My call was to help good people and organizations see changes coming, use those to create new assumptions, leverage resources, change directions, and create products and processes that could have a life in the future. Everybody won.

I always took it as a clue that I was on the right track if people didn't like my direction. There's something wrong with a new idea. It's new.

You don't think that college's faculty, staff and alumni liked those chartreuse publications, do you?

At 40, my non-profit media think tank (appropriately named New Directions) was awarded millions to take on forecasting possibilities for media. Pointers for media had to be the lack of coverage of women and minorities (society's change agents) and the huge power any individual was going to have in a wired world. The first online newspaper was invented in my roundtables long before technology arrived that could deliver it. When the future arrived, the news service was already ready! It ushered in a new direction for news for media all over the world.

Hundreds of media and tech executives gathered at my four live events a year. Brick and mortar companies resist believing they won't be important in the future. After all, they have buildings. Death by assumption. Some executives could climb over being currently successful so they could see humans changing directions. Those leaders reinvented all kinds of new products and services, from the Wall Street Journal to Yahoo.

Together, in my "upstream" roundtables, we used my systems to helped shape what was coming for them AND for their customers. They were my ideal clients – working to make the world work for everyone.

Not every executive took on the investment of time, money and thinking.

Those who did not act on placing actions "upstream" simply discounted the fast, vast change and dealt with "downstream" problems. They did not take charge of their future. Those problems quadrupled x 100. They had heard the call, but ignored it. People got hurt. Communities suffered.

To see the difference in "upstream" and "downstream" actions think of how working "upstream" helps people plant crops so they have abundance, using the right amount of water, nutrition and planting at the right time. All systematically thought through and executed. Taking "downstream" actions means trying to feed people with no food supply in the winter and being shot at by robbers.

"Upstream" action gives a different tomorrow.

Today, using Position the Future's HINTS™ system I help global organizations create new futures and move into them. In 2013, after working with a global defense team to future-plan, their CEO said, "You saved us months, money and morale. You helped us do what we could not do ourselves." The global computer company we are positioning now reaches professionals and individuals throughout the world. Our HINTS™ system can explode opportunities for them *and the people they serve* as the world reorganizes. This benefits the whole human race.

Pretty exciting.

It's even more exciting that individuals can change their futures using HINTS™!!! You and other leaders in Australia, India, Brazil, China, Norway or any of the other 170 or so countries in the world can take these learnings, apply them and imagine what's coming for you to adapt to, shape and use, to step forward. Only 2 billion people have smartphones now. Huge changes are on their way.

INVENTING YOURSELF TO MATTER IN THE RECESSION-ROLLING FUTURE – USING HINTS™ TO SAVE YOU MONTHS, MONEY AND MORALE

What companies and careers have you noticed disappearing? The "hints" were there before their collapses. My HINTS™ system helps you decode what influences, technology and global culture change will shape our next year and our future, as we understand "History Now" and what that "Indicates." This provides the fuel for "New Offerings" that can be "Tracked (and will) Travel" to new successes and "Stimulate" new categories of service to people.

Here are some hints about HINTS™ just to give you an idea of the wealth waiting when you future-plan. Of course, the specific examples will already be out-of-date by the time you read this because new ingredients for the future keep popping up.

History Now

Understanding what may be new to us is already history. Digging deep into current realities such as these gives us real insights into where our industry, country and age are going:

- 1/3 Coca Cola executives are not Coke employees.

- 3-D printing gears up to take over clothing production, house construction and cooking.

- 57% of U.S. college students are women.

- International banks stake entrepreneurs to build businesses for and with the poorest of the poor in Africa and South America, then those become investments for stockholders.

Understanding where our very own business is in the arc of *growing or going* gives us a fresh look at today's opportunities.

Indicates

- What's the predictable-almost-certain outcome of 12 industries and what does that mean to me, my business, my bank, my geography?

- What are the new opportunities for the 2 billion humans on smart phones to reach me and my expertise? What will we use when email goes away?

- How could every one of these global trends benefit me and how could every one of them make my business obsolete?

New Offering$
- How to take the History Now discoveries, plus what those could indicate for me ... what New Offering$ can I create to expand and increase my business and my service to others?

Track & Travel
- How to design and track new inventions and systems as they travel across cultures to see how they change and make my very environment.

Stimulate
-Just as Lisa Sasevich brings a new category of services to entrepreneurs using her own and others' breakthrough thinking, technology and systems -- what are the whole new categories of service you can matter in that technology, culture and global change make possible?

No matter whether you and I are a parent, college president, health worker, top executive at any world's largest company, student, president of a start-up, inventor, Fortune 500 executive, business owner with no employees or thousands, we face the same thing as we wake up every day:

What do we need to *consider and create* today that makes us, our children, our patients, our employees, our company and our education CRITICALLY USEFUL in the next five years?

No other question matters as much, yet it gets covered up in our busyness in our business. Sometimes the strategy we used five years ago captures us. Sometimes it feels so good to be currently successful we forget that only rolling strategies keep us winning tomorrow.

MY BEST HINT?

While huge sweeps of jobs have become obsolete in the past decade, there are never-before-used new tools to fashion whole new connections. Almost every human now can re-frame her/his possibilities. It just takes discipline and a system to build that future.

Because I've been helping organizations and individuals re-frame their core actions and plans for more than 25 years, it's obvious any currently successful person or organization needs to step into the forecasting game and re-frame. Kodak did not. The once-powerful photography company declared bankruptcy in 2012. IBM did re-frame, re-defining itself to fit into the future, regaining its premier status on the Fortune Top 20. (IBM hosted my future-planning roundtables five years in a row in their New York headquarters.)

Any individual's thriving depends exactly on the same thing as any company's – investing in seeing what could be coming, with discipline and structure. That's my call – to find the truth as early as possible about what reshapes us all. Then, to help get that in the hands, eyes and minds of excellent humans who can work to make the world better for all.

If it is true that world peace may occur when everyone is an entrepreneur, getting the "hints" early makes all the difference.

BTW, I think my road to the future opened up the day when I was 12, and the ophthalmologist gravely said to my mother, "Hold your daughter's hand when you leave here and cross the street. She cannot see the cars." My mother, a nurse, cried.

In that one-room school I attended in rural Missouri, no one noticed I could not see the chalkboard! We did not know what we did not know. The prescription, thick glasses arrived the next week causing wracking headaches, nausea, clumsiness … and wonder! I saw leaves on trees! I had lived in a world where leaves only showed up on the ground; I dreaded being sent on an errand to find anything; and, I learned to bat a baseball by sound.

And, I've been thinking ever since about …prescriptions, seeing, not seeing.

What are we not seeing even when the hints are right in front of us?

About Jean

Jean Gaddy Wilson helps clients change upstream... where huge possibilities for expansion and impact exist. She works with clients to position themselves, and their clients, to profit from change – where they invent new possibilities for themselves and their businesses. Downstream change focuses on fixing current problems – a limited lifetime. Upstream change provides clients with a system to purposefully move forward with unlimited possibilities as the future unfolds with all its slides, slippery surprises and shocks.

Her HINTS™ system positions leaders to re-frame, envision what's coming, explore possibilities in change, create new products and thrive. Her company, Position the Future, is a proven catalyst for change in established and entrepreneurial companies. In 2013, one of her clients in national defense said it best: "Jean, we could not reshape us on our own. You saved us months, money and morale!"

Her insights on *Where Your Tomorrow Is* have taken her around the globe – Europe, Asia, South America, Australia, Middle East, North America -- as a keynote speaker and facilitator in more than 300 venues.

Her live events – *How to Make Sure You and Your Clients End Up on the Right Side of Tomorrow* – are three-day turn-around events. Clients come in believing the problems keeping them up at night are the right ones. They go home reinvigorated with the REAL issues to address and ways to meet them head on. The result: clients are constantly ready with products and processes as the future unfolds.

Jean's clients "get it." You see THE GAP -- the space between where you and your business are today and where you need to be to ride through the rapids of change. She challenges you to make YOUR UNIQUE MAP – between today (where your machines, clothing and systems don't talk to each other) and your future (where one of your business partners is in China, your work is play and your "tribe" provides expertise for entrepreneurs in new businesses not yet invented).

Jean's international reputation for entrepreneurship, innovation, creativity and insightfulness rests on successful facilitation of bold new business development and rapid culture change in organizations. Clients prepare for their future and success no matter what the future holds for them. You have a front seat in the hard-charging reorganization of the world.

Founder of New Directions for News, a news media think tank at the University of Missouri where she was a Journalism faculty member, Jean created new systems for executives and owners to meet their futures, take action and create products ahead of the curve. The first electronic news site was created in Jean's national roundtables anticipating the technology that could deliver it.

Jean judged the Pulitzer Prizes, received the University of Missouri's 2008 Faculty-Alumni lifetime achievement award, was named the 2013 Hot Momma's History Maker Award for her case study of "It's Not About the I – It's about the US," awarded in the George Washington Business School. She co-authors *Working With Words*, eighth edition, 2013, published by Bedford St. Martins.

She played a lead role in founding these major institutions: Journalism & Women's Symposium; National Women & Media Collection, and the International Women & Media Foundation.

Connect with Jean Gaddy Wilson:
www.positionthefuture.com
jeangaddywilson@positionthefuture.com
www.linkedin.com/pub/jean-gaddy-wilson/6/493/706

CHAPTER 15

WELFARE TO WEALTH

BY KIMBERLEY BORGENS

Imagine being young, naïve and falling in love in high school to your knight in shining armor. Ah the life of a young woman in love! Graduating and working a full time job, life was bliss. After a short while imagining yourself saying "yes" when he said, let's get married. The fairy tale – or was it!

Married at eighteen, gave birth at nineteen and getting divorced at twenty. Married life began, transformed and ended all in a few short years. Does that sound like the fairy tale to you?

This is where I found myself at the age of twenty. Heartbroken, single, no real skills and now a single mom to a son who had no clue what it all meant.

After he left and I had no money for rent, I found myself and my son living in my 1978 Honda two door hatch back. I had way too much pride to ask anyone for help. I didn't want people to see me as a failure. What would people think of me – the girl they warned that she was too young to get married and who was now a young single mother with no money. If only I had listened to them when they all were telling me how to live my life!

First big lesson I had to learn – Get out of my own way and ask for help because it was unsafe staying in my car at grocery store parking lots!

I finally reached out for support. I got state assistance and found a one bedroom apartment. My welfare check was $529 a month and I received $107 a month in food stamps. My rent for my one bedroom apartment was $495 a month leaving me with $34 a month for electricity, wall phone and a bus pass. Let me just say that cheap candles, sitting in the dark a lot and being frugal with everything was the only way to survive this time in my life.

After being on welfare for a year, I enrolled in community college for some skills learning and training. I put my focus on majoring in Business Management and Administration of Justice. I worked hard in school while my son was in pre-school and kindergarten.

I did some crafts in my spare time and sold some for a little extra money. I took on a couple jobs here and there, working for small businesses in trade for something I could use for my home that they had to offer. I found ways to get some gifts for my son for birthdays and holidays that I could not have paid for on the money I received from the welfare department.

I put myself through the Police Academy and during this time I met a recently honorably discharged Marine. We began dating, and even though I was a single mother he did not run away and hide like others – who had acted interested until they saw what my offering was.

After several years of dating, as I was not going to jump back into anything looking like marriage, we decided to start a business together. That was a smarter idea than marriage I thought! We both pulled together our knowledge and skills and formed a partnership in what seemed like a business that was ideal for the both of us. We started a Private Security business. After working together for about eight months we go married!

I thought it was difficult being on welfare! At least with a welfare check I knew when the check would arrive and I knew how much was coming each month! When we started the business we had nothing steady coming in. We were frugal and I took a part-time job in retail to put food on the table. The business needed to get more clients so we could sustain our growing family.

I will be the first one to say right to your face that starting your own business is a lot of work, little to no money and in many cases, little to no sleep either! Yet there are a lot of lessons that you can learn along the way. There is also a lot that we had to learn about ourselves and about being a business owner.

Here are a few of the best lessons I learned along the way:

- No-one else can be more committed to your success than you! People may tell you that they want you to succeed more than you do, but you truly have to have the desire for more to find the solutions, when you are faced with the challenges and problems that come with being a business owner.

- No-one is going to hand you success on a silver platter. You actually have to work hard and smart to create long term success. Don't let anyone ever tell you that any business is easy to do! It may be simple to start a business, yet it takes daily effort and diligent work to make any business a profitable and sustainable success.

- Reach out and get support. You do not have to know everything to be successful in business. What you do need to know is how to find the best people to support you in your journey to success. Oh, and sometimes you have to just get out of your own way and be willing to ask for the support you need to make it all work out.
  - Connect with your local Chamber of Commerce for networking and support.
  - Locate the closest Small Business Development Center (SBDC) for low to no cost business support.
  - SCORE - (Service Corps of Retired Executives) provides no cost to low cost mentors to help you and your business discover what you need to succeed.
  - Small business incubators and co-ops can be a valuable resource.
  - Go to local business meetings, mixers and networking events to build connections.

- Share your goals with people who want to see you succeed. Keep your goals close and protected from the naysayers and those who do not believe you can do it. Share them with those who are excited for you and want you to be successful. Many times just by sharing your goals you are more likely going to reach them because you risked yourself and shared them. You do not want to look bad to those people you shared with, so you are more likely going to reach the goal.

- Be willing to do whatever it takes to be successful. Keep your integrity intact! Take on an extra job, work hard, make mistakes, be unique and take risks. Without these lessons you are likely going to quit, walk away or get crushed by your competition and then think you were not meant to be an entrepreneur.

At some point in the process of being a successful entrepreneur, you will discover who your true friends are. Sometimes your friends will vary based on where you are in your life, not who you are. Sometimes you will have friends that are only meant to be in your life for a short time. If you allow yourself to really take a look at that friendship, you will discover the lesson they brought to you to learn. Some friends are meant to be there long term. They are committed to the friendship and are some of your biggest supporters in your success. They may not even understand your business, yet they can see how passionate you are and are willing to ride that train with you without ever needing to understand. Some people will disguise themselves as friends, but they only really want you to be there for them. They want you to teach them what you know and then they are out of here! You will have to learn to recognize the signs of your friendships and release those back into the world to find the right fit for them. Remember that you have a business to run not a popularity contest!

Business can go in cycles. One year everything will feel hard and challenging – okay, the first few years may feel like this! Some years feel like everything running smooth allows you to catch your breath and relax a little. Then it all shifts again. Some things that may create the shift include; economy, tragedy, disasters, new laws, life changes (divorce, birth, marriage, etc.) and many unforeseeable obstacles can create cycle changes in your business and your success.

Simple steps to getting the support you deserve for achieving your goals and dreams include:

- Find support from people who have a positive attitude and can motivate you.

- Know that you are the only one responsible for becoming a success. It is up to you to be successful and it is up to you to look for the solutions to the challenges you face.

- Enroll people along the way to help hold you accountable for the actions you are committed to taking.

- Forgive yourself for the mistakes you have made and start new each day ready to take the next step in your future.

"You will never change your life until you change something you do daily. The secret of success is found in your daily action."
~ John Maxwell, Leadership Expert and Author

One of the most valuable lessons I have learned from being on welfare to being a successful entrepreneur with five concurrently running successful businesses, is the importance of accountability. I have been named the "Queen of Accountability" because I believe in being able to account for actions. If I said I was going to be successful then I made my actions match what I was going after. I found temporary accountability partners to keep me on track with what I said I wanted to create.

Here are some tips for utilizing and creating great accountability partnerships:

I. CREATING ACCOUNTABILITY PARTNERSHIPS

- Find someone who has similar interests with you and has the same kind of desire to succeed.

- Enroll two people to hold you accountable. That way, when one is distracted you still have someone to support you in your action steps.

- Look for people who have different strengths to yours. You both will learn from each other.

II. MAINTAINING SUCCESSFUL ACCOUNTABILITY PARTNERSHIPS

- Decide how and how often you and you partners will connect. Via phone, skype or in person? Will you get together daily? Once a week? Once a month?

- How long are you committing to this partnership? Three months? Six Months? Create a start and end time for your partnership. Once it comes to an end you get to re-evaluate and choose to continue or move forward in a different way.

- Decide what level of confidentiality you both will commit to. What is okay to share and what is not? Set this up with each other in the beginning to prevent problems later.

- Set specific and measurable goals and share them with your accountability partnerships so they know what to hold you accountable for.

- Write down the action steps you have agreed to hold your accountability partner to. This way you can ask them if they completed them when you next connect.

- Be supportive not bossy! Criticizing and bossing will lead to frustration and is the fastest way to break up accountability partnerships.

No matter where you are right now in your life, you can do something today towards what you want to create for the future. No excuses! I often say "Choose and Move" – make a choice and take an action towards that choice. If it doesn't work out the way that you thought it should, make a new choice and take a new action!

Are you ready to take action? If so, reach out to two people and see if they would be willing to be your accountability partner for thirty (30) days. Put yourself into action and keep moving forward to find your own level of success.

About Kimberley

Kimberley Borgens, CBC
"Queen of Accountability"
CEO - Be A Legacy
"Don't wait to leave a legacy, be one now and you will automatically leave one."

Kimberley Borgens is an award-winning entrepreneur, Professional Speaker, Certified Business Coach, Trainer and Author. She is a leading expert in business and personal accountability. She helps home-based business leaders focus on reaching their goals and build on their personal and professional development. She accomplishes this in a fun and empowering way through discovering limiting beliefs, competing commitments, building confidence and clear accountability.

With 20 years experience as an entrepreneur, and ownership in five companies, she has the skill, from trial and error, to help you to be successful faster. Kimberley's signature topic is *Accountability In Action*, where she speaks in a way that encourages, empowers and gets people into action. Kimberley has the ability to coach, consult and train in a wide entrepreneurial arena. Kimberley believes that without accountability in business, it creates more struggle and a feeling of not get getting where you want. When coaching, clients create tangible results through accountability and compassion. Her training helps people to gain skill, improve communication and save money.

Kimberley is an accredited WABC Certified Business Coach and Coach Trainer. A former facilitator with Klemmer & Associates, former Faculty with DSWA Coach Excellence, she majored in Business Administration and Administration of Justice and is a graduate of Leadership Stockton and Leadership Lodi. She has earned business awards from the Greater Stockton Chamber of Commerce – Small Business of the Year and the Small Business Administration (SBA) Small Business of the Year Northern California Region, as well as many extraordinary service awards in business and development.

Kimberley lives in California with her husband and is a mother of four children. Her passion for people has given her the ability to work with clients in Uganda, Mexico, Australia, Canada, Korea and the USA. Kimberley believes every household would benefit from a home-based business. The leadership lessons you learn as an entrepreneur are a huge benefit for families and personal growth and development.

CHAPTER 16

BIG DREAMS
— A SMALL WORLD

BY BRENDA R. McGUIRE

Looking out as my plane descended into the twinkling lights of sleeping Osaka, Japan, a wave of emotions hit me. It was the start of the Japanese New Year 1998 – the Year of the Tiger. Yet for me, I was touching down with little more than a backpack, some money and a dream. I disembarked without a job, contacts or even a place to sleep that night. I was not a stranger to establishing a new life in a foreign country; I had moved overseas several times before. In the past, I had found jobs, housing and friends in Australia, Ireland and the U.K. However, this journey to Japan posed my greatest obstacles-to-date: cultural and language barriers. Jet-lagged from the long flight and navigating a forebodingly-long customs line, I began to question this adventure. The reassuring voices of my parents swiftly diffused any doubts as I reminisced about our conversation as they drove me to the airport two days earlier. My parent's strong conviction in my ability to make things work resonated within me as I cleared customs and my new adventure unfolded.

Throughout my childhood in rural Iowa, I had told my parents I wanted to travel the world. At first they weren't sure if this was a childhood dream like being a movie star that would pass as I matured, but it only persisted. I started small, traveling in the U.S. with youth organizations, and later on a six-week student exchange to Switzerland. During my junior year of college, I saw a poster for *Semester at Sea*, a whirlwind educational trip aboard the *S.S. Universe,* which would take participants through 12 countries, 4 continents, 25 bodies of water and 27,000 miles over three months. Now *this* was the type of world travel I craved! My parents, who didn't even have passports, provided their unconditional support as I transformed my dream into a reality through intense work and financial sacrifice. I boarded the ship as a naïve girl and disembarked three months later a different woman. Over the course of the trip my heart soared as I saw the Nutcracker Ballet in Russia and broke as I walked through a destitute village in India. Completely in awe of the many cultures so different from my own, I vowed to return to my favorite locations to truly immerse myself.

Now, the *S.S Universe*'s first port of call, Osaka, was calling me back. For a year, I had lived with my parents and worked to save money and acquire expertise that could help me land a job in Japan. Within an hour of landing, I had connected with a Japanese woman, Akiko Furuya, who was returning from an exchange trip to Indiana. She invited me to her family's home for the night. Thanks to the hospitable nature of the Japanese and their commitment to relationships, this became my home; her family became my extended family, as we lived together over the next two years. She provided me with connections that quickly led to a corporate training position where I experienced challenge after challenge operating in an unfamiliar business environment and culture. During my stay in Japan, my parents came to visit me and began their love of international travel, which later culminated in the fulfillment of my father's childhood dream of going on safari in Africa.

After a decade spent living, working and traveling abroad, my international experience led to a job in New York as the Director of Global Workforce Development overseeing one of the world's largest intercultural and global workforce divisions for a Fortune 500 company. Yet, my home state was finally drawing me back and I negotiated a working arrangement in order to be closer to my roots in Iowa. In time, I founded my own company, *WorldWide Connect*®, training business people and their families from around the world as they navigated unfamiliar cultures. I didn't want others to needlessly suffer through the culture shock and *faux pas* as I had while living in six countries and traveling to over 65 countries. All of my experiences—whether living in Asia-Pacific, working in the Middle East or visiting an indigenous village in South America—served to solidify my desire to help others develop cultural competencies. Additionally, starting *WorldWide*

Connect® allowed me to continue my jet-setting global career and enabled me to stay connected with colleagues around the globe.

In 2013, my international business was thriving; my client list included numerous companies worldwide and I had a network of trainers and consultants on six continents. On February 19th, my world was rocked when my father was diagnosed with stage 4 lung cancer. I went from focusing on people around the world, to focusing on one man in rural Iowa receiving hospice care in the home we built together. While caring for my father, we reminisced about the adventures he had taken around the world, and what they meant to him. As news of his diagnosis spread, messages came flooding in from around the globe. It was then that he realized how many people he had met and the impact he had on them. I too, came to fully realize the crucial role he played as a constant cheerleader and advocate for all of my dreams. Shortly before he took a turn for the worse, I was in San Diego listening to Lisa Sasevich talk about following your dreams, and giving your gift to the world. Though I lost my greatest supporter on March 6, 2013, I realized that because of all that my father had given to me, I had another gift to give. As a legacy to him, I created a new company, *Global Gals®*, to help other women achieve their travel dreams. Following the example my father set forth, *Global Gals®* has the goal of empowering and educating women who want to live, work and travel around the world.

My passion is to help other women to be successful in "answering the call" of their travel dreams. I hope the below strategies can help you reach your travel goals, no matter whether you're male or female, if you just take the first step.

SIX SUCCESS STRATEGIES TO ACHIEVE YOUR TRAVEL D.R.E.A.M.S.

1. Decide - Where in the world do you want to go? Who might be a good travel companion or do you want to venture forth on your own? When will you travel and what would you like to do/see/learn/experience? Is your goal education, professional development or volunteering? Do you want to learn a new hobby or experience other cultures? What do you want to take away from the experience? Don't let your dream stay just a dream. As Mark Twain said, "Twenty years from now you will be more disappointed by the things you didn't do than by the

ones you did. So throw off the bow lines. Sail away from the safe harbor. Catch the trade winds in your sails. EXPLORE, DREAM, DISCOVER."

2. Research - Once you've picked out the "who," "where," "when" and "why," focus on the "how." Research the requirements, such as visas or vaccinations that you will need to visit your country of choice. Put together a budget for your travels. If you don't do your homework ahead of time, your dream could turn into a nightmare. I recently met a bride who arrived at her "dream destination" honeymoon in the Maldives, only to be turned away at passport control because she didn't have the necessary full six-months validity left on her passport. Even though she still had a few months left and her passport hadn't expired, they denied her entry into the country and sent her home.

One of the goals of *Global Gals®* is to educate women on what they need to do, consider and plan for in order to become more confident and safe travelers. By planning ahead, you can save valuable money and maximize the time you have in your dream location. Preparation doesn't mean everything will go perfectly (so don't forget to pack your patience, flexibility and open-mindedness before you leave), but many disasters can be averted with a little forethought.

3. Explore - You've picked your location, done all of your preparations and have finally arrived! Now what?? Be careful not to over-schedule yourself, especially at the beginning of a trip. I often give myself a day to acclimate to my new environment before I have set plans. Once you do head out, go off the beaten path and throw away the guidebook. Take a risk and try something new. Never been salsa dancing? Jump up and join in the fun at the local dance club. If you move away from the tourist centers you'll get more of a "true" experience of the country you are visiting. As you bring your own *cultural baggage* with you, make a conscious effort to observe behaviors and attitudes that are different from 'home.' Be a cultural detective as you explore. Learn the cultural do's and don'ts. Be aware of the culture's communication style and pay attention to *how* something is said, not just what is said.

4. <u>Ask, Ask, Ask!</u> - Don't be afraid to ask questions. Speak to the locals, asking them for the best places to shop, eat and visit. If someone came to your town, you'd be able to give them much better advice than anything they could read online or in a 4-year-old guidebook. Even if you don't speak the language fluently, you can often find a way to communicate and you'll be surprised how many people speak English around the world. Certainly, if you are going to a non-English speaking country, you will earn the respect and create a comfort level with the locals if you at least try to use a few basic phrases from their language such as "hello," "excuse me" or "can you help me?"

5. <u>Make it a priority</u> - We can always find excuses why this isn't the "right" time to travel. Whether it is fear of the unknown, concern about traveling alone or a lack of funds, we are constantly creating roadblocks. Finances are one of the biggest concerns I hear from would-be travelers. Through *Global Gals*®, I'm helping women around the world design their dream trip on a dime, just like I did so many years ago. You may need to be creative and think outside the box on how to finance the trip, whether it is volunteering in exchange for room and board, or staying in hostels instead of five star hotels. The key is to put together a budget and be prepared to sacrifice in order to achieve it. Look at travel as an investment you make in yourself, your future and your career. If traveling is truly your life's ambition, make it a priority because, as I learned from my father's early death, you never know how much time you have.

6. <u>It's a Small World After All</u> - When you return, you'll have pictures and mementos, yet what you will remember most are the people you met. I have countless stories of the people whom I first encountered during my adventures and I never cease to be amazed by the ways our paths continue to overlap. In 1997, I moved to London without a job. Within a few days of arriving, while walking through a bustling Piccadilly Circus, I ran into my former boss from Australia whom I hadn't seen in two years. She had an opening at the company she owned and within an hour, I was gainfully employed! Serendipity seems to have a way of bringing the people that we need into our lives, but it is up to us to take advantage of the opportunities that present themselves.

It may be a cliché, but travel is a gift that never stops giving back to you. Today I challenge you to take the first step to reach for that dream. Don't let your fears, or doubts act as a roadblock – no one I have met has ever regretted their travels, but so many have regretted not taking their dream trip. Later in life, we often realize that the obstacles we found so daunting in our younger years were not so insurmountable after all. So what are you waiting for?

The *Universe* is calling....

About Brenda

Brenda McGuire helps teach people how to successfully live, work, and travel the world. With a record of travel that would leave most in awe—and an impressive professional history to match—Brenda has the expertise and the know-how needed to help others succeed internationally. Whether training corporate executives on cross-cultural business differences, developing global leaders, or educating women on how to travel the world independently, Brenda is passionate about sharing her experience, expertise, and of course, her travel secrets. An avid globetrotter, entrepreneur, and cultural expert, Brenda's global journey has taken her to over 65 countries on 6 continents. Wherever she is in the world—backpacking Europe, trekking the Himalayas, exploring the Amazon Rain Forest, or traversing the Australian outback—she feels right at home.

Growing up in Iowa, Brenda had limited opportunities to see a world beyond her small town, but that all changed after she participated in the whirlwind *Semester at Sea* program, visiting 12 countries in 102 days. She returned home a "citizen of the world," and with a keen sense of wanderlust, spent the next 20 years turning her global dreams into reality. She successfully lived and worked in Japan, the UK, Ireland, Switzerland, Australia, New York City, and Washington, D.C. before settling back in Des Moines, Iowa, where she now resides.

During her international career, Brenda has held positions in the corporate, non-profit, academic, and government sectors. She worked in diverse positions as an educator, travel director, corporate trainer, international recruiter, cross-cultural coach, and global workforce development specialist. As an expert in her field, she has worked with thousands of individuals and companies in over 50 countries teaching them how to effectively live, work, and travel across diverse cultures, time zones, and language barriers.

Brenda is the Founder & President of *WorldWide Connect®*. With their extensive global network of consultants, they deliver cross-cultural coaching, global business effectiveness programs, global leadership development, and expatriate support to international companies. In addition, Brenda founded and became Chief Global Gal of *Global Gals®*, which empowers and educates women to reach their travel dreams through workshops, retreats, cultural training, and networking events. *Global Gals®* equips women to overcome real, or perceived roadblocks, and is a resource and support for women whether they want a backpacking adventure, dream getaway, or expatriate experience. Whatever a woman needs to fulfill her travel dreams, *Global Gals®* tailors the help and support given to meet their individual needs.

She has an MA in International Communications from Macquarie University in Sydney, Australia, and a BS in Psychology and International Relations with Distinction from Iowa State University. Furthermore, she is a frequent international speaker at conferences, corporate meetings, and industry events, and has served as a guest lecturer aboard several cruise ships around the world. Brenda has won many awards in her community, is recognized for her contributions in her field, and has been selected as one of America's PremierExperts®.

You can connect with Brenda at:
BMcGuire@worldwide-connect.com
www.globalgals.org
www.worldwideconnect.com
www.facebook/globalgals

CHAPTER 17

ACCEPTANCE OF LIFE AS AN INNER GAME

BY KAY LAM

From the outside, my life is truly blessed and envied by many. I came from an educated middle class family, went to college, have a Master's degree certificate on the wall, got a corporate professional job immediately, married a most generous husband of 28 years now, who has always supported – or at least stayed neutral to – my many ideas and projects. Thanks to him, my bank account has always been comfortable enough to do whatever I wanted within reason. And neither of us came from families of such fame, fortune and tradition that I had to be careful of maintaining someone else's reputation. We have no children. We created our own schedules and travelled the world regularly. I seemed so footloose and fancy free that friends assumed I was retired through my 30's and 40's, when in fact I was working really hard at my construction business.

On the inside, I had never felt satisfied, or fulfilled. Satisfaction and fulfillment are very different feelings, one more from the head and the other from the heart, one driven by worldly sources and the other by an unworldly source. But for decades I did not know the difference. I conformed to expectations from the world without satisfaction. I challenged expectations from the world without success. I was not fulfilled. I felt incomplete, and never accepted my life. Just before age forty seven, I hit bottom with breast cancer.

Without obvious responsibilities to influence my decision, it was truly my conscious choice to continue my journey on Earth, and give myself to whatever mission the universe had designed me for. I had already diligently followed the concepts of spirituality for nine years by then. That harsh blow allowed me to start a new chapter, unwaveringly say yes to the call from within.

My health quickly recovered, surpassing the strength and energy that I ever had before. Inner self development continued, and soon blossomed hand in hand with a new coaching career. Six years after I was diagnosed with breast cancer, I am deeply committed to my clients – to help them move from annoying ailments to long term fabulous health and harmony as I have – and happily swamped with opportunities to propel my business to the next level. My husband and I still travel regularly. While he spends his energy on his favorite outdoor activities, I spend my energy enthusiastically "working" on my passion. I am not satisfied with the results of my new business yet, but I fully accept the process, and I feel wonderfully fulfilled that I am living out my destiny.

******

It was a serene December morning. Gingerly I went to answer the door bell. Any sudden muscle contraction would send an unbearable pain reverberating through my entire body. The scars were barely two weeks old from mastectomy surgery.

"Registered mail Ma'am." I looked down at the return label on a large thin envelope in his hand, and my heart sank. The thought of refusing it dashed across my mind. Somehow I managed to scribble my signature and closed the door. Unexpected mail from a corporate lawyer is never good news. What was it this time? I slit open the envelope carefully, as if it might need resealing and returning. I glanced at the content: A claim.

My worst nightmare. A claim against my company was essentially a claim against me. Breast cancer was much easier to face. My breath quickened. A group of condominium residents were angry with the quality of their building, the usual stuff I had seen many times before. But I did not recognize any of the parties involved, including the claimant. This was not my building, these were not my customers.

This was clearly a mistake. Why were they suing my company? After a long hour, I connected with the lawyer. I explained the mistake, and my health situation, hoping that he would agree to talk the other side into sensibility. "Do you want me to file a statement of defense for you?" he asked unsympathetically. "Can you not just speak with their lawyer casually?" I reiterated. "No, we have to follow proper procedures."

A statement of defense meant legal fees. More expenses. I had to conserve energy for my life. I saw no way out of this, so I agreed and hung up. My heart raced in anger. I felt hooped, again. When would they stop squeezing me? For fifteen years in the home construction business, I was constantly on edge defending myself, and it always came down to money – my money. After risking my life savings over and over, worked 7 days a week, and barely got a salary at the end, I was still not pleasing my customers, my contractors, my team. Eventually I had enough and wound down the business. And then I was diagnosed with breast cancer.

I cringed, and was jolted out of my thoughts by pain. I fell back in exhaustion. What happened to the serenity an hour ago? For the sake of my body, I could not let this bother me.

Or so I tried for four months, until the first invoice arrived from the lawyer: $4000. My company was still nowhere near release from the lawsuit. Someone had used my company name to file a document for the condominium, illegally without my knowledge and obviously without my consent. Instead of defending for me, the lawyer spent hours verifying that I was in fact speaking the truth to him, and billed me for his time. At the end he never figured out who had done it, but insisted that I pay his bill anyway.

A month later, while I was reluctant to pay yet another legal bill, I decided I must approach my regular real estate lawyer about this mystery. She recognized the name right away. My company had sold a fee-simple piece of property years earlier, and this culprit – the lawsuit's true defendant, was my purchaser; I was not privy to information behind the transaction. With compassion and knowledge, she submitted a ten page defense document on my behalf, completely free of charge to me. I could not have been more grateful. She literally saved my day, and my life.

Toward the end of that summer, my husband and I spent a most enjoyable vacation week in St. George, Utah, then travelled on to Giant Sequoia

National Monument – one of the most peaceful and powerful places I have ever visited. Having been on the road almost two weeks, my husband decided to phone home for messages, in case of emergencies. After he listened, he passed the phone to me. A few unimportant messages, and then … the corporate lawyer. My heart sank. It had been nine months since the initial claim, and five months since his first bill. He had not done anything to advance my position, yet constantly sent reminders to pay his bill. I had been avoiding his phone calls like the plague. Upon hearing his voice, the tranquility of the giant trees, the mountains and the stream instantly vanished. Every muscle in my body tensed. Every cell shriveled. My shoulders felt like lead.

One week later, I walked into my room at Summerhill Ranch, home of the amazing teacher, healer, author Denise Linn. I was there with a dozen others to take her Soul Coaching® certification course. Inside a beautiful gift bag on the bed of my choice was an oracle card from her deck: "Acceptance." It had been pre-picked by Denise for the person who would sleep on this bed. I had no idea what it meant, I didn't think it belonged to me. But in the coming weeks, months, years, I would learn of the significance of this word. It was no mistake. Its wisdom soon began to heal my inner pain.

Two months of being a Soul Coach, it was time to clean up this nagging item in my life. As I waited for the lawyer to call back, I closed my eyes. Suddenly, images flashed across my mind of being tied to a stake… and garbed men patrolling with long weapons. I could clearly see faces of the crowd, including many whom I had considered friends. They wanted to help, but dared not speak out, fearing for their own lives.

Every cell in my body buzzed. I had the same feelings throughout my construction career: I felt no one was a true friend; I felt I was left to defend myself.

In an instant, I knew this was where all my troubles had originated. It was I who put out a signal no one could be trusted, therefore my team and customers showed up for me untrustworthy. It was I who was defending against the world, therefore even my own lawyer felt obliged to attack me. Suddenly I was at peace. I knew how I had caused my problems, and therefore I could cause them to disappear now. I accepted my assignment.

The phone rang. I jumped to answer in joy. It was the corporate lawyer as I had hoped. With a kind yet firm tone of voice, I talked facts with him. He agreed to find out the state of my defense, request the claimant pick up my legal bills, and would get back to me in two days. It was a surprisingly pleasant and professional exchange. Suddenly I felt he was a very reasonable guy!

Two days later as promised, he called back with a discharge in hand. The other side would not pick up my legal bills, so I started negotiating with him. Twenty minutes later, he wondered why he was even considering reducing his bill for me, which by now would amount to over $6000 had he invoiced fully. Jokingly I reminded him that while I enjoyed debating back and forth with him, he'd better agree to my proposal quickly, as every minute of his workday ticked with a dollar value. Did I say I "enjoyed" talking with him? Yes, I genuinely meant it! Was this the same guy who up to three days ago was my worst enemy, my nightmare? And now I considered him my friend! He voluntarily reduced his bill to $2000.

******

Life is just a game: an inner game with yourself! Imagine standing in a space surrounded by mirrors. Every person and situation out there in your world of consciousness is a reflection to you – for your understanding of yourself, and for monitoring your progress on your journey.

What do you do when you don't like a person or situation? You could consider the classical mechanics route, which is to annihilate it: blow it up, pound it down, or go around it. But the atoms and undesirable energy will always remain, albeit dispersed. The more you sneer at your reflection, the more it sneers back at you. Or, you could take the quantum mechanics route, and see everything as flexible waves, including yourself. Everything shifts as you shape-shift.

CLEAR YOURSELF, CLEAR YOUR SITUATION

1. *ACCEPT* the situation in front of you as a product of something inside of you, regardless of how ridiculous it may seem. Acceptance softens your mind, prepares you to flow with your environment.

2. Use the opportunity to *CLEAR* your inner self. At every feeling of discomfort, make a mental note to do Item 3.

3. *SAY* to yourself, *"Whatever it is inside of me that is causing this situation to show up, I am sorry. Please forgive me. I love you. Thank you."*

4. Relax and *ALLOW* the miracles to unfold!

When you feel called from within, choose to follow your heart and answer the call with positive action. It will always involve discomfort, which is simply the universe's curriculum to guide you to new heights. You are given challenges only because you are strong enough and ready! If you respond the quantum way, nothing will stay stressful for long. Stress occurs only when you believe your situation is outside your control. But there is nothing outside, they are simply reflections. The control is completely within you.

Accept life as a fun inner game. Clear yourself to uncover your sweet spot. Harmony, health and success are waiting for you!

About Kay

"Wholistic Wellness Catalyst" Kay Lam is known to help clients get out of annoying health issues. Having journeyed through breast cancer, she has a special interest in helping breast cancer survivors. Kay brings you to wellness with an all-around approach. Her work is thorough, no-nonsense, and shifts you from core to surface.

Kay is the original recipient of **Superintelligence Wellness Activation,** an effortless technique that strengthens your connection to your inner wise guidance. She received this gift from the universe suddenly on 11/1/11, and affectionately nicknamed it "Show Up, Shut Up, and Get Shifted." Kay is creator of **The Ultimate Health System**™ – seven keys to long-term health through physical, mental, emotional and spiritual balance.

Kay came from a conventional family background of western medical and science professionals, but followed her inner calling to venture into alternative healing. She is a Zhi Neng Herb Practitioner, certified under Dr. Zhi Geng Sha. She is also a Soul Coach and Past Life Coach, certified under Denise Linn. Kay has a B.Sc. in geology and physics from the University of Toronto, M.S. in operations research from the University of California at Berkeley School of Engineering. She worked in mainstream society for 23 years, first as a geophysicist with Chevron Canada, then created her own business as a condominium developer and builder, despite being a petite woman not even 5 feet tall and 92 pounds soaking wet.

After a decade walking the spiritual path, late 2007 she journeyed through breast cancer in peace and confidence. Following her lifelong philosophy to seek lasting resolution, she turned her diet upside down within weeks when it was found to be her physical sabotage, then diligently worked on her mental and emotional aspects, which resulted in dramatic improvements to her health and happiness. Kay doesn't believe we get annoying health issues for no good reason. She operates under the attitude that when the universe whacks her, it means they are priming her for new awareness for her highest good, therefore it is her duty to figure out what she needs to do – and do it now – because life is too short to suffer repeated unpleasant reminders.

Kay hosted a weekly internet radio show for one year, inspiring audiences to explore various psycho-spiritual aspects within themselves for transformation. She was a world competition level art quilter, naturally gifted in the visual arts and home design. Kay was born in Hong Kong, and has lived in Canada for forty years. She calls Calgary, Alberta her home, where she lives with her husband and helps clients around the world via the phone and Internet.

You can learn more about Kay's work on: www.SuperintelligenceWellness.com

and connect with her at:
kay@SuperintelligenceWellness.com
www.facebook.com/kayklam
www.twitter.com/kayklam
ca.linkedin.com/pub/kay-lam/36/84b/5a8/

CHAPTER 18

FINALLY FULL: A CHRISTIAN WOMAN'S JOURNEY TO SPIRITUAL SATISFACTION

BY LAURA FULFORD

Losing weight is a poorly understood endeavor. Just to highlight what I mean, here is a quiz: Write down everything you know about weight loss *that has not come* from advertising or from another commercial source like *The Biggest Loser* or other extreme weight loss programs.

In my experience as a weightloss coach, I find that people harbor many unhelpful beliefs about losing weight and few if any helpful ones. There are two extremes. On one hand, the process is overly simplified; eat this, not that, and voila, there you are sporting a bikini. At the other extreme, weight loss requires deprivation, extreme amounts of exercise, and an inexplicably angry (and annoyingly buff) trainer screaming at you, reminiscent of scenes from the Exorcist.

With each new client I work with in my practice as a weightloss coach, I encounter misinformation that must be set aside before success (short term and long term) becomes possible. Most clients have snippets of the truth - not nearly enough to help them achieve permanent weight loss and improved health, but just enough to give them false hope and set them running off in the wrong direction.

No one's problem with excess weight is what it appears to be. Now that obesity has become a health crisis, and officially a "disease," there is more noise than ever about what we must do to fight it:

- No more sodas over 16 oz.
- No more toys in happy meals.
- Let's tax junk food.
- Let's take vending machines out of the schools.

I understand the implications on us as a nation. I suppose the thinking is that because obesity will cost America in immeasurable ways – more disease, heightened healthcare costs, reduced productivity, shortened lifespan for us and our kids– that we must somehow come up with a culturally impactful solution. The social impact is huge. The collective response? Sigh. Yawn. Let us know when you figure it out, but for now, pass the mayonnaise.

Which is more concerning to you – the fact that 2 out of 3 people in America are overweight or the fact that you are a few sizes removed from the size you were in high school?

Obesity occurs in us as individuals, one by one, bite by bite. If you trace obesity back to its start in each individual, it would start with a bite of something and a reaction in the brain that said – whoa! I want more of that - now! With every bite consumed, we get to choose whether or not to take another. With certain foods, we notice the next bite is nearly impossible to refuse. Even while your mind is saying I should not be eating this, your hand is shoving it in your mouth.

I have observed myself in this very conundrum many times over a bag of Candy Corn, or a can of cream cheese frosting. All I am lacking is some surgical tubing and a hypodermic needle. I am an addict. I say I can stop anytime I want, but I don't want to. I just have to decide which is worse – the siren call of my daily fix or the growing cascade of fat rolls on my torso, which by the way, is so depressing it just makes me want to eat more.

I am the ultimate guinea pig when it comes to weight loss. I have tried every diet, every pill, excessive exercise, and even liposuction. Been there, done that, rebounded and got the fat pants. I have given every form of weight loss product known to man a run for the money. I have had my share of temporary successes. In every case, I was one cookie away from backsliding. All these methods had one thing in common – none of them addressed why I was overeating in the first place. None of them eradicated the sleeping giant within me, poised to be awakened by the scent of chocolate, and willing to snatch an old lady's purse to get at her Junior Mints.

After all I had tried, all the time and money I had spent, nothing had changed. The real problem was untouched. I didn't really want to touch it. I was hoping it would magically go away. But I saw the enemy, and it was me.

The problem would have been so much more obvious to me if it was drug use, alcohol, or pornography. In a way it was most like pornography – although it wasn't sexual, it was sensual. My weight was a reflection of the extent to which I abused the pleasure of food – a measure of my appetite for gratification. It just so happened that food was my drug of choice. There was nothing that a warm brownie couldn't fix, at least temporarily.

As a Christian, I learned that my own battle with my weight went a lot deeper than my concomitant enjoyment of chocolate and my sense of despair that I would never be thin enough. Never being thin also meant (to me) I would never be worthy. How had I so deeply connected thinness and my own self worth? I think the connection of weight to worth is a separate problem from the abuse of food, but related. If you feel better about yourself because you lost weight, what have you really solved? I had two problems to solve – to stop abusing food as a drug and to decouple my weight (at its highest or lowest) from my perception of my value. Both of these were incongruent with the truth. Food has a God-given purpose, and my value is defined by God, not my waist size.

Diet and exercise have nothing to offer to either of those problems. All diets have one thing in common – the key operating mechanism is your willpower. No diet is any more effective than your own ability to apply willpower to yourself. Good news, bad news. Bad news first – there is no good news. No one's willpower is strong enough by itself to overcome addictive behavior. It wasn't meant to be.

At its core, the battle with weight is a flesh versus spirit battle. Until I saw it for what it really was, all my weight loss efforts were futile.

In my relationship with God, if I have this stronghold, an appetite that is unrestrained, did it matter whether it was drugs, alcohol, porn or Twinkies? No, not really.

At this point in my life, I lacked absolutely nothing in terms of knowledge to solve the problem. Theoretically. I knew what to do, I could even explain why it should work using really big words I learned in college. But why wasn't I doing it? I was being out-wrestled. By what? By whom?

I was powerlessness to win the war. What is it that I'm really fighting in this battle that never ends?

I realized that it was time to stop avoiding God and ask Him to help me figure this out. He reminded me that someone we knew had a similar issue, albeit not over food.

ROMANS 7:18-19

For I know that nothing good dwells in me, that is, in my flesh. For I have the desire to do what is right, but not the ability to carry it out. [19] For I do not do the good I want, but the evil I do not want is what I keep on doing.

Reading through Romans, and other studies in the Bible, I realized I was allowing my nature, my flesh and its appetite to have its way, to dominate me. There was something in me that was entitled, spoiled, and demanding, albeit easily appeased by a treat. So what does one do about this?

Fortunately, God did not leave me hanging.

ROMANS 8: 5-8

[5] For those who live according to the flesh set their minds on the things of the flesh, but those who live according to the Spirit set their minds on the things of the Spirit. [6] For to set the mind on the flesh is death, but to set the mind on the Spirit is life and peace.

This certainly explained my lifelong battle more clearly than anything I had ever heard, seen, read, etc. The Apostle Paul explained - "the mind set on the flesh is death, the mind set on the spirit is life and peace." Diet and exercise would never work for me – they kept me focused on battling my flesh, but with my own power. It was like trying to arm wrestle myself.

Now that I knew the answer, or at least the nature of the answer, how would I make that work for me? How would that solve my problem? My desire for sweets didn't just disappear.

As I worked on figuring that out, I learned more about my faith. The pursuit of this answer took me deeper into my relationship with God. He became more personal to me. I was amazed that He was answering my questions. I knew Christianity is about relationship, but I never realized I didn't have a close relationship with Him until I began to develop one. One that was alive and personal, as opposed to a belief that I accepted but had not experienced.

The only power strong enough to overcome my flesh is the Holy Spirit. In order to have the power of the Holy Spirit, I need to accept and surrender to certain truths. I needed to understand what surrender was. I needed to understand what to do about not wanting to surrender. I needed to know God well enough not just to trust Him, but to entrust myself to Him. I had questions like - what happens when I surrender? Do I love God enough? How do I love Him more than I love the things I don't want to surrender? Like my independence. I don't have time to wait for Him. What if He doesn't answer?

God has been gracious and merciful to me. All those questions arose from selfish fear, from the same part of me that craves pancakes. Somehow, in spite of all the noise my flesh was making, my relationship with God grew. I knew I needed Him. He knew to ignore my self-interested questions and instead was answering my soul's deeper call – I need You, Lord. Will You help me? Please help my unbelief.

The biggest change in my weight came from the biggest shift in my life. I knew I needed to trust God more than I trusted myself. I believe that solving any kind of besetting problem starts by finding the middle of the rope in the flesh and spirit tug of war, and deciding which side to pull from. I knew I needed God to help me desire Him more. It is not "normal" to desire God more than our own way. When I do, I know it is because He answered my prayer – Lord help me to desire you more than all else and to be fully satisfied in you.

If you are struggling with your weight, I pray that you will allow God to draw you to His side of the battle. Ask Him to increase your soul's hunger for Him. These are prayers He loves to answer.

Thank you for taking the time to read my story. I am praying for you, that it becomes clear that Jesus Christ saves us, and not only from eternal separation from God. His power saves us every day from being overpowered by the nature in us that opposes God. When the choice is between a natural life embattled with your flesh for meaningless purposes or a supernatural life in Christ, walking in the works He created in advance for us to do, which do you choose? The decision was hard for me – my flesh was strong from a lifetime of being in charge. But what is not possible with man is possible with God.

At **Stop Dieting For Life**, our mission is to equip you to understand your unique challenges with weight, to help you learn how to shift your trust to God, to allow the Holy Spirit to work, and to learn all you need to know to live as a steward of your body, His Temple.

About Laura

Laura Fulford, Weight Loss Coach to the Christian Community, is a refreshingly honest, practical and seasoned wellness expert. Whether one-on-one, or in her group programs, Laura connects her clients to permanent success by teaching them how to get it done, once and for all. The Stop Dieting for Life Program is a comprehensive approach designed to support you to your goal and teach you how to sustain it.

Laura is the author of *Lose It For Good: 7 Ways to Slim Down without Dieting.* Contact information: www.StopDietingForLife.com. This guidebook offers seven things believers in Christ must do to achieve permanent weight loss.

The Bible says "There is nothing new under the sun," and this is certainly true of weight loss programs. Spin them any way you want to and they are all the same. No product or program in and of itself can make a person lose weight successfully. So what does?

Laura's passion for helping people overcome their struggles with weight arose from her own experience. Her battle with her weight began in childhood and continued throughout her life. In spite of all the time that the struggle plagued her, she recognized gratefully that it was this struggle that drove her deeper in her relationship with God.

The answers she discovered ultimately shaped her not just physically, but more importantly, spiritually. She learned that her deepest issues were spiritual, yet they showed up in physical ways, like overeating in response to stress or for comfort, and then over-exercising to try to compensate.

As the answers unfolded and she began to make real changes in her life, Laura realized she had discovered a system for permanent weight loss that could help others as effectively as it had helped her. Her *Stop Dieting For Life* system is a biblical, practical and responsible approach to overcoming the strongholds that make losing weight seem like a never-ending battle.

Laura graduated from Wake Forest University with a B.S. in Exercise Science, and holds certifications as a Life Coach and a Wellness Coach. Her educational background includes studies in physiology, nutrition, sports psychology, and exercise science.

CHAPTER 19

CHANGE YOUR MINDSET — CHANGE YOUR LIFE

BY LINDA ALLRED

It still amazes me that I did totally insane things revolving around food for years and years yet somehow still managed to appear "normal" to the outside world.

At the age of 46, I was 40 pounds overweight, resided in a daily state of unhappiness, and my overall life was pretty much in shambles. The only thing that brought me any semblance of comfort was food, and in particular, ice cream.

Every night after finishing a full-course meal, I'd ask my husband Don if he'd like to have a bowl of ice cream as a tasty dessert to end our meal. Of course, it was me who was secretly craving that cool delicious iciness, but I'd "trick" him into believing that it was HIS desire to partake of the treat, just so I could have a heaping helping myself. Little did he know that later on that evening after he went to bed, I'd run to the freezer, take out the container of the flavor of the night, and gorge myself until I felt sick to my stomach. Heck, I was so addicted to the stuff that I would even "nuke" the container in our microwave just to be sure I didn't waste a single precious drop of that soothing mind-numbing nectar. I was running myself ragged, tearing out to the grocery store on a daily basis, to replenish the carton of ice cream that I'd devoured the night before. I didn't want my husband to catch on to the fact that the gallon of ice cream we'd taken our dessert from the night before had mysteriously disappeared before the light of the next day!

You see, I was eating my way through my unhappiness, but it wasn't until I'd practiced this insanity for a few years that I stumbled upon the one key element that would forever change my life for the better.

I got caught up in a vicious circle while trying to just survive. My average day went like this: alarm went off at 5:30 am; I dragged myself to shower, dress and get ready for work; grabbed a cup of hot tea (laced with sugar and cream) and tore off to my office. The 10:00 am break would roll around and I'd consume a couple of doughnuts or muffins, another cup of tea, and keep going. By the time my lunch hour came around, I was starving, but I'd told myself, "I'll just eat a salad. That way I won't consume too many calories and will lose weight." Right? Like lunch was my only problem! By the time I'd get home after work, I'd be too tired to even think about cooking dinner so the meal would often consist of take-out foods or whatever happened to be in the freezer that was quick and easy to prepare. And, of course, dessert was the always beloved ice cream. Let's not forget the anti-depressants that my doctor has prescribed as well as the sleeping pills that I took nightly just to be able to get some peace.

At the time, I had a very successful 17 year career in Human Resources... but something was missing from my life. One morning around 3:00 am, I started experiencing a severe tightness in my chest. I panicked and made a rush visit to my doctor that day, as I was terrified I was having a heart attack. Much to my chagrin, he told me to go home and relax, that the pain I was experiencing was simply stress. But, being a workaholic, I continued to suffer pain and anxiety for at least another year.

One night as I lay in bed, I prayed to God to send me a solution to how I could finally let go of my stress, shed the weight I'd gained, and help me solve my general unhappiness. Acting on the advice of a trusted friend, I decided to go see a hypnotist, even though I thought that practice was a bit 'woo woo' and not totally real. I made an appointment with Dr. Arthur Winkler and went to my first appointment pre-convinced that he wouldn't be able to help me relax.

To say I was skeptical that hypnosis could help me would be a gross understatement! I'd seen television shows of people supposedly being hypnotized and turned into clucking idiots on stage during the program. While that was an entertaining show, I certainly didn't want to start barking uncontrollably if I heard a 'trigger' word at work.

However, something powerful happened at that first session. Even though I was certain that I was totally un-hypnotized and awake throughout our session and that this practice was bogus, I made the decision to give hypnosis a month and see if I noticed any changes in how I felt.

Here's where things got a bit magical. During that trial month I noticed that I was losing weight almost effortlessly, I felt calmer, and I was sleeping better at nights. Plus I seemed to have more self-confidence and my sense of self-esteem was rising as well.

I had a major 'Aha' moment when I realized how hypnosis was improving ALL levels of my life! That's when I made the decision to take back control of my life, quit that cushy job I'd had for 17 years that was making me literally sick with anxiety, and decided to become certified as a hypnotist and pay forward what I had learned.

Studying and adopting the practice of Self-Hypnosis opened up other avenues for me to creating total wellness for not only myself but also my many clients. By learning to tap into the power of your subconscious mind (which, by the way, makes up 99% of your mind and is where all of your good/bad habits and beliefs are stored), you have the opportunity to accelerate your results on any goal you undertake. I also learned that our subconscious mind serves two purposes:

1) To keep our autonomic nervous system functioning twenty-four hours a day, and

2) To listen, listen, listen, to our conscious thoughts and then do everything within its power to makes our thoughts our reality. That's why your mindset plays such a pivotal role in creating a happy, healthy and vibrant life.

I decided that I'd use what I called back then the 'power of self-talk' and literally talk my way back into being slim, trim, and mentally healthy.

Every day on my way to work I had to cross over the Amite River Bridge, which was about five miles from my home. So I'd say to myself, "Okay, Linda. You know your mind is listening and responding to your thoughts, so what do you want to think about?" I made a pact with myself and decided to repeat about 12 positive statements that I wanted to bring into my life for 28 days in a row every time I crossed that Amite River on the way to work.

As I crossed the bridge, I would tell myself:

- I am okay.
- I am happy.
- I am important.
- I am special.
- God loves me very much.
- I am having a wonderful day.
- I am successful.
- I am confident.
- I am slim and trim.
- I am learning to like and love myself more and more each day.
- I am intelligent.
- I am getting better and better in every way, day by day.

Well, I'd hit that bridge every morning, and in a *weak, depressed, low, squeaky voice*, I'd tell myself, "I am happy." And then I'd think "Linda, you don't sound happy." So I'd say, "I am happy." And once again I'd hear that 'inner critic' say "Linda, you don't sound happy." So I would make myself start screaming these positive affirmations to myself three times in a row in a loud, boisterous, forceful voice, "I am happy. I am happy. I AM HAPPY! I am having a wonderful day. I am having a wonderful day. I AM HAVING A WONDERFUL DAY," until I repeated all 12 positive affirmations. Once I'd get across that bridge I could feel the endorphins kicking in and all of a sudden, I felt so good, so alive and HAPPY! Then the next day when I crossed the Amite River Bridge, I'd be down in the dumps again, but I was so determined to form this new habit of saying positive affirmations to myself that I just kept it up. Don't forget: I was so used to beating myself up that I wasn't sure this would even work, but I would start screaming again "I am happy. I am happy. I AM HAPPY!"

I did this for 28 days. People probably thought I was crazy going over that Amite River Bridge screaming at myself, but did I care? Nope. I literally started to talk myself back to good health from doing this every single day on the way to work for 28 days.

So I opened my own business using self-hypnosis as the cornerstone to teaching people what I had learned, which in my opinion, is the best-kept secret on planet Earth.

Along my journey to wholeness and living well, I put together a simple yet highly effective system, which when practiced regularly, is almost fool-proof to creating amazing happiness, health and prosperity. I call them my 5 *Surefire Steps Change Your Mindset, Change Your Life*, and I'd like to share a brief overview of them with you in this chapter.

STEP ONE: Learn the greatest secret on planet Earth, namely harnessing the power of subconscious mind goal-setting and make it work for you.

STEP TWO: Discover the art of Self-Hypnosis/Creative Visualization – the all natural 'mind booster' that no drugs, pills, or portions can even come close to helping you break any of your bad habits.

STEP THREE: Adopt the Accelerated Change Template (ACT™*) a powerful belief-change science using the energy work of kinesiology to easily eliminate old limiting beliefs that are holding you back from achieving your goals, including that of creating amazing happiness, health, and prosperity in MINUTES.

STEP FOUR: Gain the invaluable knowledge of how to 'Connect the dots' between your thoughts and actions to tap into the life-altering Laws of Attraction by using the powerful, *Willingness Mantra***, to let go of your fears/anxieties and start living in abundance and prosperity.

STEP FIVE: Learn to use Positive Affirmations to achieve anything you desire easily, and learn to access the hidden influence that this step provides to train your thoughts to attract what you want.

---

* Created by my ACT™ mentor, Nikkea B. Devida: www.fastresultsformula.com.
** From my mentor, Sonia Miller's book, *"THE ATTRACTION DISTRACTION...*
Why The Law of Attraction Isn't Working for You...and How to Get Results – FINALLY!"
www.SuccessForTheSoul.com.

When I practice these *5 Surefire Steps*, my life goes a lot smoother, despite whatever obstacles may come my way. For example, in 2000 within a span of 4 months, my husband Don suffered a debilitating stroke and I lost my beloved eldest son Wade, when he was killed in a horrible car accident. I can't tell you that I easily coped with these two life-changing events as that would be a bold-faced lie. But I do thank God that by the time I was faced with these events, I was much better equipped, mentally, physically, and emotionally, to cope in a relatively calm manner. Self-Hypnosis and positive affirmations brought me comfort during this emotional time, and I will be forever grateful to Dr. Winkler for sharing these life-saving tools with me all those years prior to this happening.

I also want to share with you that recently I went through another trying period in my life. For three years I was a caregiver to my beloved husband of 54 years, Don, who unfortunately lost his battle with cancer in March of 2013. There were many times when I just wanted to stay in bed, pull the covers up over my head and cry, and not have to get up and face another day of watching him suffer. I was able to persevere, put one foot in front of the other and keep going because I continued using everything I'd learned from my *5 Surefire Steps*.

Today, my own personal mantra is *"I am willing to do today what most people want so tomorrow I will have what most people want."* I have learned from studying with Nikkea B. Devida, that by harnessing the power of our subconscious mind through Self-Hypnosis and the practice of ACT™, we can create amazing changes in our lives.

By the way, I almost forgot to tell you one very important thing about this entire process of my learning how to practice Self-Hypnosis. Pound-by-pound, inch-by-inch, I lost all of those 40 pesky pounds 20 years ago AND I've never regained that weight! Imagine that! Plus, remember those nasty chest pains? I'm happy to say that they disappeared as well. I invite all of you to map out a plan of action that includes the thought process of 'change your mindset – change your life!' today and see the wonderful things you can achieve simply by following my *5 Surefire Steps*. Not only will they help you create amazing happiness, good health, and prosperity in your daily living, but they'll also allow you to learn to squash any limiting beliefs you may be subconsciously carrying around in your head that could be sabotaging your levels of success.

And that, ladies and gentlemen, is a winning recipe for living well and enjoying a delicious life!

About Linda

Heralded as "The Bad Habit, Belief Breaker/Certified Hypnotist Expert/Accelerated Change Template (ACT™) Master Practitioner," Linda Allred is one of only a few people in the USA that is trained in ACT™ - a powerful belief-change science using the energy work of kinesiology that will forever uproot the single biggest fear or doubt you have about achieving your goals... and replace it with positive belief statements that free you to move forward.

And you don't even have to 'try hard' to do it! Her proven programs deliver a powerful 2-step punch - Self-Hypnosis and Accelerated Change Template (ACT™) that are designed to help you break your bad habits and limiting beliefs in MINUTES so you can achieve ground breaking success in all areas of their life. And guess what?

It's as easy to change your Bad Habits/Limiting Beliefs as it is to edit a single word document on your computer! You edit... you save... and you're done!

Creator of the *Weight Off NOW! Get Healthy – Get Happy Self-Hypnosis Bootcamp Home Study System™*: www.lindaallred.com/package, Linda is an expert in the art of Self-Hypnosis, Creative Visualization, Accelerated Change Template (ACT™), Laws of Attraction, Positive Affirmations, and whole-food nutrition. She received her certification in hypnosis in 1992 from St. John's University, Springfield, LA, and holds additional certifications in hypnosis from the National Guild of Hypnotists, Merrimack, NH. She has actively practiced hypnosis for 20+ years blending the latest discoveries in science, spirituality, and psychology thereby creating amazing accelerated results that last for her clients. Linda also became an Accelerated Change Template (ACT™) Master Practitioner in 2010, further adding to her profound toolkit to help others live happy, healthy and fulfilling lives.

Here's how to connect with Linda:
Linda@LindaAllred.com
www.LindaAllred.com
www.facebook.com/LindaVAllred
www.twitter.com/LindaVAllred

CHAPTER 20

THE BATTLE FOR DIGESTIVE HEALTH — THE KEY TO FEELING WELL

BY DR. LIZ CRUZ

"Doc I'm just not digesting well," this is something I hear day-in and day-out as a Gastroenterologist. I have been practicing Gastroenterology for over a decade now and it seems I am getting busier and busier with each passing year. From the time I started practicing medicine, I have had a very strong desire to spend time with my patients – listening to them, examining them, and really trying to get to the root of their issues. Around 2007 when I started my own practice, I noticed my patient panel start to shift. I started seeing many more young people in their 20's and 30's with the same digestive issues I was used to seeing in 50 and 60 year olds (including having pre-cancerous polyps). I was running tests and doing procedures on all ages only to find nothing medically wrong which made treating the patient's symptoms difficult. I was telling more and more patients they were going to have to be on prescription or non-prescription drugs indefinitely. This does not sit well with most, especially the younger patients.

My staff will tell you that I am the type of doctor that truly cares about the patients' well-being. When the answer is not there, Dr. Cruz will find it. But I have to admit, what was happening with my patient panel was stumping me time and time again. One day I approached my Office Manager, Tina Nunziato, who is also my life partner, and I asked her what we could do for these patients that were having digestive symptoms with no known cause. Her response was, "I don't know, but let's find out." That led us on a two-year journey to discovering some pretty interesting facts about three key industries – food, healthcare and pharmaceuticals. After reading a ton of books, going to seminars, and talking with industry experts, I realized very quickly how little my medical degree actually taught me about nutrition and digestion.

Please know that I feel honored and privileged to have gone to medical school, but knowing what I know now I feel sad that our medical schools are so focused on teaching us to find the symptoms and treat with drugs or surgery instead of really trying to get to the root cause. On average, my patients are on 12 – 15 medications and we think this is how medicine should be. Unfortunately, we are not healing patients like this; we are merely putting band-aids on very simple issues. In addition, by treating patients with this methodology, we are causing bigger issues and even more symptoms. Most of my patients cannot even remember what it feels like to be well. The question is: when will it end? When will patients realize enough is enough, and actually want to feel better again? Tina and I felt it was our mission to teach our patients what we learned, so they could make more educated decisions for themselves when it came to their health and their body.

Tina and I started incorporating our learning into our own life and the lives of our children. We felt if we were going to promote a better way of living, we'd better be models to others. We started to shift what we ate, what we drank, what supplements we took, how we approached stress, etc. Although it took us a full two years to transition our lives, I cannot even begin to explain what it has done for us as individuals and as a family. We are healthier than ever, no more aches and pains, no more foggy brain, no more trips to the doctor, no more time off school and work. We have more energy than ever; the kids are strong and well-developed both physically and mentally, and we all continue to desire healthy food and drink.

In order to help me deliver our message to patients, Tina went back to school for her Holistic Nutrition Certificate. She helped me to craft and deliver our 12-week wellness program to any patient that was willing to listen and learn. Within two years we had helped dozens of patients eliminate their digestive issues, get off some or all of their medications, regain their energy levels, and in some cases even lose a considerable amount of weight. We noticed that as we taught, patients would grasp for more, and the more they grasped, the more we offered. We began partnering with service providers to offer colon hydrotherapy, infrared sauna treatments, lymphatic massage, etc. We partnered with dozens of vendors to provide healthy food and water to patients at a discounted cost. It seemed like everyone who was introduced to the concepts we were teaching found a golden nugget that changed their life. And what was interesting was the golden nugget was different for everyone.

As many of you know, with every great accomplishment comes an even bigger challenge. We were having a hard time keeping up with all the people we helped – we realized how difficult only having two educators can be. We noticed that if the patients didn't have someone encouraging them or making them accountable they were having a hard time staying on track, no matter how bad they wanted good health. We have learned when it comes to eating, drinking and stress; the habits of Americans are very addicting and very hard to break away from. Without constant support and guidance, it makes living a healthier life very difficult. We were spending so much time on the upfront education we weren't able to be there for everyone on the back-end to help them keep up the good work. In addition, due to constant reimbursement cuts year after year from the insurance companies, I was being forced to see more patients in the office during the day, which was making it more difficult to present our concepts to patients in the exam room.

This was a very difficult time for us and there were many times we wanted to quit. Although we were helping people we felt like we were not making the lifelong impact we were hoping for. In addition, we were not able to reach as many as we were before and it just seemed like we could not talk fast enough to enough people. No matter how frustrating it was at times, Tina and I both felt God continuing to push us forward in our mission. When we finally came to terms that quitting was not an option we realized we had to put some major thought into what we were doing and how we were doing it. We needed to come up with a way to deliver our products and services to take "US" out of the equation so we could spend our whole time supporting and guiding. This thought process took us almost a year, until after attending a couple seminars by Peak Potentials and Lisa

Sasevich, we were able to craft a delivery model that would allow us to make the biggest impact and change the most lives for good.

We decided to package our teaching into a comprehensive 3-step program called the *DNA for Digestive Health*. We knew we had a lot to share with people and we did not want to leave anything out; however we wanted to make it as simple as possible. The D stands for Detoxification and Digestive Restoration. The N stands for Nutrition and Necessary Hydration and the A stands for Activating Mind, Body and Soul and Action Plan. All of which are crucial to changing a persons' digestive health. Aside from the fact that the acronym works well with the concepts we teach, the *DNA for Digestive Health* is the structure one needs to follow to experience lasting results. And what we have found personally is that once you begin on your path to digestive wellness it is almost like the DNA in your body actually does start to change. You begin craving the right foods and being disgusted by the wrong foods. You begin being negatively affected by the bad things that never seemed to bother you before (until you had symptoms that is). You literally will be able to connect with your body again and feel when something is or is not good for it.

At a high level the concepts are simple, but diving deep is where the true revelations appear. Detoxification is the first thing we teach because one of the main reasons why people are so sick today is because their body is toxic. Keep in mind that detoxification is a bit of a taboo word in the medical field. Although when you think about it, our bodies are naturally detoxifying all day through our urine, stool, sweat and breath. The problem is we are exposed to so many toxins each day in what we breathe, what we eat and drink, and what we put on our skin, that our body cannot eliminate the toxins fast enough. This toxic build-up in the body is the cause to many of our aches, pains and symptoms. And when we do not listen to those aches, pains and symptoms and treat them like warning signs, things get worse – we end up on medications, in the hospital, having surgeries, etc. Medicines only add to the toxicity of the body, which is why when many people start on one medicine it is not long before they are on another and another. We have to learn how to detoxify the body on a regular basis to avoid the symptoms all together.

Digestive Restoration is the rebuilding of the body or providing it something it no longer produces on its own; digestive enzymes are a perfect example of this. Many patients present in our office because they are experiencing gas, bloating, and acid reflux after they eat. And it is not uncommon for people in their 20's and 30's to present with these symptoms. This is because their body is producing less than optimal enzymes to digest their food properly. When we eat a poor diet, a majority of our life we rob our body of the ability to produce proper enzymes to digest our food; when this happens we are left with undigested food and a whole lot of new symptoms. Just by supplementing with a digestive enzyme before every meal, the symptoms go away and there is no need for acid reflux, gas or bloating medicines. As part of Digestive Restoration, we also discuss the importance of probiotics among other supplements that are critical to the body digesting food properly.

Nutrition and Necessary Hydration are the most important lessons we teach. This is the part we live on a daily basis and the part that is absolutely critical to long-term digestive health and overall wellness. The concept of Nutrition covers many topics, one of those being eating less processed white foods like sugar, flour, salt, rice, bread and eating more living greens like red leaf lettuce, Bok Choy, avocados, and cucumbers. Necessary Hydration covers the concept of water and why it is so important and that not all water is created equal. Americans tend to drink everything except water and when we get people drinking half of their body weight in ounces they say it makes the biggest impact on how they feel.

The Activating Mind, Body and Soul and Action Planning is all about learning how to move the body to keep the lymph system moving freely, how to feel less stressed, get proper rest and how to take everything you learned and put it into an action plan that you can actually live. Once you learn the *DNA for Digestive Health* we invite you to participate in our online community called: "www.DigestiveRevolution.com." This is where Tina and I spend most of our time adding resources, supporting and guiding those that desire life-long health. By delivering our key teachings online through home study materials, webinars, tele-seminars, and videos, it frees us up to help and support more people change their lives for good. I cannot tell you how amazing it feels to be answering my life-long call to serve patients.

Whatever your call is, never give up – you never know how many lives you will change forever!

About Liz

Dr. Liz Cruz graduated from college in 1988 with a B.S. in Medical Technology. Prior to Medical School, she taught English for one year in Bangkok, Thailand. In 1989, Dr. Cruz began her formal career in medicine by attending Loma Linda University School of Medicine in California. During medical school, Dr. Cruz was part of a student / staff physician team, which provided relief work to the natives along the Amazon River. She graduated from medical school in 1993 and then went on to do her Internal Medicine Internship under the auspices of the U.S. Navy at the Naval Hospital, Oakland, California.

Upon the closure of the Naval Hospital in Oakland, Dr. Cruz transferred and completed her internal medicine residency at the University of California, San Francisco. In 1996, she was deployed to Guam to fulfill her commitment to the U.S. Navy. While in Guam, she served as a Staff Internist at the U.S. Naval Hospital. During her active duty years in the Navy, she received the Meritorious Unit Commendation Medal as well as the Humanitarian Service Medal and the National Defense Medal for service during Operation Desert Storm. During her last two years in Guam, she was the Head of the Internal Medicine Division at the U.S. Naval Hospital.

In 2000, she went back to the University of California, San Francisco where she completed her training in Gastroenterology (GI). In 2004, Dr. Cruz moved to Arizona to join the Arizona Medical Clinic in Peoria. She served as a full-time gastroenterologist in both the outpatient and inpatient settings doing the full range of general gastroenterology including endoscopic procedures as well as hepatology. In January 2007, she opened the doors to her own practice, Digestive Healthcare Associates, LLC in Phoenix, Arizona: www.digestivehca.com.

In 2010, Dr. Cruz along with her life partner, Tina Nunziato began offering the Dr. Liz Cruz Wellness Program to educate patients on the very things that were causing their digestive issues. After helping hundreds of patients eliminate their digestive issues through detoxification, digestive restoration, nutrition, and proper hydration, Dr. Cruz decided to launch her products and services online to the masses. Her *DNA for Digestive Health* 3-step program and the www.DigestiveRevolution.com online community she created are changing people's digestive health for good. More information about her products and services can be found at: www.drlizcruz.com and through her "Digest This" podcast at: www.digestthispodcast.com.

Dr. Cruz was born in Los Angeles, California and was raised in Orlando, Florida. She speaks fluent Spanish and enjoys her family, traveling, jazz music, and photography.

Dr. Cruz is a Diplomate of the American Board of Internal Medicine and the American Board of Gastroenterology. She is a member of the American College of Gastroenterology and the American Society for Gastrointestinal Endoscopy.

CHAPTER 21

WE BUY HOUSES AND SO CAN YOU!

BY LORI DAWSON

Is it possible to buy and sell houses without using your own money or credit, and make a lot of money doing it? The answer is YES! I know this, because my family and I have done it.

When we started, we were living in a one-bedroom apartment with very little money, no credit, a flicker of hope and a big dream. Just three years later, we owned 28 houses worth $7.5 million and had a consistent monthly income of $50,000.

Looking back, there were three primary keys to our success:

1. We invested in an experienced Mentor.
2. We became students of Marketing.
3. We developed step-by-step systems.

When we first started hanging out with other investors and going to workshops, we used to hope that this would be the person with the "magic solution" that would help us "crack the egg" or "get over the hump" so we could be successful. At first, we always left disappointed and discouraged.

Then one night (after we had been buying houses for about a year) the guest speaker at our local real estate investors club meeting was a guy from Atlanta. Within ten minutes, my husband and I knew we'd found the mentor we'd been searching for. This guy had **SYSTEMS!** We were so excited! He had been a management executive for U.P.S. and he brought that expertise into the world of real estate investing.

For the next two-and-a-half years, we travelled from Phoenix to Atlanta every other month to learn from our mentor. While other investors stayed home and messed around with the idea of investing, we were serious. We were willing to do whatever it would take to learn, get results and make money. That's exactly what we did! Fumbling around on our own that first year, we made about $150,000. By the end of our first year with a mentor, we made $300,000. That was double our income for the previous year! The next year we doubled it again.

After working with our mentor for about six months, I finally "heard" something he'd been telling us from the very beginning. Your income will always be directly proportionate to your ability to market yourself. He told us that if we suck at marketing, our income will suck. If we're ok at marketing, our income will be "ok." We decided to learn marketing, and our income continued to grow. He was right!

As good as our mentor's systems were, his market was Atlanta, not Phoenix. We had to learn our market, what worked and what didn't. Our real estate attorney was a huge help. He kept in touch with the Attorney General and what was happening in the courtrooms around the Phoenix area with other real estate investors. Several times, he called us into his office and told us our paperwork needed a major overhaul to keep us out of trouble. We happily complied. Gradually we developed, refined and perfected our own systems for finding, buying, fixing, renting, lease-optioning and selling houses.

There are four different methods we've used for buying houses without using our own money or credit. No doubt there are several more, but these are the ones we learned and used.

1. Downpayment Partners (who get conventional loans)
2. Wholesaling
3. Subject-To
4. Cash Partners

The first three houses we bought were deals we found, but because we didn't have enough money to pay cash or good enough credit to go to the bank for a loan, we brought in partners who did. The first one was a great deal that had just come across our desk. Another investor had gotten it under contract and was going to fix it up himself, but got hurt and was scheduled for shoulder surgery. That night some friends came over for dinner and were telling us they'd just sold a rental property for cash and didn't know what to do with the money. "I think I can help you with that," I said happily! "How would you like to buy a house with us?" We bought it with their money and we did all the work. After fixing it up, we rented it out for a couple of years and then sold it for a nice profit!

The next two houses we bought from a local shyster who saw "newbies" written all over our foreheads. He charged us full market price, telling us all the while what a "good deal" we were getting. We learned. We had a different partner on each deal. Both went to the bank for a traditional loan as their contribution. We fixed up one, rented it and then sold it. We moved into the other one and lived there for about a year before we sold it. We did ok on both properties only because the market value went up significantly. Whew!

Meanwhile, we were busy learning some new strategies! We ran some ads in the local newspaper that looked like this ...

WE BUY HOUSES
ALL CASH
QUICK CLOSING

When the phone started ringing, we were terrified. We didn't know what to say. We didn't know what to do. We didn't know a good deal from a bad one. The first caller was an older man who had lost his wife, found a new home to buy and was anxious to sell his existing house quickly. It had not been updated since the 1950's. It needed a complete makeover! He owned the house free and clear. After agonizing and spending a lot of time with my calculator, I made him an offer that was about 60% of what he was asking. He was NOT happy, but he was very motivated. He finally said YES and signed the Purchase Contract!

Now what? We were excited and panicky at the same time. We had heard about wholesaling, and that is what we were planning to do. The basic concept was that if we could get a house under contract, and if the deal was good enough, we could sell our contract to another buyer who did have the money to close the deal. That's exactly what we did. We walked away with $3,000 cash! An old-timer told us that the deal was so good, we could have asked for $10,000 for that contract and gotten it all day long. Really?

Soon we put another one under contract and when a prospective investor came to look at it, she asked how much we wanted, we managed to choke out, "$9,000 please." She wrote a check immediately, using the hood of her car for a desk. That house was in a really bad part of town. It had been boarded up. A homeless person had made a nest of old clothes and rags in the bathtub. We even found an abandoned car in the back yard. Not our problem. We walked away with check for $9,000. We didn't fix it, and we didn't close on it. We just found and negotiated the deal, then sold our "piece of paper" to someone else! From then on, we were unstoppable!

We kept learning. The next strategy we learned about is referred to as buying a house "subject to." This means that we buy the house by taking over the payments on the existing loan. A guy called one day, begging us to come and buy his house. We would look, I assured him, and make him an offer if we could. I felt horrified as I pulled up to his house in my little beat up brown Honda Civic. This was a $500,000 house that looked like a mansion to me. Great. The guy would laugh me away from his door. He didn't. He invited me in and told me that his ex-wife was on her way over. Of course, I thought. SHE will order me out of the house. She didn't. She told him that if he didn't sign the house over to me, she would kill him. She sounded like she meant it. Both sellers signed my paperwork on the spot and handed me the keys. I left in shock. It was a beautiful 2-story home in a wonderful neighborhood. It was painted with designer colors, had wooden shutters on all of the windows, and had a beautifully-groomed backyard with a pool, water feature and outdoor kitchen. It was immaculate. We sold it to a cash buyer.

That experience opened up a whole new world to us! We did somewhere between 75-100 more subject-to closings over the next 2 years. We actually lost count. By that time, we had done nearly 200 deals. Of those, we kept 28 and rented them out, using a Lease with an Option To Buy. We helped our tenants repair their credit and get bank loans. Some did, some didn't, and we kept making money...until the market crashed!

Our game plan was to own 30-50 houses, pay off the mortgages, rent them out for $1,000-$1,200 per month and retire on the rental income. It was a good plan. However, we learned one very painful lesson: NEVER HOLD PROPERTY IN A DECLINING MARKET. The time to buy-and-hold is when the market is strong and property values are appreciating, not when it's going soft and values are dropping. Ouch.

It wasn't pretty. In one month, 17 of our tenants stopped paying their rent. Over the next two years, we sold, gave away or lost all of our 28 investment properties one-by-one, plus the beautiful horse property we'd bought for ourselves the year before. We survived for the next year by selling appliances, construction materials, tools and anything else we'd accumulated and no longer needed. It was horrifying.

After the dust settled and we began to emerge from our "comas" we started over. The market had bottomed out and the deals were amazing. We found a Cash Partner with enough money to buy 1-2 houses at a time who was willing to not only pay cash for the purchases, but also pay us a fee to us for each house we bought. He also paid for the fix-up and holding costs. When we sold them, he got part of the profit. We did several deals together and both did very well.

Next, an old acquaintance came to us who had some family money he needed to invest, wondering if we could help. We bought 22 houses for him. He paid cash for the houses, paid for the fix-up, paid us a fee for each house we bought, paid us another fee for fixing up each one and then we rented them out for him. Part of our deal with him is that we get paid again when he's ready to sell them. That little "piggy bank" is currently worth well over $3 million.

As you can see, there are a lot of different ways to structure deals and get paid. Real estate is the only vehicle we've found that allows such tremendous opportunities for making money without using our own money or credit. It becomes like a game to see how creatively we can structure deals and make them a win-win for everyone involved.

The world of real estate investing is constantly changing. The techniques and strategies that work one year, don't work the next. The market changes and the economy can be volatile. In order to be successful in this arena, it's very important to follow market trends and continually work on our education. It certainly keeps us on our toes! It makes all the difference to have an experienced mentor, consistent marketing and good systems.

By facing our fear and uncertainty, and by following our dream, we've accomplished some extraordinary levels of success. Even though we've had some very difficult experiences, what we learned can never be taken away from us. We've stepped up and Answered The Call, making a difference for many local families, and that feels really good.

About Lori

Lori Dawson and her husband Jim have been entrepreneurs for over 35 years. Three of their businesses have produced millions in income: a construction company that went from $0 to $12 million in four years, a real estate investment company that went from $0 to $8.1 million in three years and a buy-and-hold partnership currently worth $3.8 million after just 18 months.

Lori is passionate about marketing, systems and creating consistent income. She loves helping other business owners prosper, and enjoys being a business coach and educator. When working with any small company, her goals are to get the business profitable and allow its owners to experience a wonderful sense of personal freedom.

In addition to teaching real estate investment courses and boot camps, Lori coaches real estate investors and does business coaching. She will even partner with owners of businesses (usually e-commerce, chiropractic clinics and manufacturing) that have enough potential to dramatically increase the profitability and then sell them in 3-5 years.

Lori and Jim have been married for over 33 years. They have two grown children who are twins. Their son and a daughter are both married and have their own wonderful families; so the Dawson's have two adorable grandsons, a granddaughter on-the-way and a grand-dog. When Lori isn't busy working, she loves spending time with her two horses.

For contact information: please visit Lori's website: http://thesavvyrei.com.

CHAPTER 22

NOT JUST ANYBODY, YOUR BODY

BY DR. MANON BOLLIGER, ND

ANSWERING YOUR CALL DEMANDS TOTAL HEALTH

When getting rid of your symptoms is not enough, when taking more drugs or changing your prescriptions no longer has any effect, it is time to start listening…NOT just to ANYbody. It is time to start listening to YOUR body.

Before I share with you what it means to start listening to your body, there are three common misconceptions that keep people struggling with their health. Do you share any of these misconceptions?

I speak from personal experience as well as professional expertize while sharing with you what led me to create the necessary gap between my diagnosis and my complete recovery from both MS and Stage 4 Cancer *in situ*.

To tell you that it was difficult would be a lie as I was blessed with a deep listening skill to hear and trust my inner guidance and the courage to withstand the trappings of the diagnosis. I had to overcome all my objections and look at my belief system, investigate the operating presumptions before I could "surrender" into any therapeutic approach at all.

It became evident that I found myself to be the "variable factor," the "player" that would make all the difference on how the statistic about "me" would fall. I became particularly attuned to both the process of disease and the process that leads to health.

At this point with over two decades of clinical experience as a Naturopathic doctor, I would have to say that what I primarily do is empower people to own their health choices. My passion is to help people avoid the dangers of the *diagnostic* trap.

I have treated thousands of patients – from rural farmers in Nova Scotia to corporate stressed out CEOs in Toronto, to Tri-Athletes in BC. I have helped people eliminate their pain, reconfigure their thoughts and behaviors around health to live constructive positive lives and to embody the mind-body-spirit connection.

So let's look at the first misconception. The first misconception is that being symptom-free is the same as being healthy. This occurs when people limit their definition of health. Most people have decided that good health is simply a lack of noticeable symptoms.

It is common to say, "I'm healthy. I have low back pain every morning. But, it's normal – I'm over 40!" Or, "It's normal to have gas after a meal." Or, " I'm tired when I wake in the morning, but so are most people my age." We have become accustomed to a "normal" that is actually not normal. It is not normal because it is not natural! Being stiff in the morning, or gassy after a meal, or being tired upon waking is not natural. People have become so disconnected from how good they really could feel that they settle for much less than is possible. It's the difference between surviving and thriving.

The truth is, the majority of people either accept their symptoms as normal, or know their symptoms are not normal and so try a quick-fix with drugs that mask the pain for a short while but really don't resolve the issue. Along with the pharmaceuticals, we have been sold the definition that health is the absence of symptoms. *We have forgotten that our functioning body and lack of symptoms is not synonymous with health.*

Health has been defined by the World Health Organization as: "A state of complete physical, mental, and social well-being; and not merely the absence of disease or infirmity." As I've illustrated, most people don't define health in the same way as the World Health Organization.

If your goal is merely to get rid of symptoms, then go ahead and take drugs, because some drugs are effective. If you are looking for optimal, thriving health, then you need a different process – a process in which you take back your power and trust the wisdom of your body.

So, how did we get here? How did most of us disconnect and buy into this mediocre vision of health? Somewhere along the line, we gave up our power. We bought into the idea that someone else is more responsible for our own bodies than we are.

A poignant example is the medicalization of the birthing process in the late 19th and early 20th century: Women were given chloroform and later morphine and scopolamine, in order to remove the experience of pain during childbirth. These women were directed to see pain as the enemy, rather than encouraged to use methods that support the natural process of childbirth. They somehow became disconnected from their natural body process and empowerment and adopted the concept of birthing in a semi-conscious state – putting themselves and their infants at risk.

In one way or another, we've all been conditioned to stop trusting our innate body wisdom – but this can change! You don't have to settle for symptom-free living. I invite you to contemplate what optimal health would look like for you. How would you feel? How would you look? What kind of energy would you experience day to day…and what could you do in your life if you went beyond 'symptom-free' to vibrant, energetic, and feeling amazing?

The second misconception that keeps most people struggling with their health is the idea that your symptoms are the enemy. Ask yourself: When your body is "acting up," are you inclined to get upset with your body? Do you tell yourself, "Oh silly old body, what's wrong with you?"; "This pain is going to kill me"; "Why on earth are you betraying me like this?"; "What did I do to deserve this carcass of a body?", etc.

Let's be frank, sometimes things start with one ailment and if it is not addressed properly, it leads down a slippery slope – let me share with you what I mean through the experience of one of my patients.

Before she met me, this patient suffered from terrible back pain for close to five years of her life. Due to the continual back pain she was in, her family life suffered as she could not participate in certain outings. Her morale also suffered as she could not always fight the pain her body was experiencing. She sought out help and was prescribed muscle relaxants, and other prescription analgesics (painkillers). These sometimes had her feeling better temporarily… but eventually she needed stronger pain-killing drugs, to which, over time, she became addicted.

On top of her back pain, and her new addiction to painkillers, she began to develop indigestion. It got so bad she started taking Pepto-Bismol regularly. Then, when that wasn't strong enough, she turned to ranitidine – a powerful medical antacid. Finally, she received an official diagnosis of GERD: Gastro-Esophageal Reflux Disease. Did she have GERD? Or was she just suffering from prolonged use of pharmaceuticals – which were supposed to help her get healthy, but instead were making her sicker?

In addition to this, as she was approaching menopause and had slight osteopenia (thinning of the bones), she was given 'Fosamax' to strengthen her bones…and within 2 months was facing a stomach ulcer. Of course, the "antacids" she was prescribed were not able to address this. She went looking for help with back pain and she ended up with an addiction to painkillers, chronic indigestion, and a stomach ulcer!

These pharmaceutically-induced conditions meant she was now at risk for cancer and in her next visit to the doctor, after being informed of her predicament, she was prescribed an anti-depressant to alleviate any anxiety. At this point, she started to realize the trap she was in. Her body was screaming, and the only solutions she was offered were designed to shut down her own intuition and realizations. The worst part of this story is that it is very, very typical.

The approach she took to "deal" with her back pain had her fighting her body all the way. Her body kept reacting to the drugs she took and she kept fighting the symptoms her body was trying to express. What finally helped her out of this downward spiral was to LISTEN to her body and choose a therapy that respected the natural healing ability of the body. When she explored that path, she discovered the different factors that contributed to her original back pain. She was able to make lifestyle modifications, and correct her posture so that she could maintain the results of her treatment. Most significantly, she started to see her body as her teacher, providing her with clues to let her know where she had to pay attention, rather than seeing her body as a harmful enemy.

In my book, *What Patients Don't Say if Doctors Don't Ask*, I explore more deeply the whole notion of working with the body. On a physical level, this means strengthening the immune system and the gut flora. I strongly believe we become susceptible to viruses and bacteria because we are not in equilibrium and we have no homeostasis. These micro-organisms only flourish when we are in an unhealthy state. We are constantly housing micro-organisms of all sorts, but what keeps us healthy is beneficial micro-organisms in our gut. If we have enough of them, then we are easily able to fend off the harmful bacteria. This is also true of cancer. We constantly have cancerous cells in our bodies and we are equipped to rid ourselves of them. If we weaken our bodies with harmful drugs or foods that do not support our metabolism, we are less able to have the immune health to detect these cancer cells.

I hope you realize that taking a purely physical approach is not a complete one. There is plenty of research now that shows that our thoughts and emotions have a great influence over our immune and digestive systems. What people don't realize is that there are so many gentle therapeutic approaches that can actually boost your immune system and gastrointestinal health by supporting your body. We are better off working with our bodies rather than fighting our bodies. 'Working with' is supporting, nourishing, restoring, etc. – it is not a war on symptoms. We do have a very real ability to create a sound environment that will maintain our health. So work with your symptoms and not against them.

The third misconception common in our society is that drugs can bring about health. Let's see how this is playing out in your life at the moment.

Being on medication is not a rare phenomenon:

1. A study reported in *Natural News* states that doctors wrote over 4 billion prescriptions for drugs in America (2011). That's about one new prescription every month for every American.
   Source: http://www.naturalnews.com/037226_drug_prescriptions_medical_news_pills html#ixzz2ZtJwnhqb

2. The average American fills about 12 medication prescriptions annually.
   Source: Prescription Drug Trends, Kaiser Family Foundation, May 2010, http://kaiserfamilyfoundation.
   files.wordpress.com/2013/01/3057-08.pdf

3. How many Americans are on some form of medication? Well, according to Forbes: Nearly half of all Americans aged 55 and above are on a prescription drug, and 23% of those aged 18 – 24 are already on medication. According to the Wall Street Journal, 25% of U.S. kids and teens are taking a medication on a chronic basis.
   Source: "So Young and So Many Pills", Anna Wilde Mathews, 12/28/2010, *The Wall Street Journal*, http://online.wsj.com/article/SB10001424052970203731004576046073896475588.html

4. The elderly represent approximately 12.9% of the U.S. population, yet they represent approximately 25% to 30% of all prescribed medications.
   Source: "Who is popping all those pills" David Maris, 7/24/2012, *Forbes Magazine*, http://www.forbes.com/sites/davidmaris/2012/07/24/1-in-3-american-adults-take-prescription-drugs/

The real problem with medications is that we don't look at the effect the drugs are having on our health. I heard a doctor colleague friend of mine say: "There is no healthy drug, but some drugs have occasionally, a good side effect." What I tell my patients is, "While drugs are dealing with your symptoms - who is dealing with your health?"

What I find fascinating when it comes to signs and symptoms, is the relationship between the drugs available and the diagnosis given. Are drugs created to match a diagnosis? Or is the diagnosis being made by medical professionals to match the drugs which they have access to? If there is no drug to treat something, is that when our symptoms are labelled idiopathic (unknown cause), atypical (not what we've seen before), or psychosomatic (made-up)?

Conventional medical doctors are trained to recognize the scope of signs and symptoms that belong to what are called Merck Manual categories. The problem with this is if your signs and symptoms don't fit into these categories, you are basically dismissed! Many, many patients suffer from symptoms that don't readily belong to existing categories. What's worse, often the only insight they receive is that their symptoms might be "all in their heads" and they are then referred to therapists, psychologists, or psychiatrists and – worse yet – are prescribed anti-depressants.

This could have been an opportunity to delve into the science of the mind-body connection...instead, the entire medical system of 'classifying diseases' has stuck to "solutions" appropriate either for the body or for the mind, with no overlap between the two considered. One need only to look at the large body of research in psycho-neuro-immunology or neuroscience and plasticity to understand that science is debunking current conventional medical belief and practices.

If pharmaceutical deaths were found to be the third leading cause of death in a report published in JAMA (Jama, July 26, 2000 – Vol. 284, No.4), what is in store for us in the future? When we face the fact that drugs do not lead to long-term optimal health, we begin to see that we actually can make a new and better choice. By now I hope you understand that your body's innate wisdom holds the only possibility to turn things around...and it is all in your hands!!

I shared the three most common misconceptions that keep people struggling with their health:

- First – that symptom-free equals healthy;
- Second – that symptoms are the enemy; and
- Third – that drugs can bring about health.

When you address these three misconceptions – by expanding your definition of health, using your symptoms as a guide, and not relying on drugs to cover them up –you move leaps and bounds towards taking back your health. It is about knowing exactly how you can trigger your own body to start healing, and no longer relying on quick fixes. I invite you to consider other options for your health – actual real options for health – and not disease maintenance or symptom suppression.

So how do you L.I.S.T.E.N. to your body? How do you turn Confusion, Fear and Shame to Clarity, Confidence and Conviction?

The answer is within us: *all we need to do is LEARN TO LISTEN.*

About Dr. Manon

Dr. Manon Bolliger, ND, FCAH, DHANP, RBHP helps her patients discover that health is freedom, not only on a physical level, but on an emotional, mental and spiritual level as well. Her profound insights and passion for healing has made her one of Canada's leading classical homeopaths and BowenFirst™ practitioners. Over the past two decades, Dr. Bolliger has helped thousands of patients, from all walks of life - including rural farmers in Nova Scotia, corporate CEOs in Toronto and Tri-Athletes in BC – to allow their bodies to heal themselves.

Throughout her career, Dr. Bolliger has honed and diversified her skills by teaching and training students in health care and pain relief while creating a healing movement that embraces symptoms rather than fighting them. A collaborative doctor-patient relationship is key to her healing approach. She helps each patient understand the vital role they have to play in their own unique healing process so they can go beyond the diagnosis to experience true health.

In 2007 she founded Bowen College, the first Canadian College of its type to embrace and enhance the legacy of Tom Bowen, which offers Bowen therapy courses and certification around the world. Bowen College is the only college to incorporate Dr. Bolliger's unique L.I.S.T.E.N methodology into its curriculum.

In addition to being Director of Bowen College and the Cornerstone Health Centre in Vancouver, BC, Dr. Bolliger still finds time to capture audiences as an inspirational author and speaker – sharing her revolutionary insights into healing and the mind, body relationship.

Achievements / Accreditations:

- Award for Excellence in Homeopathic Medicine *(Dr. R. B. Farquharson Award)*
- Co-Founder of the Canadian Council for Homeopathic Certification *(2001)*
- Fellow of the Canadian Academy of Homeopathy *(1996)*
- Doctorate of Naturopathic Medicine *(1992 CCNM)*
- Scholarship for Master's study in Law and Alternative Health
  - *McGill Law School*
- LLB from Université de Quebec à Montreal *(UQUAM)*

- **Author:** *What Patients Don't Say if Doctors Don't Ask: The Mindful Patient-Doctor Relationship* (www.WhatPatientsDontSay.com)

- **Radio host:** "Synergy Dialogues™ in Health"

- **Founder/Developer:** "L.I.S.T.E.N" – *Methodology to own your health choices* "Understanding the 4 "E"s *That will change your practice forever*

- **President/CEO:** "Cornerstone Health Centre" - *where doctors promote patient consciousness in the healing process*

- **Founder/President:** Bowen College – *Teaching practitioners the renowned Bowen Therapy*

- **Chairperson:** Boucher Naturopathic College *(2004 – Present)*

- **Board Member:** DHANP *(Diplomate of the Homeopathic Academy of Naturopathic Physicians)*

CHAPTER 23

ANSWERING THE CALL TO TRANSFORM CORPORATE AMERICA FROM FEAR-BASED LEADERSHIP WITH THE OTHER *FOUR-LETTER* WORD

BY DR. MARIA CHURCH

Becoming an irresistible, inspirational leader requires more than just charisma. Irresistible leaders have the powerful combination of warmth and strength, love and courage. Charismatic personalities are thought to be born that way, you know, with the "it" factor. Yet warmth and courage are values and behaviors we learn from our parents and mentors. So this begs the question: *Are leaders therefore born or are leaders made?* Yes – a resounding yes to both!

In this chapter, we learn how to be irresistible, influential, and courageous leaders by leveraging the most powerful force on this planet—love. Before we start learning the strategies of love in the workplace, let's first look at where we've been and then understand how we got here by looking right into the face of the antithesis of love – fear.

FEAR-BASED LEADERSHIP

Fear in the workplace has been the standard operating procedure, the *modus operandi*, the way we do business for a very long time. We learned fear-based leadership and models of motivation through manipulation, scare tactics, and threats. The truth is that these strategies and techniques worked...well, sort of.

The use of fear *is* a motivator, with the resultant instant gratification of seeing people move immediately in the direction you wish to see. However, fear comes with a price. Fear is not sustainable. When we lead with fear, we immediately lose any trust our team or employees may have for us. The lack of trust from our employees or customers leads to lack of loyalty and commitment.

Employees who experience fear in the workplace plan their escape, both literally and figuratively.

– Literally, they leave organizations for safer places to work. The cost of employee turnover is tremendous, resulting in overworked employees, lost knowledge, training costs, interviewing and recruiting costs, and loss of credibility.

– Figuratively, employees leave organizations by "checking out" or planning their escape. They become disengaged, disillusioned, and de-motivated. Employees who check out are neither productive nor motivated.

Fear is tricky and very sneaky. In fact, we may not even recognize the sensation of fear because we've become so used to it. We become almost anesthetized to it, all the while knowing that something is off, making us feel uneasy. We see fear in the workplace manifested through micromanagement, threats, unhealthy comparisons and competition, bullying, belittling, depression, and anxiety. So why in the world would anyone *choose* to lead with fear? Because fear is something we've all learned; we know how to leverage fear, making it a comfortable method. Fear-based tactics are the *go-to* strategies primarily because they are familiar.

The key to shifting from fear to love is learning how to love with greater capacity than living in fear. Think of a scale with fear on one side and love on the other. Only when your love for something or someone becomes greater to you than fear, will the scale tip in favor of love. However, if your fear of something or someone is greater than your love for something else, then fear wins again.

- Do I love and respect my desire to go for that position more than my fear of being rejected?
- Do I love and value my goal to launch my own business more than my fear of stepping out and possibly failing?
- Do I value the call to write my own book more than my fear of negative response?

Do you see how easy it is to put more value onto the side of fear? The great news is that we can learn a better way to lead by employing love-based strategies and techniques with tremendous, sustainable results that are more powerful than fear-based methods. We can learn to be irresistible leaders with the power of love.

LOVE-BASED LEADERSHIP

Let's all get on the same page with the definitions of love and leadership about which I am speaking. *Love* -- the universal definition of love: *Honoring, caring, trusting, and respecting one human being to another. Leadership – inspiring one or many toward a vision.*

Love is our natural state of being, while fear is learned. Because love is our natural state, it is also the core, the very essence of who we are. When we fully embrace this concept and integrate it with our thoughts, attitudes, and behaviors, we come into the perfect balance of warmth and courage. Warmth and love juxtaposed with courage and strength are not opposed values; in fact, they are completely related. The root origin of the word *courage* is the French word *cuer*, which means *heart*. We know that to be courageous requires fearlessness; and to be fear-less is to be love-filled.

So how do we learn the concepts of leading with love and put love into practice in our workplaces? First, we start with love-based leadership. As I described in my book, *Love-Based Leadership: Transform Your Life with Meaning and Abundance*, leadership with love is built on three pillars: Love of self, love of Source, and love of others. These principles work in harmony as a framework for shifting from fear to love in the workplace, our communities, and in our lives.

I. *Love of self*, the first pillar, beckons us to practice honoring, caring, trusting, and valuing ourselves. We do this by developing and leveraging our intuition along with our logical skills. Practicing the skills of *truth telling* as well as *truth receiving* enables us to set healthy, respectful parameters in our life and teaches others how to interact with us. When we become self-loving, we are living in the field of possibilities, recognizing that we always have a choice and never see ourselves as victims.

My greatest teacher of this principle is Dr. Victor Frankl, an Austrian psychiatrist who was captured by the Nazis during the Second World War, and sent to concentration camps. While in the camps, Frankl realized that while the Nazis had stripped him of everything, he still held the unyielding power of choosing his own attitude.

When we develop the leadership principle of love of self, we develop the most powerful tool in our leadership toolbox – perception shifting. This skill will open up the world to you and those whom you lead. Along with the skills of awareness and presence, you will be a formidable and powerful leader of others.

Maintaining your health and wellness is imperative for irresistible leadership. Your physical body is the vehicle given to you to manifest your influence and inspiration as a leader. Take care of yourself with a power hour each day comprised of 20 minutes each of feeding your mind with inspirational or educational information, exercising your body, and nurturing your spirit with mediation, prayer, or stillness.

II. *Love of Source* is the second pillar of love-based leadership. I use the term Source, which to others may also be God, Universe, Higher-Self, or Spirit. Connecting with Source refuels us, filling us with inspiration and creativity. Did you ever notice how you solve problems in your sleep or are inspired in the shower? That is because we are still in a semi-conscious state before our minds start filling up with the external world. It is in this state where we find God. Like mediation, we suspend our thoughts for stillness and quiet, refueling us.

The fuel from Source is also happiness, peace, and absolute unconditional love. All leaders must fill up with faith and perseverance to lead in the great unknown of our human experience and workplace environments.

III. *Love of others*: When we self-love and connect with our Source, the natural progression is the extension of *love to others*, the third pillar of love-based leadership. In this alignment, we experience forgiveness and collaboration.

A powerful phenomenon, knowledge creation, occurs in a love-based culture. Two Japanese researchers, Ikujiro Nonaka and Toshihiro Nishiguchi, extensively researched how organizations create knowledge. They found that *ba* must be readily available for knowledge to occur. Loosely translated, *ba* is a positive energy. In order for ba to exist, four elements must be present: love, care, trust, and compassion. Without those elements, knowledge creation is nearly impossible. Love and fear cannot be present at the same time nor in the same space, and innovation cannot occur in fear.

Love of others in the workplace also looks like shared power and shared ownership. The old model of hoarding information with the misperception of *knowledge as power* is false. The ironic reality is that shared power, just like shared knowledge, increases the power of the leader. Transparency is much more attractive, irresistible, and powerful for leaders and organizations than secrecy and mistrust.

Leading with love is a conduit to meaning for yourself, as well as for those whom you lead. Through the three pillars of love-based leadership, we discover our *why* and help those we lead to discover theirs. Being a leader requires us to be both teacher and student, mentor and mentee. Leading with love is leading with wisdom. Leading with love is leading with strength. Leading with love is leading with courage. Are you ready to answer the call?

A LOVE-BASED LEADER JOURNEY

Many of my readers connected well with the following piece entitled *I've Arrived* from my first book:

> I've done it! I accomplished whatever Mom and Dad told me I could do! I have arrived.
>
> As the first-born of a pre-baby-boomer couple, my parents always told me to do what makes me happy, and remember that I could accomplish anything. They supported my desire to pursue acting.

They supported my desire to study sign language interpretation (I liked the dramatic flair), then they encouraged my business drive. My mother always had a career. She broke through many glass ceilings and earned great respect in her profession. She was my inspiration to break on through to the other side. I had arrived.

When I moved up in my organization, and took on more responsibility, I tripled my income over a nine-month period. In addition to the money, I earned respect and a place at the table with the men. Four men, and little ol' me. I had a place at the table in a predominately all male industry. I had arrived.

I changed my wardrobe, hair, and personal style. After all, I was in senior management. I had arrived.

I worked 80 hours a week. I was dealing in hundreds of thousands of dollars daily. I was getting little sleep with the worry. Yet, I felt important and needed; the men in my organization had come to depend on me and my opinion. I had arrived.

I started to show symptoms of extreme stress. On my fortieth birthday, the doctor put me on blood pressure medicine and told me I needed to exercise more. I'd been working long hours and my eating habits were atrocious. Fast food eaten even faster became the norm. I took up smoking as a stress reliever (yes, I am an educated woman, and yes, I know the hazards of smoking). I had arrived.

One day, on my back patio after a long day at work, with a martini in one hand and a cigarette in the other, I had a thought: *I have a place at the table. I have earned respect for my hard work and knowledge. I have an awesome six-figure income. I have everything the successful men have had for decades. I have 30 pounds of extra weight. I have a high-level position. I have a stressful job. I have a beautiful home. I have high blood pressure. I have a drink in one hand and a cigarette in the other. Oh my god...I do have it all! I have arrived...*

But just exactly where am I going?

I knew there had to be another way, a better way, and so I began my journey of discovery. I commenced my doctoral work with the mission of finding a different way to lead. I was looking for a holistic model that encapsulated mind, body, and spirit, one that allowed me to be authentic, and didn't require me to check my soul at the door.

When I didn't find a leadership model that addressed my heart's desire, I decided to develop one myself and committed to this intensive study. I was thrilled to receive the support from my cohort of fellow doctoral students and happily continued my sometimes-grueling research.

When the time came to form my dissertation committee, I started to get some resistance and pushback from the university. I couldn't understand the hesitation and mixed messages. I finally confronted a dean and asked her why they did not support me in my research. She told me that my love-based leadership model was too controversial for the university and that people would be confused by the word *love*. I was not going to receive approval to move forward.

I was devastated that I could not unveil love-based leadership as my doctoral work. I was exhausted from the amount of time and energy already spent on the study. However, what was even more jarring was the fact that we couldn't even talk about love in an advanced study of leadership. How could we study leadership and not talk about the most powerful force on earth?

I knew immediately that I had to bring love-based leadership forward... it was time.

However, like many times before, I became paralyzed with fear and masked it with busyness. I threw myself into other projects so I wouldn't have the time to finish the calling. That is when the struggle really began.

Then, on a rare day off in July 2010, while sunning myself out by the pool reading a book, I was struck by the beauty of a Monarch butterfly flitting around me. Then, the cloud formations caught my eye, followed by the sunrays shooting into the canyons. At that moment, and for the first time in a long time, I became still.

In that stillness, I heard the call. This time, I answered. The time is now. Fear no longer serves us in our personal lives, families, communities, organizations, or countries. It is time to shift from fear to love.

Will you join us and answer the call?

Resources

Church, Maria. (2010). *Love-Based Leadership: Transform Your Life with Meaning and Abundance.* Bloomington, IN: Balboa Press, a Division of Hay House.

Frankl, Viktor E. (1984). *Man's Search for Meaning.* New York: Simon & Schuster.

Nohaka, Ikujiro and Toshihiro Nishiguchi. (2001). *Knowledge Emergence: Social, Technical, and Evolutionary Dimensions of Knowledge Creation.* New York: Oxford Press.

About Maria

Dr. Maria Church is the voice of authentic leadership power.

As a certified professional leadership coach, professor, and author, Dr. Maria has helped leaders around the world strengthen their leadership power strategically and successfully with followers and teams that are motivated, productive, and loyal – while helping organizations create cultures that are innovative, profitable, and maximizing their full potential. Her company, *Dr. Maria Church International,* coaches, mentors, and trains individual leaders and leadership teams worldwide.

As the author of *Love-Based Leadership: Transform Your Life with Meaning and Abundance and her upcoming book A Course in Leadership: 21 Spiritual Lessons on Leadership, Love, and Life,* Maria approaches leadership holistically, integrating mind, body, and spirit. She has started a movement to revolutionize the workplace with love in powerful and miraculous ways.

As a keynote speaker, audiences enjoy and are inspired to hear Dr. Maria speak about her three passions—leadership, love, and life. This trifecta, along with her intense passion and ability to connect with people, produces talks that are compelling, inspirational, and warm, sprinkled with wisdom, and of course, humor.

Dr. Maria Church specializes in leadership development based on her more than 25-year career in corporate America, government, non-profit, and small business. Maria holds a doctorate of management degree in organizational leadership and currently teaches for several universities. She hosts Dr. Maria TV, has been featured on radio, television, in magazines, and writes a weekly newspaper column on leadership.

An ardent fan of classic rock and classic Motown, she is a formidable opponent in any rock trivia competition. Maria lives in the canyons of southern Arizona and continues delivering keynote speeches, training, teaching, coaching leaders, and working on her next book.

You can contact Dr. Maria at:
Maria@DrMariaChurch.com
http://DrMariaChurch.com
https://twitter.com/DrMariaChurch
https://www.facebook.com/dr.maria.church

CHAPTER 24

ASSUMPTIONS: A SLIPPERY SLOPE TO LOST PROFITS

BY MEG RENTSCHLER

My call toward helping other people started very early in my life and has certainly been a persistent theme in my personal and professional decisions throughout the years. I am the eighth child born into a large, gregarious Irish Catholic family. What is most significant regarding my birth order is that I am the first child born following the death of my brother, Kevin, who tragically stopped breathing when he was seven months old during his afternoon nap. The death of a child is a heart wrenching, traumatic event. Each of my siblings and certainly my parents were affected by the loss of my brother in similar yet individual ways. They each carry with them to this day, many decades later, a part of that sadness and the impact his death had on my family.

Being the first child born into the family following the tragedy has shaped who I am, and in fact I believe is part of who I am. Through many different circumstances and looking back through my life, I believe that I came to help my family deal with the pain. My mother believes this intently and tells me that I was born with a smile on my face. I am quick to inform her that from her position in the process, she would have no idea what was on my face when I was born. Yet she assures me that I was smiling when they handed me to her and have been smiling ever since.

The desire to bridge the gap between our experienced pain and our potential for happiness flowed into a natural process for me to build a profession around serving others. I began my work as a psychotherapist helping others heal and persevere through depression, grief, anxiety, relationship difficulties, and other issues. It was during those decades that the importance of communication first became clear to me. So many issues could be at least lessened, if not resolved, through clear, open, honest communication. While working with thousands of people over the past three decades, I have come to believe that strengthening communication skills is the foundation to any of the work that I do with my clients.

After spending over two decades in private practice working with families, couples, and individuals, I began to notice a new pattern that was emerging with my clients. Day after day I counseled clients who were frustrated with their work in corporate America. There was an increasing theme of unhealthy work environments, overwhelmed executives who were not feeling equipped to deal with the challenges that they faced, and a lack of clear communication within the workplace. This is when I shifted my practice from one that was psychotherapy-based to executive coaching, where I could be proactive and affect positive change in a huge system that seemed to have lost the human factor, or at least the factor that made humans feel human, productive, and happy—and which also affected other areas of their lives, including their relationships and health.

Answering this call meant that to really help my clients, I needed to go into workplaces and help build communication, tune into strengths, improve listening skills, and improve productivity through happier, healthier people. So began a new journey as I transitioned into executive coaching to open new doors of understanding and bring new perspective to a system with much strength yet many challenges, including dysfunctional patterns that mirrored many family systems.

I have had the honor of working with some of the most amazing people through my coaching practice. They are incredibly skilled, creative, caring, and as a whole have the desire to give their best and help their companies get to the next level, whatever that may be. They are brilliant strategists, planners, negotiators, teachers, leaders, and decision makers, but not always the best communicators. When you think about it, as we are learning our trades, becoming talented technically, building financial acumen, or moving up the ladder because we are incredibly good at whatever skill is needed in a particular business, there is not necessarily a focus on learning the dynamics of communication and relationship building. Yet this is the very foundation of what makes us human; of how we connect and thrive. The element of effective communication and the best way to speak clearly, concisely, and without assumption are tools that I believe every executive needs in his tool box.

When I work to help improve communication patterns within companies with the intent to improve relationships, increase flow, productivity and profits, there are several areas of focus. One area that I will share will help avoid assumption and create a path to clearer communication, therefore increased confidence, collaboration, and cooperation will be experienced in your workplace.

The dynamics of our communication are based on mastering belief systems that have developed through our life experiences (the things that we were taught, the hurts and joys that we have lived through, and the things to which we aspire). These belief systems impact the way that we communicate. To use the analogy of a computer, we have a program running within our minds that impacts the way that we interpret things and how we react to the circumstances, people, and situations in our life. The danger lies within the possibility that the person with whom we are interacting has their own internal program or software that may or may not match our own.

The words that we use to express our thoughts and beliefs are usually inadequate to truly express all the meaning that we hold within our program for any given word. For example, let's consider the word "dog." While I am pretty certain that when each of us thinks "dog," images of canines likely arise. The differences lie in the depth of meaning for each of us. I was raised on a farm, had many different dogs over the years, and am still a big fan of our canine friends. However, someone who is grieving their pet, has been bitten by a dog, or prefers cats, may have a very different set of beliefs that go through their mind when the word "dog" is mentioned. So it's important to remember that the words that we use every day can have very different meanings for each of us. Yet we tend to operate under the assumption that people understand *our* meaning when we talk.

One of the slipperiest slopes when it comes to non-productive communication is that of assumption. Assuming usually occurs automatically so we don't realize that we have done it until we are crashing down that slope at a high rate of speed. There may be times that we are not even tuned into the fact that we are assuming, but whether or not awareness accompanies the assumption, our relationships, our interactions, and our ability to make clear decisions are deeply affected by our assumptions.

Recently I was talking with an executive who was frustrated with a situation at work. There were delays in areas that were concerning to her. In discussing her frustration, I asked her how she was communicating her expectations to her team. It became apparent that while she felt that she was being very clear about her expectations (after all, she understood exactly what the depth of meaning was behind her words), she was not understood by her team. We explored the words that she chose: "I want you to take more action," and "Stop talking around people." In the first example, she explained the specific actions she wanted her team to take. In the second, she encouraged them to directly communicate with individuals on the team rather than circumvent the lines of communication. By implementing these changes in her communication and becoming clearer to her team regarding the meaning behind her words, they were better able to work as a team, meet her expectations, and increase productivity. It's important to consider that when there is not clarity about the intended meaning of words, we will apply our own internal program to those words and the results may be dramatically different than what was intended. This can be frustrating and is likely to affect productivity, teamwork, and profits. Assumptions are not necessarily intentional, but they can be disruptive.

Take a moment now to reflect on:

- How you worried about what you might have done to irritate a co-worker because she hasn't been as friendly as usual.

- When you became annoyed with a fellow manager because he did not take the initiative in something that you thought that he should.

- How you questioned your boss's belief in your abilities because a project was assigned to another team.

- When you ignored a colleague's suggestion because she never knows what she's talking about.

- How you walked up to a conversation between two co-workers but they abruptly stopped talking when you approach them.

These may sound like small concerns but they are examples of situations that are filled with assumption. From assumptions decisions are made, actions are taken, and sometimes those courses of action are not in alignment with the best interests of our teams, our companies, or ourselves. Assumptions are designed to protect our belief system. Rather than approaching these situations from a grounded, confident perspective, we often react from fear, and expect the worst. Any assumption based on fear disrupts communication, damages relationships, and ultimately affects the bottom line.

When we become clearer in our communication, avoid assumption, and work from the same understanding as our colleagues, we have the advantage. People understand our message, and even if they do not agree with it, there is clarity to work toward a solution. We get the obstacles out of the way and interactions are more productive.

Here are the steps to create clearer communication and avoid the slippery slope of assumption:

1. Awareness is the first step to making any change. Once we understand that each of us has our own internal belief system that gives meaning to our words and that they are not the same for everyone, we become aware of the need to take responsibility for the clarity of our communication.

2. Clarify meaning when sharing a thought with others. Check to make certain that your meaning is clear or there is an understanding of your request. Include examples or ask for a summary from the other person on what you need from them. This may sound as though it will take too much time, however, clarity takes much less time than cleaning up the errors from confusion or miscommunication.

3. Have the courage to ask for clarity from others. Perhaps you believe that it makes you look smarter to not ask for clarification, but taking a wrong turn will quickly dispel that. Not asking for clarification leads to assumption. There is always a chance that we assumed correctly, but there is also the chance that we were not

correct in our assumption. Many hours of wasted time, resources, and energy have gone down the path of bad assumption. When having the courage to say, "Let me clarify what you would like for me to do," or ask "What specifically do you mean when you say...?" we are letting the other person know that their message is important to us and that we have been listening to what they were saying. "Specifically" is one of my favorite words for uncovering the hidden meaning, because it encourages the person giving the message to get very clear about their meaning. Sometimes it takes courage to ask because it may not always be received well; a pattern may have been established that we do not ask for clarification. Maybe the assumption being made is that if we are in a certain role or position we should just know. Show courage and ask when clarification is needed. What is required is a willingness to stay curious and not jump to conclusions.

4. Stay mindful of the tendency to fall into assumption and committed to clear communication. Every new behavior takes practice and at first is not always comfortable. The advantages to clear, open communication are increased respect, clarity, understanding, and the time that you have earned back by not having to re-visit conversations that ended in assumption.

Following these steps will help you stay true to your message and make certain that others hear the message that you are sending. When you do this you create confidence, collaboration, and cooperation in your workplace.

About Meg

Meg Rentschler helps clients talk in a way that encourages others to listen. As an executive coach she is dedicated to assisting her clients in meeting their professional and personal goals as well as aligning the individual's goals with that of the organization. She works with her clients to identify areas of growth to build confidence, take leadership to the next level, and reduce roadblocks that get in the way. In her work as a professional coach, Meg has worked with clients at all levels of experience and age ranges. She helps her clients strengthen communication skills, manage time and effectiveness, improve relationships and increase professional presence.

Since 1986, Meg has worked with clients to improve their relationships, productivity and overall effectiveness. In her experience the core to success is in effective communication. Meg helps her clients to identify goals and desired outcomes, to maximize inherent strengths, as well as address the challenges at hand. Coming from a background of over twenty-five years as an individual and group therapist, Meg has the experience to help her clients understand and make changes in behaviors that are not serving them as well as improve relationship dynamics in the workplace. Her knowledge of human behavior and her ability to work with individuals with a myriad of issues has proven invaluable for the companies with whom she works – whether addressing the operations of the business or taking leadership to the next level.

Meg graduated with her Master of Social Work from the University of Michigan and earned her Bachelor of Science from Michigan State University. She holds a Graduate Certificate in Executive and Professional Coaching from the University of Texas at Dallas and is a Professional Certified Coach through the International Coach Federation. Meg uses a variety of assessments and tools in her work with executives and teams depending upon the needs within each situation.

Meg's experience stretches across industries, having worked with clients in transportation, technology, insurance, financial, healthcare and service industries. She is currently on faculty at the University of Texas at Dallas in the Graduate Program for Executive and Professional Coaching.

You can connect with Meg at:
www.afocusonresults.com
Meg@afocusonresults.com
www.twitter.com/AFocusonResults
www.linkedin.com/MegRentschler

CHAPTER 25

STOP THE ROLLER COASTER!

BY MICHELE EISENBERG

HOW TO SPRINGBOARD FROM DIVORCE INTO MORE LOVE, MORE HAPPINESS AND MORE PERSONAL POWER THAN YOU EVER IMAGINED POSSIBLE

As I sit cozily in my living room gazing out the window at the Golden Gate Bridge and the San Francisco skyline framed by the changing colors of the ocean and sky, I sip my tea contentedly while my husband and son sleep. I ponder the miracle that I'm as happy as I am, feel as loved as I do, and live in a magically happy family.

Because it wasn't always this way…

I thought I was happy, but the truth is that happiness seemed elusive and fleeting at best. Between 1998 and 2003 I built and ran a successful leadership development and executive coaching company. I loved my work as well as every single executive and manager I coached. I was happiest while coaching my clients and facilitating breakthroughs. And even though it was during this time that I got engaged, married, had a healthy, happy baby boy, made more money than I'd ever made before in my life and bought a wonderful San Francisco home, I'd be lying if I told you I was happy.

223

The truth is that while I was skilled at seeing patterns and helping leaders grow into their potential, I had no idea how to be happy or build a great marriage…nobody ever taught me. Did they ever teach you?

I left my marriage in early 2006 after two years agonizing over the decision. The three horrifically painful years after were not pretty. I was barely coping with the emotional roller coaster of shared custody and my young son's heartbreaking crying and pleading every time he went back to his Dad's care, not to mention a divorce process gone awry and my ailing health.

By 2009 I wasn't sure how much more I could take of my life feeling like a nightmare. I wondered if things would ever feel right again or if I'd *ever* be happy.

I knew things sometimes had to get worse before they could get better, but this was insanity.

We all know Einstein's definition of insanity: doing the same thing over and over again and expecting different results.

I was committed to different results. It's the only thing I knew for sure. I didn't date for nearly four years. My reasoning? Well, my marriage wasn't unhappy by coincidence. It was unhappy because I co-created it that way with my husband. I knew that finding another relationship wouldn't solve the problem. As long as I was the same person, a new relationship would simply repeat the same unhappy patterns, just with a new partner.

After all my years of executive coaching and personal growth I knew that I was the common denominator in all the unhappy and loveless circumstances of my life. I knew the key was to change myself and change my patterns.

NOTHING CHANGES UNTIL YOU DO

I'd already stopped chasing happiness through achievement and looking for love in the wrong places. But I needed to go deeper and replace my mental and emotional patterns that were causing the unhappiness and lack of love in the first place. I was on a mission to find out how to be happy and how to create real love, not the fairy-tale ending love, but the kind of love that is sustainable and grows stronger and matures over time.

2010 was the year that everything changed. All the inner work I'd been doing built to a tipping point. Years spent coaching, studying personal growth and energy medicine, and being a lead assistant of a year-long personal growth program – all of these things changed me and made my growth gain so much momentum that I was finally able to end the pain.

One of the tragedies of our world is that most of us grow primarily through pain. Even though that's the way most people live, you don't have to follow the consensus. You can grow through love instead.

Deepening my understanding of how to move from a paradigm of growing through pain to one of growing through love, and teaching others how to do the same, has been my passion ever since. I founded the Happy Family Academy to teach people how to end painful and destructive relationship dynamics and build the kind of marriages and families they dreamed of when they walked down the isle.

What's divorce got to do with this? In the midst of divorce is an incredible opportunity that most people waste: if you *have* to experience pain, you may as well use it to end the decades old patterns that create unhappiness and lack of love in the first place. The new mindsets and skillsets my divorcing clients need to thrive beyond divorce are the same ones my other clients need to create happy marriages built to last. It's no wonder that while the coaching is different, the results of lasting love and happiness are the same.

Through the methods I teach, clients quickly make changes to leave the emotional roller coaster behind, take back long lost power, eliminate guilt, hold healthier boundaries, and stand empowered in their relationships. This helps their kids thrive, assists in the divorce process, and creates a healthy relationship with their ex.

There's no way I can share all of my methods in the space of this short chapter, But understanding two of the important causes of pain and what to do instead, is enough to get you off the roller coaster right away should you choose to.

I hope these stories help and inspire you to think differently about yourself and understand that you have the power to change everything you dislike in your life. Nothing changes until you do. Everything can change when you change yourself.

ESCAPE THE ROLLER COASTER

"I feel like I'm on an emotional roller coaster and I can't get off."

99% of my divorcing clients utter this statement.

Take Julie, for example. She's a successful businesswoman, yet when it came to handling her divorce, she felt like she was drowning under the waves of emotion that often blind-sided her out of nowhere, and left her feeling powerless and out of control.

She cried a lot – more than she ever had in her life. While she imagined it was normal to cry about divorce, she couldn't stop. Worse still, the crying was often highly inconvenient, like when things got tense at work.

Julie tried really hard to "hold it all together" which left her feeling stressed, depressed, exhausted, powerless and reactive. She couldn't understand why her reactions were so out of proportion to the situation at hand and why she suddenly felt like she was losing it. And she couldn't stand it that she'd look forward to a quiet evening with her kids, but instead spent her time yelling at them.

Things changed when Julie understood this first source of pain.

When you don't have healthy ways to express and release your feelings, especially those feelings that are deemed culturally taboo, they build up inside.

In normal, everyday life, the buildup is slow enough that the average person can manage the destructive consequences. (They'd feel happier, more peaceful, have closer relationships and higher self-esteem if they didn't have the pain and sabotage that comes with this buildup, but they don't know that.) However, in a crisis situation like divorce, emotional buildup is fast and furious and most people don't have the emotional fluency or the skill to release their feelings in healthy ways before they build up.

Women have different strategies than men to try to release the painful consequences of the buildup. Because the feelings building up typically aren't "positive" and there's little permission for "negative" emotions, women resort to expressing a variety of feelings by crying. Unfortunately this strategy doesn't work and leaves them feeling disempowered and confused.

Julie understood why she felt out of control: the emotional buildup made her prone to overreacting so that one small thing caused her to reach a tipping point and explode. This hurt her kids and damaged their relationships, which made her feel worse about herself. It was a vicious cycle of pain.

In our work together, Julie learned to express and release her feelings in healthy ways, and avoid the buildup. I'll outline a technique to do this in a moment. First, we need to examine the single most avoided feeling, so you won't neglect it as you practice this technique.

TAKE YOUR POWER BACK

In my 17 years of coaching, I've never met a client who didn't need help taking their power back from anger. Ever!

Most people, myself included, before they're taught otherwise, think anger is a problem or something to be avoided. They may see anger as dangerous because they or someone they love were hurt by it in the past.

Good people with great intentions struggle to express their anger without hurting themselves or those they love.

Margie often felt "irritated" by her ex, Steve. A year after moving out, his stuff was still in their basement and whenever he dropped off the kids, they were exhausted and full of sugar. In addition, he'd hang around and play with them.

Margie had grown up with parents who yelled and screamed so she did everything she could to keep her cool. Understandably so! She didn't want to treat the people in her life the way she'd been treated. The problem with her strategy is that Margie's power was all tied up with her anger. Also, despite her best efforts, her built-up anger spilled out and damaged her relationships. A comment here, a jab there, the slam of a door or the silent treatment...all of these decrease the trust and the safety in a relationship.

Most people leak their anger unintentionally, instead of intentionally and powerfully expressing it.

I helped Margie realize that she was fighting herself over her anger.

She realized she was furious! She resented sharing custody with a Disneyland Dad who indulged their kids' every whim in the attempt to be their friend instead of their parent. She felt invaded every time Steve played with the kids when dropping them off. Nobody else came into her home uninvited. Her home! It was no longer their home. She got to decide who and what came into it. She didn't want Steve's stuff in the basement - she wanted a playroom for the kids.

As a result of learning to express her anger powerfully, Margie realized that she experienced relief whenever she expressed and released her anger, and that she suddenly had clarity where before she'd felt confused. Margie learned that by not letting herself get angry, she had no access to her boundaries! Now she knew what she wanted and didn't want, and she felt empowered to act on her clarity.

Anger has a very specific, positive function. Its job is to let you know when your boundaries have been crossed, help you find those boundaries and claim them.

By understanding the positive function of anger, Margie had a new sense of permission to express it. You will too. By making this simple internal change, she stopped simmering in anger and snapping into reaction, she found healthier boundaries and therefore became a better parent and co-parent. She felt more empowered and her relationships improved – her kids were better behaved and Steve became more cooperative because Margie's boundaries were clear.

How did she do it? Margie ended the pain of hurting herself and her relationships with built-up feelings as well as the pain of not having boundaries she wanted and needed because of unhealthy anger habits by using the following technique: stop storytelling.

Is this familiar? Something happens that makes you really mad. You call your best friend and tell them what happened and who said what to whom… Even though you told the story, you're still upset. So as the day goes on, you retell the story to another friend… When a family member calls, you tell the story again… Depending on how angry you are, you keep telling the story the next day and the next…

Storytelling is the most common anger avoidance strategy. We tell the story instead of expressing anger. We tell the story instead of feeling.

STOP TELLING STORIES

Avoid the story-telling trap by using two or three word sentences: "I'm angry" "I'm really furious!" I'm so mad!" Don't say why or because… as soon as you do, you're back in the story.

The key is to really let your feelings fuel your words, so that as you speak the words, you express and release your anger. Try doing this without words. If you're expressing anger, try growling or make up the sound that best expresses whatever you're feeling.

Don't limit yourself to anger. We've focused on anger because it trips people up so much. But there are plenty of other feelings. Here's a list of a few others that I recommend practicing with:

- Frustration
- Sadness
- Rage (yes, anger and rage are different feelings with different functions)
- Optimism
- Happiness

What do you notice?

Do you have easier access to some than others?

Which ones do you avoid?

Which ones do you like?

Now all you need to do is practice. Practice alone, especially with the feelings that you could hurt someone with.

There's so much more to say about this. We haven't even gotten into the really juicy benefits of healthy anger habits, like increased intimacy in your relationships. And there are so many other sources of pain to eliminate like the pain of negative intimacy, the pain caused by shame, the pain caused by getting stuck in the past… I won't list them all.

THE SYNERGY OF A HAPPY FAMILY

I had no idea, when I set out to discover the secrets of happiness and the keys to building real love that I'd succeed and find so much more than

I was looking for.

Today I live a happy joyful life with my husband and my son. We enjoy plenty of silliness and the fun of learning and laughing together. We still follow the steps that I teach my clients and we discover more every day.

Friends and acquaintances have asked us to teach them what we're doing because our relationship feels magical to be around. We've noticed it too: there's a synergy that happens in a happy family that is more than the sum of its parts. There's more happiness and more love than you'd get if you added together what each of us brings. It seems that when you minimize the sources of pain in your life the way we've done, there's a compounding magic that happens in the love, trust and safety that grow in its place.

This is what you have to look forward to. It's my deepest wish, for you, that you join us!

About Michele

Michele Eisenberg is passionate about thriving relationships. She loves teaching clients how to create healthy relationships that are built to last. She founded the Happy Family Academy to bring happiness, love, and intimacy into families throughout the world, one person at a time.

Michele believes that a person's ultimate leadership begins as a partner and parent. She knows that when a person is happy in their relationships at home, they can flourish in the rest of their life. She loves nothing more than empowering people and giving them tools to thrive in their families and beyond.

Michele is a veteran leadership and relationship coach, happiness expert, devoted wife and mom and CEO of the Happy Family Academy. She has worked with clients from all over the world and is known for her mastery in helping them transform their lives by transforming themselves. As a result, her clients become the kind of people they admire and aspire to be, who enjoy love, happiness, and success in their relationships with themselves, their partners, their kids and, of course, as leaders in their lives.

Having lived and worked in Luxembourg, France, Italy, the UK, New York and now the San Francisco Bay Area, Michele is tri-lingual—fluent in English, French, and Italian. She has a passion for her work, for children and for parenting. She is an avid student of metaphysics and yoga and loves spending time with family, friends and in nature.

Michele lives in the Bay Area with her husband, Michael, her son, Zachary, their dog, Spencer, and Ethel the turtle.

You can connect with Michele at:
Michele@HappyFamilyAcademy.com
https://www.facebook.com/HappyFamilyAcademy
http://www.linkedin.com/in/micheleeisenberg
https://twitter.com/HappyMichele

CHAPTER 26

THE DELIVERY TRUCK

BY MONIKA ZANDS

"What in the world am I doing here?" repeated again and again in my mind like a scratched record.

For seven long years, I sat in the same small, dark, windowless editing bay, producing videos about people working towards their dreams, while I was sleepwalking through life, denying my own. I had been completely ignoring myself and my hopes of being a mother and a successful business-owner. The truth was that I felt that somehow I could still make a positive impact on people's lives.

I returned to editing, eager to make progress, when I heard someone say, "You're going to get hit." I removed my headphones to see who was speaking to me, but no one was there. Consumed by my project, I continued plugging away. When I looked up at the clock again, seven hours had passed. My eyes were tired, my heart drained, and my mind exhausted after two weeks of twelve-hour workdays. Always the last to leave, I walked down the hallway, past all the dark offices, and again I heard someone say, "You're going to get hit." I turned around to see who was there, but I was still alone. I wondered where that voice was coming from. The ominous message and mysterious voice created a feeling of dis-ease that was so strong that I could not ignore it. The thought of getting hit made me nervous to drive, but my husband wouldn't be home for hours and I had no other way to get home. I felt like I held my breath for the entire ride home, but I made it back safely and let out a sigh of relief as I pulled into my driveway.

Ironically, I had traffic school that night, and was still feeling disturbed by the voice I had heard, so I asked a friend to drive me. In class I found myself again in a dark room, this time filled with strangers, and we were forced to watch gruesome videos of car accidents. My already uneasy stomach was now doing somersaults, and I asked myself again, "What am I doing here?"

It was time for our class to take a break from traffic school so I decided to grab a snack from a market across the street.

WHAT HAPPENED NEXT CHANGED MY LIFE FOREVER.

I was in the crosswalk, halfway across the street when suddenly came "THE HIT." It was so hard and so loud, and then everything went completely silent. I was no longer on the street. I was floating high above everything, watching the chaos that ensued from the accident below. I watched my body fly 25 feet in the air, land on the ground, and slide across the pavement another 15 feet.

Then I saw my body laying helplessly in Donna's lap, a girl I had just met in class. Her large brown eyes comforted my racing heart as she gently stroked my hair.

I remember hearing over and over in my mind, "please don't let me die, please don't let me die," but there were no words coming out of my mouth.

Donna remained calm and present and kept asking me to keep my eyes open to stay with her. I continued watching from above and noticed the concern and emotion in people's faces. I noticed the colors and patterns of people's movements and how alive everyone looked. It was like a painting had come to life and I was watching the scenes unfold below me in slow motion. I didn't feel my body. I didn't feel any pain. I felt warm and comforted. Deep in the seat of my soul, I could feel a pulling or a tapping that whispered, "wake up, wake up," but it felt so peaceful where I was that I didn't want to return to my life below.

Then, like a bolt of lightning, "CRASH", I was back in my body, lying in the back of an ambulance being hooked up to a myriad of machines.

Now, instead of everything being serene and tranquil, a rush of loud sounds, people, and questions surrounded me and my brain entered a panic. I felt pain shooting through my body in places I had never felt pain before.

If it had been my choice, I would never have come back into my body. There are no words to describe the deep peace and serenity I felt when I was "out of my body" and high above the accident. Now, I was in such a state of trauma that I could not speak, but I felt my brain ache as I watched the scene in the ambulance. A flash of fear entered my heart as I thought, "Am I paralyzed?"

The paramedics were talking to each other about me as though I was not even there. "She sure was a lucky one. Must have had angel wings. We usually see them through the windshield or in the axle. When we got the call, we were sure she was dead."

"Lucky" was not the feeling I was having, but rather curiosity as to why I hadn't died. I would have gone. I was ready to go. Even though I had the thought, "please don't let me die," I believe that was more of an instinctive response rather than my heart's desire. Feeling overworked, underappreciated, and empty for years, this accident seemed to be a perfect ticket off the planet. It was so graceful and so effortless, and yet somehow I was back in my body, feeling more human than I had ever felt. Why wasn't it my time to die? What was I brought back here to do?

After hours confined to the cold, sterile, white walls of the hospital, I was finally released to go home with severe swelling, road burn, bruised hips and ribs, whiplash, migraine headaches, and highly compromised internal systems. The doctor insisted that I rest in bed for the week until our next appointment.

The week turned into four long months, and with each day that passed, I grew more and more angry—angry that my internal systems were shutting down, angry that my back could not support my weight, angry that I had constant migraine headaches, angry that I wasn't healing, angry at the truck driver, angry at the doctors who told me it was doubtful I would ever be a mother, angry at myself, and angry that I was stuck in my bed unable to do anything but sleep and look out my bedroom window. It seemed to me that my life was a waste. I wondered why my life had been spared and asked myself again, "What am I doing here?"

As the days went by, I spent hours with nothing to do but watch and listen to the world outside my window: the leaves rustling in the wind, hummingbirds flittering through their daily rounds, the sun rising and setting reminding me of another lost day. Eventually something miraculous began to happen. The anger subsided and a new feeling swirled inside of me. Instead of hearing the rustling leaves as noise, I began to hear the poetry in the wind talking to the leaves. The irritating chirping of the birds I now heard as a sweet song used to pass soothing messages to and fro. Colors came alive, pulsating with radiance and life. I stopped seeing everyday minutiae as mundane, and I practiced paying attention to the smallest details of my life and the world around me. Even when I spoke to my friends, I started hearing more than their words; I could hear what they weren't saying out loud. I could see and feel what they were hiding.

As this new childlike curiosity of the world grew, a new ability to tap into my heart, the universe, and a collective planetary consciousness arose. Months passed, and my heart continued to open, allowing me to effortlessly receive what I had previously been working hard to obtain. For years, I had been a driving force, moving mountains to get things done; now I sat in silence and allowed the world and its beauty to come to me. I saw and heard things I never had before. Each day, I landed deeper into acceptance of my circumstances, my limitations, and my pain; I noticed that my pain lessened, my smile grew, and I began to attract things to me. It was like a waterfall of information, awareness, experience, and love pouring into my soul. The more I received, the stronger and more alive I felt.

I embraced that I had discovered my superpower, but I recognized this new awareness wasn't coming only from me. I started praying, writing, and talking about my dreams and plans. I began to ask for guidance, instructions, and encouragement from the universe. I was having my own personal conversations with God, and I vowed to myself that I would never return to a mindless slumber.

It became apparent that I had been ignoring messages and signs for years and that the universe had a different plan for me. It sent a BIG wake-up call to get me out of my stupor. I was awakened into the greatness that I am, and for the first time, I began to see it, trust it and be it.

Once I was healthy enough to go back to work, I knew that I couldn't return to the dark editing room. I was on a mission to learn, grow, and discover how to use my new awareness to help others. I enrolled in a Master's program in Spiritual Psychology, and I found myself moving forward one step, one lesson, and one day at a time—with courage. Fulfilling my dreams and goals no longer required me to push and grind. I discovered how to see my gifts and my contribution. I practiced being gentle and serene… just as it had felt high above the scene of the accident.

I moved out of the fear of the unknown and into the preciousness of my truth, my happiness, and my love for myself and all mankind. I began working with individuals, couples, and parents to help them see the details of their lives. I launched a program to help entrepreneurs build their businesses by cultivating their gifts and releasing their attachments to beliefs that were never theirs to begin with. I was no longer a spectator, creating videos about people working on their dreams—I was now a force of love and contribution, helping others see their greatness while finally embracing my own.

Even though my body had gotten hit, my soul was knocked back into alignment and my true calling was revealed.

Today, I am grateful that I am a mother to three beautiful children who know my story and remind me that life is most precious in the small moments that we share together. We pray together, we tell stories together, and we share our gratitude around the dinner table often. My goal is to help them stay awake in a world that presents valuable challenges and tests us so our soul continues to grow and elevate.

I continue to surrender and listen, and I am constantly building a deeper relationship with myself in new ways. I still sit in my room and look out my window daily, which brings me right back to a space of deep awareness and appreciation of life's beautiful details. I recognize that I was brought back to life to live and to pay forward all that I have and will learn on this magnificent journey.

I see every interaction as an opportunity to learn, love, and give. I see greatness in everyone and aspire to help them see it as well.

I help people stay awake on their journey by asking them these four questions:

1. Are you paying attention to the details of your life?

2. Are you wondering what your unique gifts are?

3. Are you seeing the messages that are coming your way?

4. When the call comes to you, will you recognize it and be ready to answer it?

We all have a story. And it has either plagued us our whole lives, holding us victim to our circumstances, or it has liberated us and been our life's greatest gift.

THANK GOD I WAS HIT BY A TRUCK!

When the message comes to you, will you **ANSWER THE CALL**?

About Monika

Monika Zands is an executive business consultant and life strategist who loves to help highly successful entrepreneurs tap into their greatness and build global empires. Her unique ability is to see through people's perceived limitations and help them recognize and use their true gifts and expertise to build their unique and specific LEGACY. She is a master communicator and an expert at building excellent teams, designing clear, effective business strategies and leadership development roadmaps. Her powerful intuitive guidance helps people clarify a plan for impeccable success and a way to leave their footprint on the planet.

With the nickname, Walking Love, Monika's clients often say that she gives them peace of mind while arming them with the knowledge and confidence to achieve their wildest dreams and beyond.

A graduate of UCLA and a certified Master of Neuro-Linguistic Programming, Monika uses her broad range of business experience, including a Master's in Spiritual Psychology, advanced business training, and twenty years of corporate leadership facilitation to support her clients to achieve massive results, experience joy in the process, and effectively develop deeper, more profound relationships that last a lifetime.

Monika is the Founder of The Next Level™, a business mastery program designed for people to tap into their greatness and bring their life and business to the next level of success. Selected as one of America's PremierExperts™, Monika has taught her innovative technology on stages around the country, inspiring audiences with her heart-centered approach to achieving life-altering results.

Monika loves adventure. She speaks three different languages and immerses herself in new cultures at every turn. She's traveled to over fifteen countries, has run five triathlons, and has risked her life in countless extreme sporting events. She even met her wonderful and adoring husband on the UCLA sailing team. But her biggest adventure and success to date has been conceiving, delivering, and raising three generous, loving, delightful children.

See your greatness. Be your greatness. Pay it forward™.

To tap into your greatness, visit:
www.MonikaZands.com
www.facebook.com/monikazandsconsulting
www.twitter.com/monikazands
Instagram: @monikazands

CHAPTER 27

LISTENING IS THE KEY

NICK NANTON AND JW DICKS

The email came in on a typically busy day and it made us stop. All of us move fast these days and at the Celebrity Branding® Agency, we move really fast. Like you, we are moving at the pace of business in this digital world – we're taking calls, tweeting, blogging, leading seminars and meeting with our clients. So when this simple 'thank you' email showed up we didn't think it would be a life changing event. The email was from Jim Titus and it said, "Thought you might like this article my wife wrote." The article opened with a vivid picture:

> My son Jacob's T-ball team made it to the championship game in the Floyds Knobs Community Club league tournament this year. He's four and it was his first year playing. It was awesome! Fun and exciting. But it was so much more than that. Jacob's experience was a wonderful display of acceptance and patience and love. Love of baseball and love of a child.

Rewind. Four months earlier, Nick was traveling and on a layover at Midway Airport in Chicago. He noticed that the person next to him had a shot of a cute little boy in a baseball uniform as his laptop screen. When Nick complimented the picture, Jim Titus introduced himself and the two men struck up a conversation about the boy's beaming smile. Jim said, "Jacob is an amazing blessing to us," adding that Jacob had Down Syndrome. They continued to talk – about Jim's job at UPS, about Nick being "The Celebrity Lawyer" and our unique business promoting, marketing and creating Celebrity Experts across a variety of industries from entertainment, health and fitness, law, medicine, personal development, finance, to real estate. Jim mentioned his family's involvement in the Down Syndrome Support Association of Southern Indiana and asked if there was a possibility of any celebrity items we could donate to the silent auction for the organization's annual Buddy Walk. A great conversation followed by a few email exchanges – that was it. We sent the Titus family autographed CDs by country stars Rascal Flatts and Bucky Covington for the auction.

Then the email with the article arrived to Nick's inbox. Patricia's article about Jacob's turn at bat told such a great story that these branding guys felt, well, called.

Considering that hundreds of thousands of kids across the country join T-ball teams every year, it could have been a totally unremarkable story. Jacob Titus is a four year old boy from small rural community – Floyds Knobs, Indiana, just outside of Louisville — playing T-ball in a place where, as his mother Patricia wrote, "life lessons are learned at church, home and on the baseball field." It's a familiar story. Except that as Patricia Titus' article accounts, "My youngest son loves to bat, loves to run, loves to play catcher. Jacob also happens to have Down Syndrome." Jacob's "turn" at bat and on the field was a thrill for him, but more importantly it was an event that transformed the hearts of everyone in his town. The wheels started to turn – how could we make this story go viral to help promote a charitable cause?

We knew that Jim Titus had no agenda beyond sharing his family's personal story and thanking us for putting together items for the charity auction. Honestly, we weren't looking for a new project or another line of business. At that time, we were jetting around the country doing seminars and talks on our last book, *Celebrity Branding You*. We weren't in the film business. But the seeds were there – Nick had used his student loans in college to purchase a video camera to shoot music videos of the bands he worked with and J.W.'s background as an entrepreneur perfectly positioned him to be an executive producer. Nick had spent more than a decade immersed in the entertainment industry as an award-winning songwriter and television producer, and had worked on projects and negotiated deals from large-scale events to reality television shows.

When we read the article and shared it with Nick's dad, Geoff, together we started wondering if we could turn this article into a documentary. Then it hit us – what if we could connect with our network of marketing experts and create a new model for funding and producing films? The only thing stopping us was time and money. And that's never a good enough reason not to do something that needs to be done and can make an impact on the world.

That's how we 'answered the call' at that specific moment. The amazing thing is that by responding to that one tug on our hearts, to make a film, we walked into a whole new world of ideas. First, we pursued the idea of getting people to support the project from our network of colleagues and maximized exposure for Jacob's story. Then we followed the call to create widespread awareness of special needs children everywhere by using our backgrounds and employing the same process used to launch a product in the online world. A process in which many marketers band together, leveraging their own unique customer and client lists—often to the tune of hundreds of thousands and even millions of people—to support a charitable cause instead of the typical launch of a product.

From there we caught a vision for creating films, for both the causes that we care about and the clients that we are passionate about. Our clients were coming to us asking if we could tell their stories on film like we were able to share Jacob's story. We sure could. *Jacob's Turn* was the first film released in 2010 and subsequently won an Emmy® Award. In 2011, Celebrity Films released *Car Men* a documentary about used car dealer Tracy Myers. The film has been a game changer for us and for Tracy. In fact, the documentaries which have become a movement allowing us to feature our clients on our show, airs on the Biography channel called Profiles of Success®.

When you think about answering the call, you usually think about the big stuff – what is my life's work? My mission? My purpose? We want to focus on answering the call to the small stuff. There are micro-calls coming in all day, every day that lead to huge shifts in your business, and your life. So how do you catch those micro-calls? The process of answering the call looks a lot like the steps we take when we make a movie.

DEVELOPMENT – LISTENING FOR THE CALL

When we start a movie, the first step is to develop the idea. That means being aware of all the potential ideas floating around related to the theme of the movie. To answer the call, you need to listen. Be available to the random email that might spark an idea.

The idea of making a documentary about Jacob Titus took a turn when we were talking about *how* to do it. We went from producing a film to benefit charity to connecting entrepreneurs and marketing gurus to form an organization, Entrepreneur's International Foundation. Drawing upon the expertise of the top international marketing minds of our time, Entrepreneurs International Foundation (EIF), is now a not-for-profit organization dedicated to creating unique campaigns to raise money and awareness for charitable causes. We utilize cutting edge business and marketing strategies and through EIF bring together top marketing and business minds in order to encourage and lift up those in need. All of that came about from having one conversation and reading one email.

We also used the magic of 'what if?' – a question that screenwriter's routinely ask themselves during the development stage. 'What if a pirate commanded a ship of the undead?' 'What if a giant shark was terrorizing the beach in New England?' By asking ourselves 'what if ' we used our marketing processes to produce this film, which led us to not only producing *Jacob's Turn,* but to winning an Emmy® Award for that film, to producing other documentaries that serve charities, and to creating a new business of making films for our marketing clients, called CelebrityFilms®. Developing one idea led to numerous ideas and huge breakthroughs for our business.

PRE-PRODUCTION – RESPONDING TO THE CALL

On a film, pre-production is the time when we lay out all the puzzle pieces. We scout locations, we assemble the cast and crew, and we figure out everything we need before we start filming. The CelebrityFilms® experience is a full two-day shoot. Even though a film shoot is full of excitement and anticipation for the subject of the documentary, for their staff and everyone in their community, we can assure you that it wouldn't be nearly as much fun if we used that time to figure out what shots we wanted. We come to a film shoot with our list of planned shots. Sure, we make changes on set and respond to the environment, the weather and any other factors that might make an even better shot. But we come prepared.

To answer the call that you are sensing is the next step in your business, hunker down and plan. Do the research, prepare the idea, create the plan that will ensure your success. Plot out your journey and you won't be unpleasantly surprised along the way. Instead, you will be ready to meet any challenges and to make any adjustments that will lead to the next call, and the next call, and the next one.

PRODUCTION – TAKING ACTION ON THE CALL

This is pedal to the metal time! Take all your passion for your idea, all the prep work you've done and take action. Production on a movie set can be stressful but it's also a lot of fun. This is the moment we've been working towards, so we enjoy putting the idea into motion.

When we worked on *Car Men* our documentary about used car dealer Tracy Meyers, we were blown away by the on-set atmosphere and the incredible story we were getting to tell. This is a guy whose dad was an amazing salesman but he never thought he would follow in his dad's footsteps. When Tracy came home from college his dad put him to work not as a salesman but in detailing, and made him work his way up from washing cars until he owned the business himself. Along the way, he and his dad had a lot of battles. It's an inspiring story and the theme of 'Now's your time' is powerfully revealed through the movie.

Sounds like a drama, right? Except these guys are a ton of fun. We got amazing shots and incredible interviews of the family reunion party type atmosphere that the Meyers create at their business every day. For us answering this call was pure fun. How you feel while you are answering the call should tell you that you are on the right track. Sure it will be hard work – but while you are producing your idea, your sense of satisfaction should be there. You should be having the time of your life.

POST PRODUCTION – EVALUATING THE CALL

Movie making goes back and forth between being a collaborative team sport to being a solitary deadline driven grind. In post production the director and the editor are locked in a dark room going over the details, looking at every frame of film and deciding what stays in and what gets left on the cutting room floor. When you answer a call and make a step forward in your business, make that time for solitary evaluation. Revisit the steps you took. Decide what you would 're-script' if you could. Look closely at the details that are successful. Evaluating your call is an important part in hearing the micro-calls that can lead to the many ideas coming from this one step.

DISTRIBUTION – COMMUNICATING THE CALL

Words do not do justice to the impact these films have had on the businesses of our clients – from throwing local movie screenings for all their clients at a rented out theater to being featured on Profiles Of Success® on the Biography Channel. Distributing a movie is when you can see how your work impacts others.

These steps will help you answer the call in your business, but the real challenge comes from taking the risk – stepping out and answering that first call to something new can be scary. When you see the impact that you have had, then you will know that the risk and the challenges were worth it. It can be hard to hear that call towards the next big thing in your life and your business. If you will listen and develop the idea, respond with planning, take action on answering the call, then evaluate it and re-work the idea to perfection, you will see that your call can have bigger impact than you ever anticipated. Who knows, it might even bring you an entirely new business line – like it did for us!

About Nick

An Emmy Award-Winning Director and Producer, Nick Nanton, Esq., is known as the Top Agent to Celebrity Experts around the world for his role in developing and marketing business and professional experts, through personal branding, media, marketing and PR. Nick is recognized as the nation's leading expert on personal branding as Fast Company Magazine's Expert Blogger on the subject and lectures regularly on the topic at major universities around the world. His book *Celebrity Branding You®*, while an easy and informative read, has also been used as a text book at the University level.

The CEO and Chief StoryTeller at The Dicks + Nanton Celebrity Branding Agency, an international agency with more than 1800 clients in 33 countries, Nick is an award -winning director, producer and songwriter who has worked on everything from large scale events to television shows with the likes of Steve Forbes, Brian Tracy, Jack Canfield (*The Secret*, Creator of the *Chicken Soup for the Soul* Series), Michael E. Gerber, Tom Hopkins, Dan Kennedy and many more.

Nick is recognized as one of the top thought-leaders in the business world and has co-authored 30 best-selling books alongside Brian Tracy, Jack Canfield, Dan Kennedy, Dr. Ivan Misner (Founder of BNI), Jay Conrad Levinson (Author of the Guerilla Marketing Series), Super Agent Leigh Steinberg and many others, including the breakthrough hit *Celebrity Branding You!®*.

Nick has led the marketing and PR campaigns that have driven more than 1000 authors to Best-Seller status. Nick has been seen in *USA Today, The Wall Street Journal, Newsweek, BusinessWeek, Inc. Magazine, The New York Times, Entrepreneur® Magazine, Forbes,* FastCompany.com and has appeared on ABC, NBC, CBS, and FOX television affiliates around the country, as well as CNN, FOX News, CNBC, and MSNBC from coast to coast.

Nick is a member of the Florida Bar, holds a JD from the University Of Florida Levin College Of Law, as well as a BSBA in Finance from the University of Florida's Warrington College of Business. Nick is a voting member of The National Academy of Recording Arts & Sciences (NARAS, Home to The GRAMMYs), a member of The National Academy of Television Arts & Sciences (Home to the Emmy Awards), co-founder of the National Academy of Best-Selling Authors, a 16-time Telly Award winner, and spends his spare time working with Young Life, Downtown Credo Orlando, Entrepreneurs International and rooting for the Florida Gators with his wife Kristina and their three children, Brock, Bowen and Addison.

Learn more at www.NickNanton.com and:
www.CelebrityBrandingAgency.com

About JW

JW Dicks, Esq., is America's foremost authority on using personal branding for business development. He has created some of the most successful brand and marketing campaigns for business and professional clients to make them the credible celebrity experts in their field and build multi-million dollar businesses using their recognized status.

JW Dicks has started, bought, built, and sold a large number of businesses over his 39-year career and developed a loyal international following as a business attorney, author, speaker, consultant, and business experts' coach. He not only practices what he preaches by using his strategies to build his own businesses, he also applies those same concepts to help clients grow their business or professional practice the ways he does.

JW has been extensively quoted in such national media as *USA Today,* the *Wall Street Journal, Newsweek, Inc.,* Forbes.com, CNBC.com, and *Fortune Small Business.* His television appearances include ABC, NBC, CBS and FOX affiliate stations around the country. He is the resident branding expert for *Fast Company'*s internationally syndicated blog and is the publisher of *Celebrity Expert Insider,* a monthly newsletter targeting business and brand-building strategies.

JW has written over 22 books, including numerous best-sellers, and has been inducted into the National Academy of Best-Selling Authors. JW is married to Linda, his wife of 42 years, and they have two daughters, two granddaughters and two Yorkies. JW is a 6th generation Floridian and splits his time between his home in Orlando and beach house on the Florida west coast.

CHAPTER 28

GETTING TO YOU 2.2*
— LIFE SUCCESS BY DESIGN™

BY ROBERT WARREN HESS

DO YOU KNOW YOUR LIFE'S DESTINATION?
CAN YOU ACTUALLY GET THERE?

Answering the Call is about helping people reach their life's goal and, along the way, helping others do the same, because none of us succeeds alone.

Successfully reaching goals or responding to challenges means that you know precisely where you want to be and have a workable plan for getting there. Yogi Berra famously noted, "If you don't know where you're going, you might wind up someplace else." Sometimes we set the wrong goals and sometimes the goal is right, but we simply don't have the assets to achieve it.

What we all need is a simple system that allows us to set a goal, know what it will take to achieve it, if we're on track, and how to adjust our goals as we move through life.

GOAL SETTING UNDER THE PALM TREES

I did my undergraduate degree at the Virginia Military Institute and I thought I had learned everything about planning but when I arrived at my first field duty assignment as a Platoon Leader with the 173rd Airborne Brigade in the Republic of Vietnam, I quickly found out I knew nothing about planning.

Over the next 12 months I learned that the mission – what my unit was tasked to do – was everything and that my job was to make certain the mission was accomplished with the least possible expenditure of resources and, if at all possible, with no loss of life.

Ensuring the mission got done meant beginning with a precise definition of the conditions that needed to exist when the mission was complete. Sometimes the mission was as simple as "secure" Tay Ninh village by a specified day and time. But there were a lot of requirements inherent in that term "secure." It meant that all enemy forces and influence were eliminated and that the village would be secure from attack – a complex task.

Military operations almost always are joint operations, meaning that artillery, air support, logistics – fuel, ammunition, and rations – need to be requisitioned, organized, and delivered to the right place at the right time. Knowing how to precisely define the end result, plan the mission, and assemble the needed resources are crucial elements in the "tool box" of operational success for the military.

Getting this done was a challenge, but the Army – in fact all of the military services – teach a structured process for ensuring that nothing is missed.

Most of our daily business and personal lives don't involve the risk to human life inherent in military operations, but the challenges we face and the tasks we need to accomplish can be just as complicated. The good news is that we can use the same process the military uses.

HOW TO APPLY US ARMY BACKWARD PLANNING TO YOUR LIFE GOALS

While relatively few of us have had the opportunity to learn the military's backward planning process - precisely defining the objective and then planning backwards to identify the necessary resources and the milestones when tasks need to be accomplished, it's a simple, quickly learned 5-step system that can have a dramatic impact on your professional and personal life.

I call my process "The *Getting to You 2.2* System." You can use it in your business and your personal life, and you can – and should – teach it to your children.

WHY "YOU 2.2?"

The number "2.0" is an adjective commonly used to denote a more advanced version of an original concept, product, or service. We're all accustomed to seeing this in the media and in software version releases.

I use the term "You 2.2" to illustrate the concept that each person, organization, business, and culture constantly evolves over time. Even our individual DNA, which once was thought to remain constant over our lifetime, has been found to be constantly changing over our individual lifetimes.

The *Getting to You 2.2* system is an easy-to-follow process of 5 simple steps, each with a simple checklist. Together, the process and the checklists show you where you are headed, show you the tools (assets) you need to get there, and give you a process for knowing if you are veering off track.

Getting to You 2.2 is the distillation of my experiences – a career in the US Army leading men in combat, conquering ADD, leading the business development and lobbying team in the Washington, DC office of a French aerospace company, getting an MBA at 54, becoming an entrepreneur, being diagnosed with cancer and becoming a prostate cancer survivor and advocate, and co-founding a unique Los Angeles-based market entry accelerator for foreign companies entering the US marketplace.

STEP 1 - REVERSE ENGINEER YOUR FUTURE – WHY IT'S ABSOLUTELY CRUCIAL

We've all heard the term reverse engineering. It's a process used to determine how a finished product was made and the materials that were used. The product, whatever it might be, is taken apart piece-by-piece, with each part being analyzed for materials used, assembly process, and how it was manufactured. The end result is a complete plan for recreating the product.

This is precisely the process we use in *Getting to You 2.2*. For business owners, you need to look at what you want your business to look like in 5 years. I use a 5-year time horizon because culture and technology changes too quickly to look beyond that horizon. For our personal lives, though, we need to begin at the "end game;" whenever you want to stop actively working – 45, 50, 55, 62, - whatever you might choose, and apply the same reverse engineering process.

For business owners, the goal always is the "exit strategy," the planned date when the business will be sold or perhaps transferred to the next generation. For the exit to deliver the desired financial outcome, the business must be built, piece-by-piece, with a specific financial goal as a target. The only way to achieve that outcome is to define the goal and then backward plan and build the processes and assets that will make it happen. Take a moment and write down these two items: the dollar amount you want to receive as you exit, and the annual turnover your business needs to be earning to generate your exit amount based on the normal multiple valuation for your industry.

The same process holds true in personal life. Every career requires a certain set of skills that must be acquired and honed. Write down the following: your target job title, the knowledge and skills you need to qualify, how long it will take to acquire them, and any sacrifices – time, family, location of residence, core personal values – that might be required.

STEP 2 – VALIDATE THE CONTEXT

This is the most crucial step in the entire process. In the business sense, I'm talking about the need to look closely at the industry you are working in to ensure that there is a genuine opportunity for the product or service you plan to offer. Start with these basic questions:

1) Is there a clearly defined market?

2) Am I solving a real problem?

3) Can the offering be scaled?

4) Do I have a special or unique advantage in the marketplace?

5) Does it fit your business's core objectives?

Validating the context is even more important in our personal lives. Reaching your goals and being content and gratified when you arrive demands that what you do be congruent with your personal core beliefs and values, whatever they may be. Pursuing a career that conflicts with core values, either initially or over time, introduces a high degree of stress that eventually will take its toll.

STEP 3 – ACQUIRING THE NEEDED ASSETS

Now that you know precisely where you are headed and that the goal – business or personal – is in consonance with your personal beliefs or business culture and capabilities, the next step is to acquire the assets needed to reach those goals.

People, processes, and knowledge are the basic building blocks for reaching both business and personal goals. In Steps 1 and 2 we described in specific terms what the "product" – business or personal life goal - looks like and confirmed that they fit the market need and our personal life values context. Step 3 is about dissecting those goals to understand the essential knowledge, skills, and relationships needed – the "parts.'"

Take a minute and write down the 10 critical assets you think you'll need. They most likely will fall into the categories of people, processes, knowledge, and physical assets – including capital. Make one list for your business, if you own one, and a second for your personal life.

STEP 4 – EXECUTION... STAYING ON TRACK

In the first 3 steps, we defined the desired outcome, made certain that the outcome made sense from a business or personal perspective, and identified the list of "parts" – the knowledge, skills, processes, and relationships – necessary to reach the goal. The next step is actually executing on the plan.

Enter "To Do List" into Google and you'll get an astounding 4,550,000,000 entries returned in just 0.26 seconds. There are hundreds, if not thousands, of different ways to track tasks – paper and electronic. Getting tasks into a list isn't the challenge. The challenge is to know the next thing that needs to get done, actually doing it, and keeping score as you accomplish the tasks and mini-projects.

Execution means putting those tasks into a priority sequence and assigning specific dates to them. Finishing each task, or group of tasks, represents a milestone along the path to the goal. Every Army operational plan has specifically defined milestones - we called them phase lines - so that everyone in the division knew when and where they needed to be.

STEP 5 – THE REALITY CHECK

The final step in the *Getting to You 2.2* system is the review process. Everything around us is in constant motion. This holds true in business and in our personal lives. Planning is fundamental, but it's even more crucial to periodically review the plan to make certain it's still our destination and that it's still possible.

One of the world's great military strategists, Prussian Chief of Staff Helmuth von Moltke, famously noted, "No battle plan survives contact with the enemy." I found this statement to be true during my Army career and just as true in my business and personal life. Things always change and the best way to survive and capitalize on change is to have a simple, effective planning and review process in place.

Step 5 is simply setting a sequence of reviews where you assess where you are in the process, reaffirm that the goals you're pursuing are still where you want to go, and fine tune your asset and task requirements.

If you're using *Getting to You 2.2* in business, you should constantly reassess your progress with all of your management team. Schedule monthly, quarterly, and year-end reviews.

If you are applying *Getting to You 2.2* to your personal life, be certain to include your significant other. Marriage or long-term relationships are a lot like business partnerships; everyone needs to have input and consensus is critical.

A PICTURE IS WORTH A THOUSAND WORDS. PROBABLY MORE...

One of the references in the tool section below deals with PechaKucha™, which is a technique developed by two architects in 2003. A PechaKucha™ presentation is a series of 20 slides shown for just 20 seconds each.

One great way to visualize your future state is to construct a PechaKucha™ presentation of your business five years in the future, or you personally at some future time. Thinking through what pictures you select to show literally will lead you through the *Getting to You 2.2* process.

I LOVE *GETTING TO YOU 2.2*. BUT I JUST DON'T HAVE TIME... !

As you should have figured out by now, *Getting to You 2.2* is all about process and simplicity. Commit just four hours to the *Getting to You 2.2* process and you will have a basic roadmap and asset requirements list.

Still not convinced you should go through this process? Make a short list of the five unhappiest people you know and picture yourself in their situation. We all arrive somewhere in life. Arriving at the place of our choosing is simply a matter of planning, choice, and discipline. And it doesn't need to be complex.

GETTING TO YOU 2.2

I created the *Getting to You 2.2* System as a simple but powerful process for people and organizations to picture their future state, construct a road map to get there, and track their process along the way.

Successfully answering your own call will give you the ability to help others reach their goals. It doesn't get better than that!

<u>REFERENCE TOOLS YOU CAN USE</u>

William Jensen, *Simplicity: Working Smarter in a World of Infinite Choices.* This isn't a perfect book, but it has lots of great insights about simplifying tasks and processes.

Steven R. Covey, *Begin With the End In Mind: Habit 2 of the 7 Habits of Highly Effective People.* This is the second habit of *The 7 Habits of Highly Effective People*, which was named the most influential business book of the twentieth century.

Dave Lavinsky, *Start at the End: How Companies Can Grow Bigger and Faster by Reversing their Business Plan. Start at the End* provides a concise, practical process for making sure your business is on the right path. I reviewed this book for the American Banking Association.

Tom Rath, *Strengths Finder 2.0: A New and Upgraded Edition of the Online Test from Gallup's "Now, Discover Your Strengths."* This is a great exercise. Research shows you are more likely to benefit from leveraging your strengths than trying to improve your weaknesses. Full disclosure: my Gallup strengths are: Strategic, Activator, Input, Ideation, Learner.

Atul Gawande, M.D., *The Checklist Manifesto: How to Get Things Right.* This is a particularly interesting book. It's all about how organizations use simple checklists to accomplish complex projects and improve cross-functional processes. I reviewed this book for the American Banking Association.

PechaKutcha™ 20 x 20. A simple but enlightening process of illustrating a concept or a future state using just 20 images shown for just 20 seconds each.

Dorie Clark, *Reinventing You: Define Your Brand, Imagine Your Future.* This is a great book filled with usable insights and practical advice. I would make it mandatory reading for every college graduate and professional. It's almost a field manual for *Getting to You 2.2.*

Dave Gowel, *The Power in a Link:* More than 80% of US professionals have a LinkedIn account. Less than 5% of LinkedIn users know why they have an account or how to use it effectively. Dave's book is an absolute must read. Full disclosure: Dave also is a former Army Ranger.

About Robert

Robert Warren Hess is a lifelong performance improvement architect, practical technologist, and public health advocate. Robert works with corporate and private clients to define specific business and life objectives, develop plans to acquire the assets needed to reach these goals, and the milestones and scorekeeping structures essential to keeping everything on track.

Robert learned the critical importance of planning and execution firsthand as a young Army officer while serving with airborne infantry and armor units in Vietnam and Germany. The critical importance of focusing on the ultimate objective of any activity was a constant theme throughout his Army career, including his service in the Pentagon and with the US Department of State. He brings this structured thinking and planning process to all of his client engagements.

He is the Founder and President of TSG Inc., a management information consulting firm based in Santa Monica, California, and a Founder of InterspaceLA, a market entry accelerator for foreign companies seeking to enter the US marketplace. TSG Inc. developed the TrakPointe™ task tracking and dashboard software solution now in use in the banking and technology development industries.

Robert also is a Senior Fellow at the Center for the Digital Future, which is part of the Annenberg School of Communications at the University of Southern California in Los Angeles. In 2009, he spent a year conducting field research and writing a report for the US Department of Defense on how military families were using social media tools to manage the extended family separations associated with US military deployments in Iraq and Afghanistan.

An author and teacher, Robert is a frequent book reviewer and blogger, and teaches the *World's Toughest LinkedIn Training Program,* along with a special Social Media Bootcamp for CEOs and senior executives. You can find links to his book reviews on his LinkedIn profile.

A prostate cancer survivor and wellness advocate, Robert founded the Prostate Cancer Awareness Project based in Manhattan Beach, California, and created ProstateTracker, the first Internet-based prostate cancer early detection system. He was honored in 2013 by the *Los Angeles Business Journal* for his role in health advocacy, was selected as a consumer reviewer for prostate cancer research projects funded by the Congressionally Directed Medical Research Program, and he currently is developing a program to help prostate cancer survivors prevent their disease recurrence.

You can connect with Robert at:
Robert.Hess@TSG.LA
Robert.Hess@ThePCAP.org
www.LinkedIn.com/in/RobertWarrenHess
www.twitter.com/RobertWHess
www.Facebook.com/RobertWarrenHess

CHAPTER 29

ARE YOU READY?

BY ROCHELE LAWSON

Imagine being a little girl and dreaming that you are helping people to feel better so that they no longer have to suffer in silence, but not knowing truly what your dream means. Imagine having this dream over and over and each time the dream occurs it becomes more vivid and real. Now imagine suffering four traumatic life-changing experiences all before the age of eight that began your journey towards your destiny. However the traumas that you suffered and held deep inside your mind began to manifest in various ways within your body. Of course the holding on to the traumas was not done intentionally but it was just your way of coping with what was happening in your life, after all you are only eight years old. You see this was the beginning of a 17-year, painful journey of suffering from a medical condition that doctors were unable to diagnose. Imagine telling the doctors that when you grow up you are going to heal yourself so that no one has to suffer in pain like you.

Now visualize the same little girl from above that knew from the age of four that she could see wellness or illness in people but did not quite understand what she was seeing or what to do with the information. When she would discuss what she would see in people with her mother, her mom would say, "that's not possible, you are only a little girl and you are imagining things" or "you always have such a vivid imagination." When the little girl would press her mother about what she was seeing her mom would say, "don't share this with anybody because you are not suppose to know things like that. If you keep talking about that stuff,

I'm going to have to spank you." So after a while the little girl did what most kids would do, she stopped talking about it and kept what she saw to herself but deep down inside she knew that what she saw in others was the key to helping them feel better.

The above scenario is a description of my life as a child. I knew from a very young age that I had a gift of seeing wellness in people. The problem was that my health and wellness began to suffer from what was occurring in my life, so that it took the focus off my "gift" and placed it upon myself. The older I got the more intense and frequent the painful abdominal episodes became. It was during this time I also developed what I call "perfectionism" and "type A personality syndrome." Now these terms are not *bona fide* medical terms, but they are a true description of me and what was occurring inside me. I was also highly but secretly competitive. I believe the saving grace for me was that I always had a connection to "Spirit" or "God" which would provide me with divine guidance and direction. You see although I could see health and wellness or the lack of it in others, I could not see how to fix the illness within myself. The external stressors in my life were making me sick and suffer in pain on the inside, but on the outside, others saw me beaming like a beacon of light. It is this that negated me from truly tapping into the divine knowledge of wellness that was being bestowed upon me.

During this time, I remained in constant communication with my source of "Divine Guidance." I began to study Herbology and incorporated utilizing herbs to soothe my discomfort. I began focusing on eating the best foods that I could possibly get my hands on. I began to get massages as often as I could afford them and I began experimenting with different types of meditation. I also began a daily practice of prayer and connecting with the "Divine." I would say that my life took on a more holistic form even though I did not know that's what it was at the time. As this way of life became a natural way of life for me, my connection to "divine guidance" deepened and more awareness about my physical and mental state was revealed. The revelation was that I had been suffering from "Traumatic Stress" and this potent form of stress that I had in my mind had manifested in my body and that is why I was suffering from the severe abdominal pain. My digestive system was the weak spot in my body.

With this information, I began to learn as much as I could about stress and how I could use a holistic approach to relieved the stress that affected every aspect of my health and well-being. What I discovered was astonishing. I discovered that I could be relieved of the excruciating pain that had plagued me for 17 years and that the way I was now living my life was nourishing and healing to my mind, body and spirit. It was a secret "cure" to restoring optimal health and well being.

I incorporated this wisdom of health and in 9 months I was completely cured and living pain free! And the doctors deemed it a "miracle."

This holistic way of taking care of myself dramatically changed every aspect of my life. I tapped into my "divine guidance" for wisdom and direction and was guided to the science of Ayurveda. Immersion in Ayurveda led me to understand that the wisdom given to me to heal myself was based on the principles of Ayurveda. It was the wisdom of this ancient, 3500-year-old natural and holistic medical science that healed me from my pain and suffering, when modern medicine could not.

Imagine how thrilled I was to be pain free, healthy, well with vibrancy, energy, clarity, focus, creativity, peace of mind and body and success in all my endeavors. It felt oh so yummy and still does! During this time, my career as a RN excelled, I started a business with my husband, and became a very successful entrepreneur. I obtained an advanced degree in Ayurveda, incorporated into how I managed my patients as a RN in the clinical setting and in my private practice.

Now don't get me wrong, I am very thankful for all the advances that we have available today with modern medicine and even though I am a Registered Nurse, I have always believed that it was better to treat the body and mind naturally than not. You see when I look back on my journey that began when I was 8 years old, I know that I was being prepared to answer the call to help heal and serve our world holistically and naturally. My theme since I was a little girl was to help others with the knowledge that was bestowed upon me. I know that even though the journey I have taken has not always been easy, I know that I was being prepared for greater things along the way. I believe that our journey here on earth is our path to bliss. We walk down this path with our own unique challenges with their own unique solutions and successes, and even though this path may not always be smooth, it is uniquely ours and no one else can experience it in the same manner as we can.

As I began to analyze why holistic medicine worked for me, I learned that there are three components that I needed to focus on. They were the mind, body and spirit. Each of these components are directly related to the other. If one of these components are out of balance, health, wellness and true success cannot be achieved. The methods I used to heal myself were based on the principles of Ayurveda. I learned that what resides in the mind, conscious, subconscious or ego, will eventually manifest itself in the body.

When I think about all the years that I suffered in pain, when I think about all the other people in the world that are suffering in pain like I did, when I think about how stress and toxins are killing our society and when I think about why this suffering is so unnecessary, I know that as a health and wellness expert it is my duty to help end this unnecessary suffering.

What I would like you to do is think about how you are feeling right now. Think about your uniqueness and how your path to optimal health and wellbeing is unique to you. Did you know your uniqueness is the secret to your success to being healthy and well? When you discover this life changing information about your unique mind and body, you will hold the key to everlasting energy, vitality, clarity, focus, no stress, abundance and prosperity. Does this sound like something you would like to enjoy? Are you ready to stop suffering in pain with poor health and wellness? Are you ready to truly end your struggle of pretending that stress isn't killing you?

If you are ready to make a change that will "up level" your life as you journey down your path to "Bliss," then I would love to help you.

First of all let me say I utilize the principles of Ayurveda to help you discover and restore your true nature. It is from within this source of information that the key to your success lies. The belief is that when you experience optimal health and wellness, you are unstoppable, and all that you want to achieve is yours to receive. The balance and harmony that exist within the mind and the body while in this state can lead to bliss and success in all endeavors.

Secondly I want to share with you that within the context of you walking down your path to "Bliss," there will always be challenges, but it is how the challenge is handled that can make such a tremendous difference in life. When you know your unique composition you become armed with the most powerful information that a person can posses. This information allows you to successfully navigate the challenges that may surface on your journey with much more ease and accuracy and a lot less pain and suffering. Think about it as having your own personal road map and GPS system. If you follow the guidance you most definitely will get to your destination.

My dream is to help as many people as possible discover their hidden secret to optimal health and wellness, holistically and naturally, so they can successfully steer their life to live their dreams. It is a systematic approach that is unique to you. First you discover your unique composition, then you can begin incorporating the first step – which is the *5 Critical Keys to Bliss*. These keys are clarifying, nourishing, restorative and peaceful for the mind, allowing abundance and prosperity to flow into one's life. The *5 Critical Keys to Bliss* are designed to balance the conscious, sub-conscious and ego aspects of the mind. Remember what exists in the mind will manifest itself in the body, so the goal is to balance the mind so that balance can proceed within the body. Utilizing these keys opens up the gateway to less stress, thinking rich and living a life of bliss!

The *5 Critical Keys to Bliss* are:

1. Finding your Path to Joy by Changing Negatives to Positive.

2. The Art of Self Love.

3. Identifying Your Heart's Wisdom to Refine Your Ego and Increase Your Power.

4. Opening to Receive.

5. Calming the Winds of Stress.

Well-being is your divine right and being successful is your divine gift. The two go hand-in-hand. You cannot experience one without experiencing the other. In fact I want you to tap into how you are feeling at this very moment in time. If you are not feeling 100% in both mind and body then you are not doing yourself justice and I'm asking you to answer the call to make a change. You are the most valuable person on the planet. When you are in a healthy and well state of being, a state of "Bliss," then you are able to magnetize abundance and success in all areas of your life. When you learn what to do the task becomes all the easier and when you get focused guidance, the sky's the limit. This is what I have done for hundreds of people and I can do this for you.

My dream for you is to be healthy, well, successful and "rich." My goal is to show you how to do this for yourself and my destiny is to help you do this successfully time after time as you travel down your path to "Bliss."

The question is: Are You Ready?

About Rochele

Rochele Marie Lawson, known as the "Queen of Feeling Fabulous" is a successful entrepreneur, Registered Nurse, Ayurvedic Health Practitioner, Holistic Health and Wellness Consultant, Best-Selling Author and Speaker. After many years as a successful entrepreneur and being named one of the Top 50 Women-Owned Businesses in Silicon Valley for several consecutive years, she decided to turn her focus to helping those that she did business with become healthy and well, holistically and naturally, and this transcended her into launching her own wellness company.

Rochele is the Founder and President of The Health, Healing & Wellness Company, founded to bring holistic health and wellness into the lives of individuals seeking a natural and successful path to wellness. Her goal is to help her clients achieve a state of well-being that transcends itself into all aspects of their lives – so that abundance and prosperity can easily flow into their lives.

Rochele's energy, knowledge, guidance and enthusiasm have helped thousands of people improve their health and wellbeing, and that has spilled over into greater success in all aspects of their lives. The belief is that when a person is healthy and well, what they aspire to achieve, as they walk down their path to bliss, is able to manifest itself in their lives much more easily. It is this manifestation that allows the gateway to more prosperity and abundance to flow into all areas of their lives.

She is a graduate of both San Diego State University and San Jose State University and has advanced degrees in business and Ayurveda. She is the author of the book *Intro To Holistic Health, Ayurveda Style*. She has her own blog and is a guest writer for Supermomceo.com blog and has her own weekly syndicated radio show called "Blissful Living." Rochele has spent over 25 years assisting people to achieve optimal health and wellness so that they can live the life of their dreams with more energy, vitality, mental clarity, alertness and mental focus – while reversing the aging process.

You can connect with Rochele Marie at:
rochele@rochelelawson.com
www.twitter.com/rochelelawson
www.facebook.com/RocheleLawson
www.linkedin.com/rochelelawson

CHAPTER 30

ON MY WAY TO ME

BY NAILAH G. BERAKI-PIERRE

When I was growing up we didn't use the term entrepreneurs, MLM, or any of those expressions as we know them today. Looking back, I would say that my parents were the first entrepreneurs I've ever known. As adults they were in the health fields when they were growing up, they were resourceful. They learned how to make shoes and furniture, built homes, and grew their own food. Mom was a farmer's daughter; both worked hard for what they got. There were no excuses in those days.

My mom's a retired nurse now; she used to make patterns, design hats and make custom clothing. My father was always creating healing oils, herbal formulas, and soaps; and had a large clientele. Like many of our ancestors, he was ahead of his time, as evidenced by today's health and market sales, equal to a trillion dollar business. He is deceased now, but he would have been proud of the recognition natural health has achieved. Both parents were active in our community, networking with our teachers and interacting with the church family. Mom was the head of my Brownie troop. I was a girl scout and a Cadet, so I experienced the joy of selling, but didn't consciously realize I was selling until later. My energy for "selling" was always related to a cause, and the monies received were an expression of support for the cause.

In my family, we also learned about giving. I worked at Harlem Hospital as a candy striper, volunteer. I visited patients and learned how to make a bed properly, using what was referred to as "hospital corners," which entailed tucking the sheet corners, in a specific fashion. I mastered it, and still use the technique today.

We got very excited when it was time for the annual Girl Scout cookie sale – as I can recall, people were happy buying cookies, giving me their money and receiving goods. This was exciting to me, and everyone was happy! And, as a thank you bonus, once in a while I got additional boxes as gifts; so at every opportunity, I wanted more of that good feeling. Since then, opportunities to share quality products, meet positive people and make money (yaay!!) have always been very attractive to me. From Amway to Tupperware to Mary Kay, I made money through selling products, back in those days. It didn't require the same kind of marketing plan or Internet access that we have today. It's hard to imagine it wasn't that long ago. It was always such a joy that my father used to say: "fair exchange, no robbery." At the time it sounded odd to me. But I've grown to appreciate his words.

It appeared that people who were selling were upbeat, happy, positive people, and I always wanted to be around people like that. I also loved helping people and solving problems, and my friends loved to talk to me. I guess I was also a problem solver. ...Definitely a problem solver! When you have a household full of brothers and there were girls seeking out your expertise as to how to reach them, you become a problem solver and negotiator.

My parents provided a lot of leadership and direction to all of us. Having positive leadership was key in my life. I have always had a lot of ideas and creativity, and wanted to see it all to fruition. I have also held a lot of positions of various types, but I was always looking for something special.

My work history included working for an advertising agency, Housing Development Administration, and as a buyer's assistant and in the hospitals. I loved law, medicine and social work and advocating for people's rights, and I loved learning, but for me, something was missing. Working at the hospital was confusing. The wisdom my Father shared about the body healing itself via natural cures was not congruent with what I was taught while attending college and working at the hospital. Just like my Mom, who is a great motivator and leader, provided steps for me to follow, I was following the steps of traditional positions that did not fit me. You would have thought I would have invested my energies in a Business degree, but Holistic Health was part of my passion, and my life's calling.

Business was natural and fun, even though I couldn't conceive the whole picture. I learned about a program to become a Naturopathic Doctor. This, I felt, was my dream come true. The curriculum answered most of my questions about health and spirituality, but licensure appeared to be pending, so upon graduation I found out licensing still wasn't available in New York or on the entire eastern seaboard at that time. I got married shortly after graduation and we relocated to San Diego, California.

When I moved to California, Naturopathic Physicians held no licensure there either. I went back to college, and to supplement my income I found another multi-level marketing program with a bigger gain; it was an opportunity to own my own house. It was exciting meeting people involved in this new venture. I met inspired people wanting to be independent and free. So when I discovered the *"no money down" real estate investing techniques* program, I was on board immediately! I expressed breast milk into a bottle for my infant son everyday so I could attend the events. It was very successful with very different ground rules, but the basics were familiar--selling and networking with people. For me it was all about creating generational wealth and being independent. There was no technology as it exists today, but people shared amazing stories of their success. I wanted that too!

Also, being home with my baby was a one-time opportunity – given how quickly they grow and change. I wanted the full experience. The ability to make six figures in six months, allowed me to be home with my baby, pay a sitter, attend classes and to research new and upcoming avenues to acquire more properties; and it afforded out-of-state family visits a few times a year. Everything was going very well; my feet were on solid ground. I was raised being part of a community and wanted my son to be part of a community as well. After all we were living in California and my family lived on the East Coast, 3,000 miles away, so I created a community for us. It was wonderful. Everything appeared to be in place; nothing was missing.

I acquired four properties in a short time, making money while working from home–before my life was forever changed.

Then, as a pedestrian, I was hit by a car, in a coma, and paralyzed on the left side. When I woke up days later, my memory kept drifting back to the dream of what had happened – or at least I thought it was a dream. One day, while in my hospital bed, I drifted above my body. Looking down at my body, I appeared to be well. It was an unusual experience, and I relaxed when I heard a small reassuring voice whisper, "everything will be all right ...according to your belief, ...according to your belief." It was completely surreal!

Once I was released from the hospital, I found that I was a Mother and wife, separated from my husband, but suddenly, I was unable to follow the marketing plan step-by-step, in the Guidelines as I had learned. I no longer had automatic recurring revenue. I knew I was great at helping other people make money but that was something that I could no longer do, after the accident. Now, I just had to learn how to save myself, heal myself, and make a living. I had to learn how to survive.

What happens to a dream deferred? How do you face life when all hell is breaking loose? You need to know how to survive when things don't go the way you planned – to stand in the rain vulnerable and alone and still have faith, without knowing which way you're going. When everything that you worked for is gone, how do you survive? For me, it was not easy, but what I was most grateful for is that my parents taught me how to pray, have faith and trust God to show me the way. Can I tell you I was put to the test energetically; I was no longer connected to my old self. This body was paralyzed on one side, and I had to learn how to navigate within the parameters of the 'new me.' I was in a spiritual boot-camp intensive! Can you imagine knowing yourself in one way all of your life, and then, suddenly operating from a new system without a manual?

I held on to the mystical experience in my hospital room for dear life, and I still do. It held a greater vision for my life than the prognosis the physicians had for me, even though I didn't have enough consciousness to sort that out, at that time. I was only able to focus and stay awake for minutes at a time and worked my way up to half a day. One day, it occurred to me that I had always enjoyed helping others. Now I asked myself the question, "have I been better at helping others than helping myself?" As I lay there, I realized that I knew what to do for others, but I didn't know how to help myself, in my new circumstances. However, the Rehabilitation team knew exactly what to do. They had plans for me, and my Angels were 'on board.' I spent two months in the hospital, and left in a wheel chair, with a prognosis of mobility via wheel chair, and doing crossword puzzles for life. I knew God had another plan for my life, and it was greater than being in a wheel chair. As a result of that experience, I have uncovered new strengths within myself, and coping techniques.

I want to share five of the lessons that I learned from this experience.

1. Begin to identify yourself--not just your name, gender, your age and occupation, but who you are, your likes and dislikes, and things that you have discovered about yourself. The more you identify yourself, the stronger the relationship that you can have with yourself, which will allow you to become a more confident person and increase your self-esteem.

2. Feel yourself in your body! I had to become present moment-by-moment, not living in the past or future--just now! The journey is a lifelong one, because you're ever growing spiritually and emotionally.

3. Become grounded in the face of adversity and joyful times.

4. Create a self-exploration sheet. Explore which belief systems are yours and become aware of those you inherited. Some beliefs and rituals you'll want to embrace, and some of them you will have to let go. It's called personal development.

5. Learn to like and accept all parts of yourself. There may be days when you don't like yourself, but all feelings are temporary. Feel your current feeling, then choose a feeling that will make you happy. Gratitude for your life is important. Know that your life's plan is unfolding. What you're seeking is seeking you. Don't do it alone. Invest in your dream. Find out how much it costs and pay for it. It'll pay you back tenfold. Be mindful of people with invisible disabilities you never knew had a challenge. Learn to pivot, shift, and learn the steps of the dance. Make the necessary steps, and learn the moves and turns so that you can become balanced in the storm when it hits, as it will. Your ability to shift will be a tool for personal and spiritual growth.

I love the evidence of my effort and the satisfaction of overcoming adversity. I'm still a work in progress--aren't we all, and I'm grateful for that. I remember being in a workshop, and the group was asked, "If you could go back in time and magically change your life, would you do it?" Well, as author Maya Angelou says, "I wouldn't take anything for my journey now!" I finished college again; relocated back to my home state and got married to a wonderful man.

What does it mean to be healthy, and who decides what it means? I do.

My life experience has taught me to transition to transformation. I moved through that challenge, and there have been many more since then. I am a Creative Strategist. I rebuilt and redesigned my life. That experience has taught me how to help myself, and others, to design a life that honors and rewards us for our efforts. Create and develop the strategies to focus on your highest income-producing activities to support your dreams, not just to get rich. Money alone will never equal wealth. Health is wealth. I was so impressed with the knowledge and wisdom of Rehabilitation and Mental Health Counselors, so I completed my graduate work and integrated my Holistic practice within this field. The missing pieces came together in unexpected ways. My profession is Natural health, which includes mental and spiritual health, wealth, and mindset. My philosophy is that it all matters – whole body-mind-health. I have also had awesome mentors, who have taught me about today's techniques for marketing. While I'm fascinated by technology, and know it is important to learn, I continue to love being in the energy of others.

It's been a very unexpected and sometimes frightening journey. I've lived through a nightmare that has enriched my soul, in every area of my life. My heart has become so much richer. I look forward to the experience of every day when I am willing to laugh out loud at myself, and see the humor of my life, and enjoy it.

Becoming the most that we can be is simply not possible without professional or spiritual guidance. And often, once we receive the help we need, we can then offer support to kindred souls we encounter, while on our journey. We can accomplish a lot alone, but we all need someone who can lift us up when we stumble, to show us how to dance in the rain. Learn the steps to propel yourself forward, and then become a beacon—to share with others what you have learned.

About Nailah

Nailah G. Beraki-Pierre, LMHC, CRC, is a Professional Healing Arts Practitioner. With over three decades of experience as a Holistic Practitioner, Nailah's mission is to help others make a difference in their own lives, and ultimately, the lives of others. Her personal coaching style and the ability to empower others is often described as Transformational!

With deep compassion, humor, and down-to-earth common sense, Nailah's full-life experiences allow her to embrace the world as a Healer and Teacher. In her personal quest for meaningful self-discovery and healing, she researched indigenous rituals of healing practices and has traveled the world to study the healing arts in more than 20 countries, and more than twenty-five U.S. states. She gained amazing tools and techniques under the tutelage of renowned teachers in various modalities.

Nailah has worked with thousands of clients – from rural farmers in Beijing, China to corporate CEOs, entertainers, entrepreneurs and many more. In this diversified experience, she implements stress management, in-depth inner work processes, Breath-work, holistic medicine, and many timeless modalities. After consistent and intensive consultations, her clients report increased inner peace, joy and the ability to identify their talents and abilities. She has helped people manage career transitions, launch new businesses, overcome significant challenges and discover their life's purpose. We all face challenging situations and Nailah helps us to uncover inner strength, unleash the passion and confidence to take action, and turn problems into opportunities. Nailah's fusion of real-life stories and her conversational techniques connect with her audience at an intimate, intense and individual level. She is able to take you from where you are and pivot you to where you want to be, with more than you could have imagined for yourself!

In addition to being a prominent therapist, Nailah has taught Business for Health Professionals and Reflexology at the New York College of Health Professions. She has conducted presentations at national conferences speaking on the topics of alternative healing, stress reduction, disability/ability issues, career, wealth building as well as spirituality and life design. She has appeared on Lifetime television and been called on as an expert for publications such as *The New York Daily News*, *Essence Magazine*, *Massage & Bodywork* magazine, and a book titled *Body and Soul* and the *Rehabilitation Medicine Journal*.

She contributed ten years at various conferences including the: National Black Women's Health conference, annually at Conference Women of Color as Warriors of Light held all over the U.S. She holds the following degrees and certificates: MSEd. Counseling Education, from Hunter College in New York, ND, Educator, Certified Iridologist, and Certified Health Coach and Tunia at the Training Center of China Academy of Chinese Medical Sciences, Beijing, China. Nailah is the creator of Pivot Now™ – a dynamic group program to help burgeoning entrepreneurs build a business, attract more clients with step-by-step guidance and accountability to grow their business, taking all of the guess work out of it, and providing support and real talk, with real results.

For those committed to accomplishing their goals. Nailah believes that mind, body and health is wealth – they are not separate and apart.

You can connect with Nailah at www.nailahberaki-pierre.com
www.nailahberakithemindsetmentor.com
www.pivotnow.com
www.twitter.comshakeraywellness
www.facebook/pivotnow.com

CHAPTER 31

THE SEVEN SECRETS TO LASTING, PASSIONATE LOVE!

BY EVA LOVE

Fortunately for me, years ago I answered the call to create a passionate, committed, fun relationship where I continue to be "in love" as a part of my everyday life, and I get to teach others how to do that too!

Today I am married to the love of my life and after 18 years of marriage (20 years of being together), my heart still does a little flip when I see him walk into a room. We have the love and fun that other's long for yet can't seem to achieve.

But it wasn't always this way.

PICKING THE ROTTEN APPLE

I got married at 17 to escape from my physically and emotionally abusive Dad. Even though I knew it was a mistake, I don't regret it because I have two amazing daughters from that marriage. After my first marriage, I was engaged four times! I always seemed to pick the 'bad' ones. All of these men were just another version of my ex-husband, i.e. womanizing addicts. After the fourth break-up, I realized that the one thing all of these guys had in common was ME! So I decided that until I fixed my "picker" I'd forget men and just focus on my children and work.

EVERYTHING ON MY LIST

I obsessed about what I did wrong for 11 years before marrying my second husband.

According to my list, he should have been Mr. Right, and his last name was Love! But that relationship was a total disaster. I came home early from work one day to find him beating my 16 year old daughter. I came unglued.

I found out that he had been beating both of my girls the entire 4 years of our marriage. I felt like a complete failure. How could I not know what was going on with my own daughters? How could I have made such a terrible mistake?

There I was, 35 years old and twice divorced! I didn't even believe in divorce! I had horrendous guilt for the damage my second marriage caused my girls. I was devastated. I felt I didn't deserve to live, and everyone would be better off without me.

EVA ... STOP THE CAR

As I rounded the corner to drive off a 1000-foot cliff, I heard a voice from deep inside say, "Eva, you're sick. It's like you have the flu. You'll get well. Stop the car." I'm so grateful I listened to that voice and was able to steer the car to safety.

To heal my deep emotional wounds, I spent thousands and thousands of dollars trying different types of therapists, healers, workshops, study groups, churches and spiritual paths. **Nothing helped!** Not only was I miserable, but I was making everyone around me miserable, too.

One night in total desperation, not knowing what else to do or where to turn, I cried out, "God, help me." A warm peace came over me, the weight of my agony lifted, and even though I didn't know how, I knew everything would be all right.

MY MIRACLE

The next day the techniques that I later named *The Love Miracle System*™ came to me. After using this system for only three weeks, my life changed radically. I became truly happy. I was healing my relationships and learning to love myself. I was becoming a new Eva!

My friends wanted to know what I was doing. My roommate asked me to teach her and a few of her girlfriends my system.

After that first class, things snowballed. I was so busy nights and weekends teaching workshops and working privately with clients that nine months later I quit my high-level executive position.

GOODBYE, CORPORATE WORLD

I was working for a billion dollar national auto-parts chain, had two departments reporting to me, with a $5.5M budget. I was the only woman on the executive team. I had a big, beautiful, top-floor corner office, nice salary, and all the perks. People thought I was crazy for leaving.

I never looked back.

As exciting as achieving that level of corporate success had been, it was nothing when compared to helping people out of their relationship misery and finding genuine happiness and fulfillment.

I was having the time of my life teaching classes and mentoring private clients, all by referral. I never marketed or advertised.

THE MOST IMPORTANT THING WAS MISSING

It looked like I had it all: beautiful home, snazzy sports car, loads of wonderful friends, lots of dates with fun guys, great income, exciting world travel, and an effervescent joy that bubbled up from within me. What I didn't have — had never had — was a passionate, deeply committed union with the love of my life.

MAMA WAS RIGHT!

Mama always said, "The greatest thing in the world is to love and be loved." Although I had lots of dates, I was lonely for "The One."

I longed for someone to share my life with and to play with. I didn't want to grow old alone.

WHERE WAS MY PRINCE?

One night while teaching a class, I noticed a gal who was radiant. In just 3 weeks she had attracted a gem of a guy. Though early in the relationship, I saw a solidness about them that gave me confidence it would last.

Never having had that sureness in my own relationships, I thought "Why can't you do that for yourself?" That night using my *Love Miracle System*™ I began working through the obstacles that were keeping me in superficial relationships.

WHO WAS KEEPING MY PRINCE AWAY?

I discovered I had never committed to myself. My focus was always on helping others. In that moment, I deeply embraced committing to myself – to treating myself with the same love and sweetness I wanted from my man.

I became a student of love, fabulous marriages, and healthy relationships.

I ATTRACTED MY PRINCE

Shortly thereafter, I met my husband, Will. He lived in San Diego, CA, and I lived in Scottsdale, AZ. For months we burned up the phone lines and kept the airlines profitable. When we hit a major problem, I wanted to run (an old pattern), but instead of running, I faced my fear and learned to stay.

We learned how to work through our disagreements and problems rather than fight. We learned how to find solutions that worked for both of us. Mostly we learned to look inside ourselves when it looks like the other person is at fault. And we learned how to share this process with others.

We committed to keep our love for each other 'front and center' in our lives. And that is where it has stayed. It has made me confront my ego and become a better person. Will feels the same.

MORE IN LOVE THAN EVER!

We've created a life together that is better than I ever thought possible.

We've learned a lot about each other and even more about ourselves.

We've gained enormous insight into how relationships really work (and don't work!).

As friends and family observed our relationship, they would constantly ask us to share our secrets. They always say, "You give us hope."

THE ENEMY OF LOVE

It upset us to see so much bad relationship advice in the media leading people down the road of disappointment and heartbreak.

Men are taught how to seduce women but not create a real relationship in the process, and women are being taught to manipulate men.

These and other popular ideas get traction in the media, but they are dead-end paths for those who long for a loving, deeply committed relationship.

A NEW RELATIONSHIP MODEL THAT WORKS!

With a 50% divorce rate and so much heartbreak, it was obvious there was a tremendous need for life-changing tools, skills and a model that really works.

We began sharing our relationship model in the *Magical Relationships Weekend Retreat* in 2001 which has helped hundreds and hundreds of couples gain the skill set, tool set, and mindset to create happy, lasting relationships. An equal number of singles have learned how to attract the right mate for them, sealing the deal with marriage. We're invited to so many weddings and vow renewal ceremonies, we can't attend them all!

In my 24 years of deep inner work with over 6,500 clients, 87% of my single clients are now either married or in a committed relationship within a year and 91% of my couple clients are like "love-birds", (some for the first time), and their relationships continue to thrive!

THE SEVEN SECRETS TO LASTING, PASSIONATE LOVE

Secret # 1 – The Basis for a Happy, Love-filled Relationship
Having a happy, fulfilling relationship starts with two happy people who genuinely love and respect themselves. Too many people want to fix

their unhappiness with a relationship. It doesn't work! A mate can only love you as much as you love yourself! In working with clients over the years, I realized this was THE most important step. I dug deep to discover how to teach others to really love themselves and out of that came my 10-module program *How to Be Loved Like You've Never Been Loved Before*. It has made all the difference in my client's relationships.

Secret # 2 – Removing the Biggest Obstacles to Your Happiness

Relationships (and life) are an inside job. You've got to build a solid foundation before you build a house. The same is true for your life! All the time and energy that you put into making money, building your career or raising your kids is like building a house on the sand. It won't last if you haven't done the inner work first to lay a solid foundation. All the issues that you blame your partner for have their origin within you. I know, it sure doesn't seem like it, but when my students work through their deep inner issues, they are amazed at how their mate automatically changes into their prince charming or princess of their dreams.

Secret # 3 – The "We" Mindset

Often we think about other's needs before our own, especially if we have children. Yet, somehow when we get into a primary relationship our need to be right and get our way dominates and we don't even realize it. The key to getting to the "We" mindset is to really listen to the needs of your mate before explaining your own needs. Then when you speak back to your partner what you heard and they see that you are really listening, then they will be willing to hear what your needs are. From that understanding of each other, you can come up with solutions that work for both of you.

Secret # 4 – If He Loved Me, He Would Know

I'm talking to the ladies here. As women we have learned not to ask for what we want. We were taught it isn't polite. Yet, when we drop hints and our guy doesn't get it, we get frustrated. I hear women say, "Well, if he loved me, he would know." That myth causes a lot pain. When we don't get what we want, we can get demanding (even though we think we're being nice). When he still doesn't respond, we become disappointed in him and our relationship. The solution is to learn how to ask so that our men are inspired to give us what we want. The key is for us to receive with pleasure. As natural givers, women usually aren't good at receiving because we have to let go of control to allow others to give to us.

Secret # 5 – Making Her Happy

This one is for the gentlemen. The one thing I consistently hear from my divorced men clients is "There was just no making that woman happy. No matter how much I did, it was never enough." Here's the biggest gift I can give you. Giving her "stuff" will never hold a candle to giving her your attention! Women crave attention. So men, stop working so hard to give her all the "things" she wants (because you will never satisfy her with things). Give her your attention. Listen to her. Let her know that you care about the things she cares about and, soon she will be smiling and feeling understood and loved like never before.

Secret # 6 – Making Him Happy

This one is for the ladies. You cook, clean, and take care of the kids, plus you may have your own important career. Making time for your husband (or boyfriend) may be a lower priority and you don't realize how far down the list he has become. He feels it. He's working hard to make you happy and if you don't show appreciation for it, he's likely to feel that no matter how much he does, it isn't enough. This is extremely discouraging for a man and will drive him away. (See Secret # 5.) Here's the biggest gift I can give you. Show him appreciation for everything he does. Now you may be thinking, "Why should I give him appreciation? He doesn't give it to me." Only give it to him if you want a great relationship and a happy man. When you do, then he will leap tall buildings to give you everything you want. The key to giving a man appreciation is to tell him specifically how his actions make a difference in your life.

Secret # 7 – What About the Kids?

One of the biggest mistakes that couples make is they put their children first. I'm sure you just re-read that line, because isn't that what you're supposed to do? No, it's not! It's not good for your children or for your relationship. More than anything children need parents who love each other and provide a strong family environment. Your relationship is the imprint for their future relationships. If your children are brought up in a loveless home, where you and your mate are either openly fighting or silently cold, it will affect their relationships for the rest of their lives. The one consistent component of a happy and long life is a happy marriage. So put your marriage first. Show your children how it's done. And if you're having problems in your marriage, get some professional help.

My mission is to show mostly women and some lucky men how to have the "in love" relationship that they've always wanted. So whether you are married or single, just know that you can have a juicy romantic relationship. It may feel like it will take a miracle to achieve this, but all it really takes is laying a strong foundation within yourself and putting the proper tools to work. You don't need to figure it out by yourself. You can have someone who has helped thousands of others take your hand and walk you into living your dream relationship.

About Eva

Eva Love is known as the Relationship Expert Extraordinaire by her clients. In the last 24 years, 87% of her single clients have either gotten married or are in a committed relationship within a year of working with her. And 91% of her couple clients are like love-birds, enjoying a happy, thriving relationship.

Today Eva is married to the love of her life, more in love than ever. After 18 years of marriage (20 years of being together), her heart still does a little flip when she sees her husband. They have a loving, fun partnership that has withstood terribly difficult and stressful life events that often end relationships.

After graduating *Magna Cum Laude* from Business School, she worked for Proctor and Gamble as their first woman Field Representative. She then started the first Women's Center in Tulsa, OK, in 1975, enrolling a diverse field of professionals to volunteer 7200 hours of time in the center's first year, giving a hand-up to women who had been abused, raped, were homeless or had special unmet needs.

Committed to helping women knock down career barriers, she was the first woman hired in a management position in a 90-year old transportation company. As the first woman to ever manage long-haul teamsters, she actively mentored women in clerical positions to be promoted into management.

She held a special ombudsman position with Citicorp where she lead the marketing, legal, and IT departments to work together to create the highly successful launch of their first mortgage program.

She broke the glass ceiling in a billion dollar auto-parts chain becoming the first woman to sit on the executive team. With two departments reporting to her with a $5.5 million budget, a big corner office, Eva had all the perks.

She divorced her first husband before going to college, then during her career building years, she was engaged four times before marrying again. Four years into her second marriage, she walked in on her second husband beating her 16 year old daughter. After promising herself that her children would never have to endure the childhood beatings she had to bear, she became deeply depressed and was saved from a suicide attempt through a spiritual message she received as she was about to drive off a 1000' cliff.

In 1989 Eva had a profound spiritual experience that gave her the tools she later named the *Love Miracle System™*. Within three weeks of using this system, her life changed radically. Others asked her to share this system with them which launched her into teaching and mentoring students and private clients full-time.

Eva has two daughters, a step-son, and a daughter-in-law who have blessed her and her husband with three adorable grandchildren. Eva and her beloved live in Las Vegas, loving their life together and sharing her message of love and fulfillment to students throughout the world.

You can connect with Eva at:
Eva@MagicalRelationships.com
http://MagicalRelationships.com
Also find Eva on Facebook, Twitter and LinkedIn

CHAPTER 32

HOW LOSING MY HAIR GAVE ME MY PURPOSE

BY ROSANNA SAVONE

I moved to Hollywood with the big dream of becoming a screenwriter. At the time, I was bursting with confidence. I felt like I had everything it took to make it. I was smart and creative with a hard work ethic.

I had also recently run two marathons and consequently, I looked the best I had in years, having slimmed down to my lowest weight since college. Although I thought I knew true beauty comes from within, I discovered in time that I had a hidden belief – *the hotter you look, the easier it is to get what you want, especially from men.* And Hollywood is ruled by men. So I moved to LA armed to conquer Tinseltown.

But things didn't go quite as I planned. Just two months after arriving, I looked in the mirror and discovered that my life had taken an unexpected twist. That fateful morning in October 2004, I pulled my hair back only to discover a large crescent shaped bald spot behind each of my ears.

I instantly took a double take. This is odd, I thought as I stared at the pale crescent moons, utterly confused. They were so symmetrical that in my complete shock, I started to question myself. *I always had hair there, didn't I? But how could a 28-year-old woman lose so much hair literally over night?* All I knew for certain was that the answer couldn't be good.

I decided for the obvious reason to wear my hair down instead of the originally planned sleek ponytail. As I stared into the bathroom mirror at my thick head of wavy hair easily covering the bald spots, I noted that the ponytail would have indeed looked better with my outfit.

However, what I didn't know at the time was I would never be able to wear a ponytail again. Because that morning was only the beginning of my journey with *Alopecia Universalis*, a rare autoimmune disease, that caused every single hair on my body to fall out within the coming year. To make matters worse, it all fell out less than six months before my wedding day, causing me to consider postponing it until all my hair grew back.

It wasn't long before I realized that the bold confidence I once had evaporated when my fiancé, Howard, shaved the straggly remaining strands of hair I desperately hung on to for far too long. I stopped networking and to relieve stress, I quit the job I loved at a bustling top Hollywood talent agency, WMA. I stopped going out with friends. I even stopped writing for months.

I felt like everyone expected me to write about my experience but what woman really wants to announce to the world in writing that she's bald? That definitely wasn't me at that time. I had despised the thought. I didn't want my work or myself to be pigeonholed by being bald.

But I chose to not even write at all. In retrospect, that wasn't a great choice. I had gone from being a vibrant, ambitious woman going all out for her dreams, to an isolated, depressed person putting her life on hold. In reality, my hair loss was defining me whether I wrote about it or not.

In time, using my 7 Step FLY System™ that I developed through disciplined study and life experience, I learned that it wasn't being bald that made my life less colorful. Rather, it was my hidden belief regarding beauty mentioned above that determined the choices I was making in allowing my hair loss to press the pause button on my life.

I realized that my hair loss caused a deep emotional impact, which shifted my self image from one with confidence to one with none. Since I believed I was no longer as "hot" without hair, I concluded that I could no longer get what I wanted in life as easily. Consequently, my life did indeed become much harder because my new self-defeating image in essence dictated all my opportunities and choices.

This occurs because in the words of the now famous author of *Psycho-Cybernetics,* Dr. Maxwell Maltz, "Human beings always act and feel and perform in accordance with what they imagine to be true about themselves and their environment." For instance, since I believed I was no longer as beautiful without hair, I concluded that I couldn't have an amazing wedding day until my hair grew back. So I acted accordingly by pushing the date.

Yet, right in front of my eyes, I had a gorgeous man eager to marry me as soon as possible. But remember Dr. Maltz said that humans always act in accordance to what they *imagine* to be true. Your belief doesn't have to be actually true. Rather, it can be a limiting or false belief. All that matters is that you believe it to be true. So it didn't matter what was in front of my eyes because I could only see those opportunities that were in line with my self image. Everything else not in line with it is always either unseen, ignored, or rejected.

Here's the kicker - much of your self-image is hidden from you! It's hidden because you've accepted many of your beliefs as true for so long that you're operating on auto-pilot in regards to them. So you don't even notice how they influence your decision-making, let alone think about questioning them for accuracy.

But there's good news! Despite being hidden, you can discover these self-defeating beliefs and change them to ones that are true and empower you. The *key* is to fearlessly love yourself! Hence, the reason my entire program revolves around this concept. Here's how it works with my 7 Step FLY System™.

STEP 1: FEARLESSLY LOVE YOURSELF

When you love and accept (unapologetically and unconditionally; hence, fearlessly) those things about yourself that you find most unlovable and unacceptable, a counter argument within you will crop up quickly in its defense. That counterargument will tell you the reason you don't deserve or can't get the love and acceptance you're giving yourself at that moment. That counter argument is your hidden belief! Hence, your reaction to this fearless love for yourself will expose the belief you've accepted as a truism for all this time.

For example, when I decided to love and accept myself as a bald woman, a voice within said, *You can't love and accept yourself! You are a bald woman and bald isn't beautiful. Without beauty, you can't get what you want. Everything is harder in life.*

Now question whether your counter argument is even true. You may notice that it was true about you at one time but no longer has to be true about you today. However, more likely than not, you will discover this counter argument is actually nothing more than a limiting or false belief about yourself or the world around you. In addition, you'll find that this belief wasn't even yours but handed down to you from other people.

STEP 2: CALCULATE THE COST

Then take a moment to reflect on the costs this belief is essentially charging you in time, money, happiness, love, etc. It's important to do this because without understanding the cost, you won't be sufficiently motivated to take action. Keep in mind, you are only to acknowledge the costs but not dwell on them. Dwelling on them only defeats the purpose at hand.

Once I questioned whether having hair was necessary for an easy life, I started to see many examples of men and women that were having an amazing life despite hair loss. I discovered that I was carrying a false belief about beauty and it was costing me things like my writing career and getting to marry the love of my life.

STEP 3: MAKE A DEFINITE DECISION

Now that you have this information, it's time to make a decision about it. Are you going to continue believing that flawed limiting or false belief? My desire for you is to answer a resounding NO!

Choosing to see the belief for what it is (i.e., limiting and/or false) is a must; however, you do need to take it further than just rejecting it. You must decide what your true belief is and then replace the flawed belief with this truth. This is vitally important because if you don't decide to replace it with a belief based on truth, it will be quite easy to slip back into your *status quo*.

I decided to replace my flawed belief with the true belief that it's our inner light that makes us beautiful, not the shapes, sizes, and colors of the vehicle we were given to house it. It's what we do with that light that truly defines us and determines how easy or hard our life ends up.

STEP 4: IMAGINE YOUR FLY VISION

Although every step in my system is equally important, I have to admit creating a FLY Vision is my personal favorite. I love it because it allows you to use your imagination for what it was meant to do – directing your subconscious mind so you can build your life by design.

Once you've made a definite decision, you focus your imagination on what your life would look like as a person with this new true belief. How do you react to things? What opportunities arise? What choices do you make? Play out your new possible scenarios on the TV screen of your mind. Then commit it to writing and read it a minimum of twice a day.

For me, I started to imagine my June wedding in Malibu, California – overlooking the ocean having the time of my life with my new husband amongst friends and family.

STEP 5: CREATE YOUR FLIGHT PLAN

Your Flight Plan consists of writing down every idea that brings you a step closer to your FLY Vision. Once you've completed your list, pick only those ideas that excite you and make a plan to move forward on them. Then organize the tasks by priority and place them directly into your calendar.

Two important points here:

1) Don't worry if your plan is incomplete. Just jot down anything you have at the moment even if it's only the first step. Your Flight Plan will appear as if out of the sky as you continue with Step 6 of my system.

2) Take action immediately. You need to do something, even if it's only a small five minute task. This will immediately put the Universe in motion to ultimately align the necessary elements needed to achieve your FLY vision.

For me, I had created a plan for my dream wedding taking place in less than six months, and the first action step I immediately took was confirming the date in June.

STEP 6: TAKE CONSISTENT ACTION

This step involves taking consistent action – every day – by affirming your new true belief and following your plan. You will find because you have replaced your limiting/false belief with truth, your new self-empowered image will allow you: (i) to see and act upon a much wider range of opportunities, and (ii) to maximize your creative power because you're no longer boxed in; thereby giving you better results that stick as surely as your initial undesirable results did.

For instance, I found planning my wedding to be utterly enjoyable – our families got along, solutions for challenges appeared, and everything came together seamlessly.

STEP 7: SAVOR VICTORY

The best way to begin to savor victory is by taking hourly moments of gratitude for what you already have in your life. Everything you have to be thankful for is an example of a victory you've experienced. Essentially, it's proof you've manifested your desires successfully! Not only are these great reminders that you've done it in the past, so you can do it again but this step also gets you on the frequency of abundance because you are focusing on what you have, versus what you don't.

You then continue to savor in delight each new victory as they come with a sense of expectancy at once again manifesting your desire, due to your new true self-image.

I began by savoring every detail I found for my wedding, including the perfect wig to create the exact look I desired for my big day.

In the end, my hair didn't have any magical source of self confidence but rather, it was the thoughts, feelings and beliefs I was holding about my hairless situation that were producing the dismal results I was experiencing in my life. It wasn't until I learned how to fearlessly love myself despite my inability to wear a sleek ponytail to match my outfit that I was able to shift my negative self-image into a true self-image; thereby allowing me to enjoy the wedding of my dreams.

In time, I also used my 7 Step FLY System™ to expose other limiting and false beliefs allowing me to write freely about my experience with hair loss. Since doing so, a new world filled with love, happiness and abundance has opened up for me. Most importantly, it led me to my purpose, which is to support you in fearlessly loving yourself. I love witnessing how discovering your true self-image can give you wings allowing you to soar to your own new world and for that opportunity, I am forever grateful.

About Rosanna

Rosanna Savone is a Self-image Expert, Author and Speaker that supports you in fearlessly loving yourself. Her upcoming book, *Memoirs of a Bald Bride*, shares her personal struggle with a rare autoimmune disease, *Alopecia Universalis,* that caused her hair to all fall out at 29 years old within 6 months of her wedding day. This caused a deep emotional impact that caused her self-image to change over night – and not for the better. She uses her experience in overcoming her self-image struggles to offer her top notch program, Fearlessly Love Yourself.

Using her own 7 Step FLY System™, her latest screenwriting project is currently represented by a top Hollywood talent agency, WME, and has an Academy Award Nominated Producer attached. Her clients also gain similar results through discovering their true self-image allowing them to take flight towards their long-awaited dreams!

CHAPTER 33

LISTENING TO THE CALL OF YOUR SOUL, YOUR GREATEST UNTAPPED RESOURCE

BY FLO MAGDALENA

MY SEARCH FOR MY CALLING

As far back as I can remember I have searched for answers: *Why is it so hard for us to love deeply and forgive easily? Why are we unable to co-create a world where the heart and soul guide us in every moment so that we all experience harmony, love, and peace?*

To find these answers I looked into religion, science, and medicine to find the keys to unlocking the human psyche. As I studied societal conditioning, I found that the laws and dictums of the established and agreed upon ways of believing and behaving are based on the premise that there is a right and a wrong, a good and bad—dualistic thinking.

I kept questioning because the answers provided by others didn't make sense to me. Religion and spiritual practices teach us that we are all one, that we come from the same light, and that there is really no other. But when it came to practicing this, I couldn't find ways that worked. I wanted to learn to live oneness by actually connecting with others through the heart and soul. I sensed that this was the only way that we would actually be able to change the ways things are.

As I explored alternative medicine and healing, I delved into the connection between our body, emotion, mind and spirit. I had experiences where I felt the alignment and union of these aspects of myself, in oneness. I began to realize that in order for the world to feel these things, or for me to feel this oneness with another, I had to first find this oneness within myself. I had to come to my center.

I could actually feel my heart and the love that is there always, only, when my mind was not in the way. Only when I experienced this "inner heart" could I actually learn and grow beyond what the outer dictums held as "true." Only when I began to explore how the inner world of the heart and the deep understandings in the soul come together, could I recognize "my truth." Only then could I answer questions like, *Who am I?* and *What I am here for?* As I learned about the calling of my soul, I understood that it was the perpetual questions that kept me up at night that had led me to find myself and my work.

THE SEED OF LIGHT

Coming to the heart and soul with individuals and groups became my focus and my urgency, and I taught what I had learned. But, my soul had more in store for me. In 1989, an experience with Mary Magdalene led me to write a book about Mary's life with Jesus and how she lived her calling, entitled, *I Remember Union*. Writing this book was the key to opening my understanding about how I might contribute knowledge to the world that is timeless and all-inclusive.

My unfolding relationship with Mary deepened me immensely. She brought me an understanding of how union could be experienced individually through connecting with the Seed of Light within us.

Our soul seed or seed of light is a point of light that connects with our spirit. Located below our heart in the Xyphoid Process, it is the pointy piece of cartilage at the base of the sternum. Opening this point of light is one way to access the blueprint or design held within our soul. This design is our program for our life or what we have chosen to learn, teach, express, and create in this lifetime.

To connect with your soul, place your fingertips in the center of your chest, on the Xyphoid Process. Breathe deeply into this space, imagining, sensing or feeling that you are opening a gateway to your deepest self, the center of your being.

Then, ask a question. Breathe the answer or sense or feel the guidance there. Take a moment to steady and feel the connection. Your soul will "speak" with you in a language that you will recognize, but most probably not in a linear or loud way. This is a subtle message that, over time, offers you your calling.

Breathe into the environment around you and feel your connection to all that is. An in-breath can connect you with yourself, and an out-breath connects you with all that is. Breath in and out to establish a rhythm and resonance with yourself. Feel the opening that happens when you can ask and receive your own answers from within. Feel the peace that connecting with your most precious asset, the soul, brings to you and those with whom you relate.

Connecting with our soul supports us in living authentically. It opens us to remember that we have chosen certain lessons and teachers. The soul knows who we are and why we have come and is our greatest ally and friend. As we relate to our soul, we learn to give ourselves the benefit of the doubt, to forgive and understand more fully what those lessons are about. It becomes clearer what our pathway will be. We can respond rather than react to events, situations and people. We realize that beliefs are what separate us, and recognize that our individual truths can be woven together instead of keeping us separate. As we let those beliefs go, we join with others through the heart and soul.

We learn to settle into our body, being fully present, facing what comes into our awareness instead of jumping up into the mind to defend or attack, rationalize or pretend. As we deepen our relationship with ourselves there is less projecting onto others, blaming is no longer an option, and we begin to take full responsibility for our actions and reactions.

Our relationships begin to reflect this understanding. Living with others in a deeper harmony is our intention, and we fully respect and honor each person, the earth and all creatures.

SOUL SUPPORT SYSTEMS

In 1994, Soul Support Systems, a non-profit organization was created to guide individuals to follow the calling of their soul. Deep experiential processes, like **Soul Recognition** are offered, where the clearing of patterns, judgments, beliefs and traumas are witnessed in a group setting. As the soul's expansion fills the spaces of loss and grief within us, we are filled with joy, connection, understanding and resolution.

An individual process to bring the soul's essence and spirit more fully into the body, emotion and mind, is called **Circuitry Alignment.** Here we are reunited with our original energetic signature so we have access to the destiny and design held within us. Connecting with this signature supports us to be more authentic, clear, and directed. As this design comes to rest fully within us, our path and our calling become more conscious. "It feels like things fall into place."

Another program offered is **HeartThread**, an easy and effective way to shift the unconscious patterns carried in the body. Tension, stress, and fear are released as the body relaxes, bringing healing and resolution.

To experience releasing old, unconscious patterns and to establish a deep heart connection, place your right hand on your heart and your left hand on your right hand. Breathe through your heart so that your hands feel warm and united with your heart energy. Practice placing your hands on your heart whenever there is angst or challenge, either existing or anticipated.

Breathe deeply and imagine your heart expanding throughout your body, an energy of light and love.

Because we are not taught in western society about energy, we usually try to change our lives through thinking differently. Instead of resting in the resonance of all of our levels relating in oneness, or listening to the voices of our body, soul, or unconscious, we respond through the conditioning and beliefs of our upbringing and society.

When we realize that we are energy, a whole new world opens up for us. There are so many opportunities available for flowing and releasing what is held; opening and expanding to what makes us happy; and healing and growing as we express who we are.

To experience your energy system, imagine that your energy is inside a garden hose that is flowing through your body. Any clog in the garden hose and your energy stops flowing. There is congestion exactly where the energy isn't flowing, and that causes pain. Feel into this flow and see where your energy stops and starts. Where is the flow easy and where is the flow more congested? As you connect with your energy, you can practice deepening the flow within you.

To direct the mind to listen to the heart and soul, and to bring union within, practice the **Four Level Meditation.** This exercise takes about twenty minutes, and brings peace to your body/emotion/mind and spirit, as they vibrate at the same rate of speed. There is a calmness that is possible when the levels relate in the same rhythm and communicate non-verbally as energy. At the end of the meditation, open to your light and expand, becoming all that is. The union that you feel will then make it possible to understand the difference between these levels. Once that is clear, you can see which of the levels is asking for balance and which ones are contributing to balance. This opens many doorways for you to then feel the spirit alive within you. (Meditation available by going on my website.)

BECOMING A SASSY

From 1994 to May of 2013, these programs were spread by word of mouth and referrals. As we brought these understandings to others it became clear that we have a great gift to give to humanity, but very few people knew about it. Also, our way of offering the work did not truly reflect its value. As we became more aware of this, we decided to market our work and offer it at a value consistent with its contribution. But we didn't know how. It was then that I found Lisa Sasevich.

As I listened to Lisa speak at her Las Vegas event about being "on your dime" and offering your greatest to the world, I was very moved. I sat there thinking that this was exactly what I needed, but I was not going to commit to a large-scale one-year program that would take a lot of time and resource to initiate. As I sat and listened, however, there was a diving in that happened, similar to when one is ready for a **Soul Recognition journey**. I went down the shute-shute and the part of me that wasn't logically engaged found myself completely on the path of being a Sassy as a path of my soul.

Since becoming a Sassy I have had limited access to the calls, the retreats and the support. Previous engagements for work and family have taken me away from the scheduled events and, in some ways, the expectations of what I should be doing as a Sassy.

The interesting thing is that just being a Sassy has increased my income, given me the underpinnings of success in advancing my work and brought numerous individuals to study with me and to accomplish next steps in their lives. I have more confidence that I bring value and am looking at patterns in myself where I give more than I receive, and have an imbalanced sense of caregiving. I am opening to bring more wealth into my life and the lives of those with whom I work so that I can do more good in the world.

There is a culture to being a Sassy, but there is also a way of being that offers us each a clear pathway to embrace and embody what the clarity of "being different," successful, and holding the space for the utmost value of our calling, brings forth.

To answer your calling is to listen to the soul, regardless of how and where it appears, and to trust that when the mind goes to sleep the essence will speak to us, guide us, and direct us.

As you come to the fullest flow of your energy, you understand that you are a field of light connected deeply with your soul's essence. As you listen to the voice of your destiny, you are guided more fully to live the dream within and to trust the yearnings that arise within you. You let go of what was and what might be, are present in the moment of your knowing, and relax as you bring the gifts of your heart and soul to the earth.

You realize that the soul is your greatest untapped resource. You live the fullness of your design and make your utmost contribution to the world, in full acknowledgement of the uniqueness of your gift—the gift you came here to bring.

About Flo

Flo Aeveia Magdalena is a respected visionary, author, channel, healer, teacher, and spiritual mid-wife. She has worked throughout the world for 35 years with individuals and groups, guiding them to connect to and access their soul's calling.

Through listening to and connecting with the soul, we catalyze our potential and open to inner understanding, which assists us to live our congruent vibration. Living in this vibration keeps our interactions, choices and decisions compatible with our purpose, which links us to our part of the design. This process is supported individually through programs Flo has developed, such as Soul Recognition^{SM}, Circuitry Alignment^{SM}, Heart Thread^{SM} and The Accelerated Thinking Process^{SM}.

Soul Recognition (SR) is an ancient and shamanic journey that aligns and anchors the energy, purpose, and patterning of the soul consciously into the body and life. SR releases energetic and karmic blocks within the body and re-patterns the conditioning held in the physical, mental and emotional levels. This supports us to open the auric field and ground light into the cellular tissue to assist in relaxing, opening, and healing the subtle bodies. In October of 2005, Flo introduced Circuitry Alignment^{SM}, a process to unify our original blueprint within the cells and systems of our body. Recently, she has developed HeartThread^{SM}, an effective yet easy way to shift long-standing physical patterns that inhibit our full health and expression.

Flo trains teachers and facilitators to assist others to live from their soul's calling, certifying them to offer Soul Recognition^{SM}, Circuitry Alignment^{SM}, Heart Thread^{SM} and The Accelerated Thinking Process^{SM} sessions.

A Published Author

Flo has published three books; *Honoring Your Child's Spirit: Pre-Birth Bonding and Communication; I Remember Union: The Story of Mary Magdalena;* and *Sunlight On Water: A Guide for Soul-full Living.* Each brings a message of hope about humanity's capacity to create a world of peace, honor, and union.

Background

Trained as a registered nurse, Flo has a background in psychiatry and medicine. After graduating from the Patricia Hayes School in 1981, a school of "inner sense development," Flo combined her nursing experience with metaphysics, and began teaching classes in holistic health, therapeutic touch, and psychoneuroimmunology–

mind/body connection. Flo uses the hologram as a model for balance and communication between left and right hemispheres of the brain. She assists young people and adults to use their "whole" brain, create more easily, and live in harmony with their potential and their world.

"To intentionally create together and foster living from the soul utilizes our fullest potential and purpose outside of existing societal limitations. Assisting everyone to live their purpose, and changing the existing structure and dogma seems like the same thing to me. It fires my heart and intention."

To Contact Flo:

Flo is married and has two children and three grandchildren. She is the founder and executive director of Soul Support Systems. To contact Flo or to receive more information about her personal work, go to her website: FloMagdalena.com. For information on facilitating programs offered through Soul Support Systems, go to: www.soulsupportsystems.org, or email: soulsupportsystems@comcast.net.

CHAPTER 34

ARISE AND CLAIM YOUR SUCCESS

BY DR. CHRISTINE ROSE

I remember the day very clearly as if it was only yesterday that my grandfather called my brother David and I to his bedside. Calling for both of us and calling us in together – well that was strange. I hoped we were not in trouble, after all we were already in our thirties and as for me, I was already married with three children.

You see my grandfather was already on his death bed and had sent for all his children and grand-children; he wanted to speak to each of them intimately and privately one very last time. He then proceeded to ask my brother and I a series of questions, including: "Have I been good to you?" and "Have I been fair to you?" You see, we have been raised in the house of Claude Ambrose, the house of integrity. Then with the deepest remorse he said, "If I have done anything to hurt you or have not been fair to you in any way, please forgive me?" And of course we both said "no" and proceeded to cry. The very last advice my grandfather gave to us was to help others and let our lives stand for something greater than ourselves. He said you have so much to give. You see my grandfather knew he was dying and not many people get the opportunity to be able to reflect and connect with loved ones during that time. This is also the man who, when I was a child, would always say to me, you are going to be a nurse, you are going to be a doctor. He went as far as referring to me with those tittles throughout my entire life.

Throughout our lives and at the end of it we are bombarded with a series of internal questions. Who am I? Why am I here? Did I make a difference while I lived? How do you know what you're supposed to be doing and who you're supposed to be serving? These are some of the most perplexing questions that each of us struggle with, and some for most of their life. I started out by becoming a registered nurse then I got my master's degree. Soon I was a nurse midwife and a Women's Health nurse Practitioner. That was just not enough; I want to give more and decided to become a professor. A few years later, I pursued and completed my Doctorate degree, hoping to make a bigger impact – all the while having three children and a marriage.

FULL BLOWN ADDICTION

This job was a dream opportunity and offered the most unique set of circumstances and most wonderful people to help me grow in a big way. This included twenty-four hour coverage, responsibility and accountability but my daily hours on paper were 8:00am to 4:30pm. I pretty much threw myself into my work. Any project, every new initiative, anything requested of me was a definite yes. If anyone knows working in corporate – yes I work in corporate healthcare , it comes with some perks and one of them being that you are given your own Blackberry. I covered seven cost centers (seven units and /or groups of people) approximately 350 staff and with no assistants. Pretty soon, my days were filled with meetings, meeting with the staff on the units, individual meetings, meeting with leaders, preparing for presentations, attending committee meetings, surveys, coaching, resolving conflicts and yes, using the staircase to run up and down to the different units Nothing could have prepared me for this experience, but it was what I wanted, it was what I needed. If anyone knows anything about having a corporate Blackberry, it is that it's just another way for you to continue work away from your office and I took full advantage of that ability. When my husband picked me up from work I was on the Blackberry, at 2:00 am when it vibrated under my pillow I took the call or text. It had gotten me. I was addicted to both The Blackberry and saying YES. But wait, if I was always saying so many 'yeses' to one area of my life what others was I saying 'no' to? That's right, I was not giving any 'yeses' to family, self, spirituality and so many other areas in my life. One day as I pulled the Blackberry out from under the pillow – this time at 3am, my husband asked, "Is there something or someone I should know about?"

THE WHISPER

Pretty soon the "WHISPER" set in, but I pretty much didn't hear it. I was knee deep in another project or initiative or saying YES to another person or project. Soon everyone had a request because I became the 'go to' person for getting things done and getting the results. I would come in to work as early as 4 am and/or leave as late as 12 midnight in order to accomplish these results. You and I know that this cannot last for too long. But after all, my grandfather had told us *to help others and let our lives stand for something greater than ourselves.* Pretty soon my family was complaining, but that did not stop me. Then one day my daughter who absolutely loved nursing and nurses said to me, " I hate your job." That shocked the heck out of me. I asked her why and she said, "Because it takes you away from me." That night I had one of the most vivid dreams ever. You see, what no one knew was that I was already way past the "whisper and the tap on the shoulders." I was already staring the 2X4 straight in the face. I was already experiencing deep fatigue, burnout, insomnia, thinning hair, change in physical appearance, a 42 pound weight gain, migraine and yes, even a brain tumor scare.

THE CALL

In my dream, it was as clear as you are seeing and reading these pages. I heard and saw it as clear as day. In my dream I saw my life as it currently was and how unhappy and unfulfilled I was. I heard a voice telling me to ARISE. It said ARISE! Claim your GREATNESS. It was the voice of GOD telling me to ARISE. Now I was confused what did that meant. Now just a little background, I was already on a journey to find my life's purpose beginning a few years back. I found out that my purpose in life was to: **Help others Claim their Value and Worth**. I honestly thought giving more of my time to others was, *"Helping others Claim Their Value and Worth."* It became quite apparent in that moment how far from the truth that my truth was. Truthfully, it made sense, but I still didn't understand what ARISE! Claim Your GREATNESS meant.

That morning at 4 am I got up and started writing frantically in the dark. What was coming through me was amazing and scary at the same time. This is how I was to start living my life. This was how I was supposed *to help others and let our lives stand for something greater than ourselves by helping others Claim their Value and Worth.*

AUTHENTICITY

A - Authenticity - being true to who you are. To live authentically is to be able to tap into who you are at the core. At the deepest level, when you show up in the world, whether at your job, with friends and or being in the presence of your family, you are who you know you are to be and are being. Some people are one way with their work colleagues, another way with their friends and a different person to their families. That is in part because they don't know who they are, or have not spent that much time with themselves, nor have they done the work on themselves. To be authentically you, the real you - that is the person that would make your customers want to buy from you, if you are an entrepreneur or make your patient more compliant in their treatment regimen and plan of care because you showed up. The real you and the real you is way more interesting and yes, compassionate, than you think.

RELEASE AND RECLAIM

R - Release and **Reclaim** are two of the most critical steps in this process. To release is to forgive. The art of forgiveness is a gift. Forgiveness is a gift to you. You have to **Release** others from the bondage in which you have placed them. But the greatest of those whom you forgave is yourself. To **Reclaim** is to accept and embrace those "parts" of yourself long ignored, forgotten or yet to be discovered. To forgive is the freeing of ones' spirit so you can finally **Reclaim**- gain access to claim the essence of who you are, who you are meant to be. The Authentic you is found beneath the pile of baggage containing the pile of grudges and unforgiveness that you carry around as baggage. The real you is buried underneath it all.

INTEGRITY

I - INTEGRITY- When you show up Authentically and finally **Release** and **Reclaim** you, it is quite easy to be in Integrity. You already know who you are. You already know your truth, and most of all, no one can tell you who you are not. When you show up in integrity, you are always in control of your internal environment and not allowing your external environment to control you. It is during this process that you have implemented both check points and set points in your daily life to ensure you become the "YES" person in the room. You have total faith in yourself and your abilities. Most of all you have mastered the art of saying NO and saying YES only to those things that are in line with your full purpose and their place in the mission that is your life.

SERVE

S - Service - To be in Service to others is one of the most dynamic and life-changing acts that we do on this earth. But if you are like most people we first think of how big and how much we can serve others. For those of us in healthcare and the business of service, serving others is equivalent to getting a free blessing every day. But most people spend very little time serving themselves. For this purpose, SERVE means to be in service to yourself, to care for yourself in a compassionate manner and without judgment. This is where we see the true transformation taking place, when each part of the SELF is addressed. After all, your body is undisputedly your temple and must be worshipped, adored, cared for and protected. This is the Basis for you living a fully inspired and transformed life. When you do not put yourself first you are out of integrity and out of service to yourself. Even the heart serves itself first. The heart pumps blood to itself first then sends the remaining portion to the rest of the body, including the brain.

EMPOWER

E - Empower - Now you are ready to go out into the world. Now you can show the real **You**. Your mission is to teach and share the essence of who you are. In this space, the purpose of your message, your service mission, is to give access to who you are through your services you have to offer, and yourself.

What are you not claiming for yourself? What part of your legacy are you not claiming? For me I found out it was my greatness. How influential and successful I can be. I reclaimed my Greatness.

When you ARISE and claim your _____ you can finally start being an authentic presence in the world. The connections made and relations that you build are grounded on a more solid foundation, thus, forming a lasting relationship. You become more trustworthy because you can first trust you. You are now free to serve from a place of abundance and allow you to serve others in a bigger and deeper way, without giving more of your physical time. This process forced me to make the only decision I could. I resigned my job to finally help serve others deeper – so they can finally have the tools necessary to ARISE!

Here is an activity that you can do right away. Here is a list of words you can chose from or you may choose to come up with your own. Go ahead and fill in the blank space. Then repeat the entire sentence at the beginning and the end of each day (morning and before bed).

ARISE! Claim you(r) _____.

Shine

Brilliance

Greatness

Confidence

Success

Power

Freedom

Autonomy

Health

Wealth

Happiness

Balance

Purpose

Mission

Vision

About Christine

Dr. Christine Rose is the founder and CEO of a company called TheNurseWhisperer.com; it is dedicated to helping Health professionals finally Claim their Greatness by reclaiming their value and worth. Here she focuses her talent on helping Health professionals leverage their expertise, position themselves for greatness, maximize their potential and serve at a deeper level. This ranges from coaching them on starting their own businesses to career acceleration coaching, to seminars and workshops on Success and Confidence.

Dr. Rose is a Doctor of Health Science, a Nurse Midwife, Women's Health Nurse Practitioner and Registered Nurse. As a Certified Holistic Health Coach, International Board Certified Lactation Consultant and is also certified as a Dream Coach. She works with clients to help them make their dreams come true. As a holistic nutritionist she has studied several dietary theories, contemporary health issues and Eastern and Western nutrition. She has been trained by some of the top professionals in the Nutrition field such as Dr. Mark Hyman, Dr. Oz, Deepak Chopra and Dr. David Katz.

Her expertise in Women's Health and Obstetrics led her to become the founder of a lactation education program and a Lamaze Childbirth Education program for adolescence at a major NYC hospital. To reframe her perception from pathology to growth, change, and a normal aspect of life, she became one of only two midwives providing care to adolescents in the teen City University of New York Clinic located in an area with one of the highest teen pregnancy rates. In addition to almost two decades years of experience in nursing, education, midwifery and lactation, Dr. Christine Rose held adjunct Professor Positions at the State University of New York, Long Island University, City University of New York and New York University.

Most recent she has held the position as the Lead Education specialist for Women's Health and Obstetrics at one of *US News & World Report's* top hospital in NYC. Dr. Rose, an international speaker, speaks on topics of Health and Wellness, Holistic Nutrition, Women's Health. ARISE! Claim your Greatness and Confidence is the new currency.

Dr. Rose is happily married to Colin, a photographer and Art Dealer, and they have three children together. Kijana is currently attending college, while Kimane and Kemba are too busy trying to figure out which one of them is the boss. Oh, and then there's Queenie, the family's hamster, who doesn't know she is a girl.

CHAPTER 35

STORY SECRETS!
NOTHING CREATES MORE POWERFUL BUSINESS CONNECTIONS THAN THE RIGHT STORY, TOLD THE RIGHT WAY

BY SANDRA MILLERS YOUNGER

THE BOBCAT THAT SAVED MY LIFE

At first I couldn't make sense of the orange light flooding our bedroom, or my husband's shouting. It was three in the morning. Why was he waking me? In another instant, I understood. Outside our windows, on the other side of the California canyon we called home, the mountain was on fire.

I scrambled out of bed and threw on jeans and a t-shirt.

"Oh my God! What do we do?"

"Don't panic," Bob said, but his voice sounded forced.

We couldn't find his truck keys, so we stuffed ourselves into my little sports coupe, Bob and me, our two giant dogs, a cockatiel in a cage, and a laundry basket filled with photos and negatives. At the top of the driveway, we took a last look at our home and then drove away amid firelight and swirling embers.

Within seconds we hit the smoke, so dense I couldn't see the road. It was narrow and steep, cut into the side of a mountain. I didn't want to drive off the edge. At that exact moment, a bobcat jumped out of the surrounding brush and into my headlights, then dashed off into the smoke, running straight ahead of me. Somehow I knew to follow it.

Soon I could see red smears of light through the murk, and I realized: everything below us was on fire. I steered toward a patch of darkness that was the road, and suddenly we were flanked by fire on both sides.

"Maybe it's like running your finger through a candle flame," I thought. "If I drive fast enough, it won't burn us."

After what seemed forever, we punched through a last curtain of flames into clear night. Like waking up from a nightmare, I thought. But it was all too real. Our home—and more than 2,200 others—were gone. Even worse, 15 people—12 of them our canyon neighbors—never made it to safety.

I knew from the first that I had to tell the story of the Cedar Fire. How could I not? I was a journalist, a storyteller, who'd come out of the worst part of the worst fire anyone could remember.

So in the years that followed, as we rebuilt our home and rebooted our lives, I gathered dozens of stories from fire fighters, survivors, and victims' families. Piece by piece, I wove them all together, along with my own experience, to tell the whole story of the Cedar Fire. Then I found an agent, who found a publisher—and after 38 years in journalism, I became a first-time, best-selling author.

Great stories can do that. They can inspire you to dream bigger dreams. They can enable you to achieve more than ever before. And they can revolutionize your business, no matter what kind of business you're in.

That's why now, as founder and chief story strategist at Strategic Story Solutions, I'm passionate about helping others unlock the power of *their* stories—especially in business, where the right story, told the right way, can effortlessly create the emotional connections necessary to lead, sell, grow and succeed.

WHY ARE STORIES SO POWERFUL?

Always begin presentations with your signature story, the story that connects you to your audience. That's what I teach my clients—transformational speakers, entrepreneurs, and organizational leaders.

But when I speak to groups about Story Power, I often do the opposite, opening instead with the usual laundry list of credentials—my title, my university degrees, my years of experience, my writing credits. Then I ask them to jot down the answers to three questions: *On a scale of 1-10, how well do you feel you know me? How much do you like me? How much do you trust me?* Finally, I ask them to take their pulse.

Only then do I tell my signature story, repeat my experiment, and invite them to compare their numbers, which invariably shoot up. Suddenly, just because I've told them my story, a group of people I've never met feel that they know, like and trust me. What's more, their elevated pulse rates tell me I've connected with them on an emotional level, where decision-making really takes place. That's Story Power, I tell them. It's immediate; it's measurable; and it's lasting.

(Warning! This demonstration only works with captive audiences. If I'd tried to replicate it here, you wouldn't have read past the first sentence!)

We really shouldn't be surprised that stories wield so much influence in our hearts and minds. The latest brain science confirms what we've suspected all along—we humans are hard-wired to tell, respond to and remember stories. From cave paintings to Facebook posts, we've always depended on narratives to communicate and connect with one another, to share our knowledge, advance our points of view, and pass our collective wisdom from one generation to the next. Simply put, stories serve as our cultural currency.

Now we know why. Using advanced brain imaging, researchers have found that a well-told story actually changes our brain chemistry, causing emotional and physical responses. We feel fear, anger, amusement, empathy or whatever else we'd feel if we experienced what's happening in the story in real life! This of course explains why we tend to squirm in our seats while watching a thriller or horror movie, and why we wipe our eyes during the "good parts" of a sweet romance or epic tragedy. A good story takes us into the action with the characters. We empathize with them; we feel whatever they feel.

In contrast to this whole-brain response to stories, only the brain's center of logic lights up in reaction to facts and figures, charts and graphs, which isn't enough to carry a persuasive argument. Again, thanks to recent brain studies, we now know that we base our decisions primarily on emotion, and then back them up with logic—not the other way around!

STORYTELLING FOR BUSINESS

No wonder so many business leaders are re-discovering the persuasive power of storytelling in all sorts of business tasks: leadership and strategic planning; employee development and team-building; customer service and client education; and of course, marketing and sales.

Super savvy companies, including Ben & Jerry's, Zappos, Facebook and Tom's Shoes, have turned to story-branding. For example: By publicizing the company's unique practice of donating a pair of shoes for each pair sold, Tom's has built a dynamite brand story. "People don't just wear our shoes," explains Blake Mycoskie, the company's founder and CEO, "they tell our story."

Advertising offers an obvious showcase for business storytelling, especially now that technological advances have given us ways to avoid intrusive ads. We seldom have to read, watch or listen to anything that doesn't interest us anymore. Instead, the click of a mouse or fast-forward button whisks us away in search of something more to our liking.

Advertising agencies have figured out that today's consumers will only tolerate content that actually appeals to them. And they also realize that people can't resist a good story any more than a dog can walk past a bone, or a cat can ignore a laser dot. As author Christina Baldwin puts it: "We live in story like a fish lives in water."

Case in point: Those wonderful Budweiser Clydesdale Superbowl commercials. Who knew horses played football? Or started snowball fights? But now that we know, how can we forget? Budweiser's clever horse fables stick in our heads year after year, long after we've spaced on thousands of other ads. And by the way, did anyone say anything about beer? Did anyone need to?

Budweiser brewer Anheuser Busch isn't the only global firm to discover "Story Power." Nike, Volkswagen, Intel, Coke, AT&T, Procter and Gamble, and Toshiba, to name a very few, have all turned to storytelling in branding, marketing or advertising. In fact, for the last several years, nearly every television commercial honored with a Clio award—the Oscar of TV advertising—has told a story.

Another clue to the widespread adoption of storytelling for business is the growing frequency of articles on the subject in prestigious business publications like Forbes, Fortune and the Harvard Business Review. Written for business owners, executives and managers, these pieces document the power of stories in leadership, team-building, motivation and performance.

Proving the point, some of the most successful business leaders of our time, including Steve Jobs, Sheryl Sandberg and Richard Branson, have used storytelling to persuasive and profitable advantage. Best-selling business author Tom Peters underscores the wisdom of their approach. "The best leaders," he says, "almost without exception and at every level, are master users of stories and symbols."

WHAT'S YOUR STORY?

And yet most companies haven't even plugged into their "Story Power." Author and serial entrepreneur Gary Vaynerchuk goes so far as to say, "Storytelling is by far the most underrated skill in business."

In particular, I've found that most transformational entrepreneurs are barely aware of the value of storytelling, and few are skilled in story strategy. Yet no one is better poised to benefit from sharing their signature stories!

Most service-driven entrepreneurs have chosen their work because of some life experience that triggered a passion to serve in a particular area. That life experience is their story. When well told, it can create magnetic connections with perfect prospects, establishing that "know, like and trust" factor essential to sales and profits.

So how can you unlock the power of *your* stories? Start with the five-step system I've developed for my clients. It's called the Story POWER Process™.

STEP 1: PINPOINT YOUR SIGNATURE STORY.

Whether consulting with my clients in groups or 1-to-1 coaching sessions, I always start by asking a few key questions that help uncover important pieces of their signature story, the story that can effortlessly connect them to their target audience.

(It's wonderful how many of my clients tell me the resulting big-picture view of their lives also gives them greater clarity of purpose, greater focus on their ideal clients, and even greater peace about painful twists and turns in their lives.)

So here are those illuminating questions:

1. What three problems in the world would you most like to solve?
2. Who are the three most influential people in your life, whether positive or negative, living or dead, and why?
3. What are the three most significant tipping points in your life so far?

Now it's time to connect the dots. Which of your three top problems does your business address? What lessons learned from your major influencers relate to your business? What tipping points relate to your business? And perhaps most importantly, how does all of this relate to the needs and experiences of your ideal clients?

STEP 2: ORGANIZE YOUR STORY INTO A NARRATIVE ARC

One specific story structure has been scientifically proven to create emotional connection! Neuroeconomist Paul Zak has shown that a story told in a roller-coaster curve of rising and falling action, with a crisis in the middle, actually changes our brain chemistry, resulting in empathy, trust and generosity.

STEP 3: WEAVE YOUR SIGNATURE STORY INTO THE FABRIC OF YOUR BUSINESS

Once you've nailed your signature story, there's no more powerful message to share with your target clients and customers, so push it out there every way you can. Use it in your signature speech, your marketing and positioning, your long-term planning, your employee collaborations, your leadership and development efforts, your corporate culture. Refer to it in advertising, press releases, and community outreach projects.

STEP 4. ESTABLISH A PORTFOLIO OF "STICKY" STORIES THAT HELP PEOPLE REMEMBER KEY FACTORS

Product benefits, teaching points, and organizational values all become more memorable when paired with a good story.

STEP 5. RECOGNIZE, COLLECT AND CRAFT YOUR MOST POWERFUL CLIENT SUCCESS STORIES

Stories about the positive experiences of people who achieved success with your help and methods help prove the value of your work. The trick comes in choosing the right testimonials and crafting them into memorable nuggets.

So what's your story? The story that explains who you are, the story behind your passion to serve, the story that can effortlessly connect you to your perfect audience? Whatever it is, wherever it may be hiding, there's a story inside of you. It's deep. It's powerful.

And the world is waiting to hear it.

About Sandra

Sandra Millers Younger grew up in North Carolina in the 1950s and '60s, a place and time when people still sat down together and swapped stories over fried chicken, apple pie and sweet tea.

As an English and journalism major at the University of North Carolina, Chapel Hill, Sandra studied stories—what makes the great ones great, how to find them, and how to share them in powerful ways that make a difference in the world.

Eventually, she ended up with two degrees in journalism—a bachelor's from UNC and a master's from Syracuse University. By then she'd already written hundreds of stories for newspapers and magazines.

She kept at it, telling thousands more stories about all kinds of people—from school kids to scientists, celebrities to CEOs—and all kinds of subjects—from laser beams to garden mulch, Spanish architecture to Newfoundland dogs.

Finally, Sandra told her own story, in a first-person, narrative nonfiction book called, *The Fire Outside My Window: A Survivor Tells the True Story of California's Epic Cedar Fire.*

Now, as founder and chief story strategist at Strategic Story Solutions, she helps others discover their story power. And use it to change the world.

You can connect with Sandra at: www.strategicstorysolutions

CHAPTER 36

IT'S ALL ABOUT THE FOOD, AND NOT AT ALL ABOUT THE FOOD
— LIVING A HEALTHY LIFE WITH TYPE 2 DIABETES

BY MARY COSTA

I picked up the phone in my office and answered the way I usually do: "This is Mary, how can I help you?" There was a long pause. I was almost ready to hang up when I heard, "Mary, I'm going to lose my driver's license. What am I going to do?"

The voice sounded familiar. I'm usually pretty good at matching a voice to a name, and just as I was about to figure it out I heard, "This is Tanisia."

I took a deep breath as our very first conversation flashed through my mind. It had been pretty rocky. As a Registered Nurse and a Certified Diabetes Educator (CDE) for over 20 years, I speak to people with diabetes every day, but when Tanisia first entered my office, she said defiantly, "if you're going to tell me to 'diet and exercise', you're wasting your time and mine too. I hear that every time I go to the doctor and I certainly don't need to hear that from you. I know I'm overweight and I don't like to exercise!"

At the time I remember wanting to burst out laughing but I knew that wasn't the best response. I had to admit to her that very early on when I started working with people with diabetes, that is *exactly* what I said and recommended. I kept writing the same advice over and over, but it wasn't until I decided actually to try living like someone with diabetes that I fully understood what I was asking. For four days while wearing an insulin pump, I did everything I instruct my diabetic patients to do. What a lesson *that* was.

My memories were interrupted when Tanisia began speaking again. "My doctor reported on my work physical that my diabetes is not in good control, and the report went to the DMV. They can take away my license if my diabetes is not in good control. What am I going to do if I can't drive? Who will take my daughter to school? How will I get to work?"

After a long pause, I said, "Tanisia, can you come in to my office today? Let's figure out what we can do about this."

As I hung up the phone, I remembered how hard it had been to change my thinking and habits during those four days I had lived like someone with diabetes. I found myself thinking, "Shoot, I ate without checking my blood sugar—and what about the insulin I forgot to program into the insulin pump *before* I started eating?" And, "What the heck, it's a wedding: surely one piece of cake and some ice cream won't hurt." After that, I finally understood how hard it was to follow the very lifestyle I had prescribed so unthinkingly to my patients. Heck, I couldn't live up to my own expectations! That experience began to change my thoughts about managing a chronic disease. While diabetes management has everything to do with what you choose to eat, there's something even bigger and more important than food.

While I waited for Tanisia, I recalled someone telling me that the word "crisis" in Chinese is made up of two separate characters, one associated with "danger" and the other with "opportunity." I believe that the diagnosis of diabetes is a crisis that also combines danger and opportunity. And as in life, danger is often preceded with warning signals. When the memory in your computer is reaching its capacity, for example, you may get messages that there isn't enough disk space to save a file. If you ignore the warnings, you may soon see the "blue screen of death," and you'll know you need to get your computer fixed, or purchase another. However, if the new computer has an updated operating system, usually the old programs won't work anymore.

When you've been diagnosed with diabetes, you too need a new, healthier operating system (beliefs), and new "programs" (practices) to replace the ones that created the problem. This requires deliberate action and some hard thinking about why you eat and do some of the things you do. But if you examine the "programs" that no longer serve you, you'll understand the situations that created those believes and practices no longer exist, or were faulty to begin with. That's the danger side of crisis. The opportunity is to decide what actions and beliefs can bring you a healthier body and better quality of life.

As I sat at my desk, I thought, "Could this situation that has endangered Tanisia be her opportunity for a better life?"

When Tanisia entered my office a few minutes later, she was very different from our first encounter. She seemed overwhelmed, and as her body slumped into the chair, shoulders down, the usual spark in her eyes missing, she looked hopeless. "Opportunity," I kept repeating to myself, "I hope she can see opportunity in this situation—that she can, and deserves to be, healthy."

Tanisia sounded defeated and frustrated. "I know, you warned me the last time we spoke that if nothing changed that I'd begin having complications. But I just want to be normal, to do what I want, when I want, and to live my life MY way. I don't get it, I feel perfectly fine, I don't feel sick!"

"I know, Tanisia. What would be most helpful for you? What would you like to focus on?" I asked.

"Just tell me what to do, I promise I'll follow every word you say," she answered.

That should have been music to my ears, but it wasn't. I've found that when people are in the midst of crisis, any change that is made to get out of it usually disappears over time.

"I'm not going to tell you, you're going to tell me," I said. "What changes can you see yourself making to what you eat that would improve your health?"

"I know I eat too much fast food, but that works for us as a family since we have very little time to prepare meals...but I guess I have to change... it's going to be hard to change those habits, though," she sighed.

We discussed a few tips that would minimize food preparation for the week. But that's just one new "program," and I knew we needed to address the operating system. We needed to have a deeper conversation.

"Tanisia, do you remember when you were pregnant, and had a very strict diet to keep your diabetes in good control? Was it hard to do that?" (I wanted to point out that despite the fact that her environment and habits needed to change, she had already done the same work before, successfully.) She shook her head no.

"Why not?" I asked.

"I wanted a healthy baby—I was willing to do it for the baby."

"Don't *you* deserve the same health as your baby? Would you be willing to make changes so you can have a healthy body?" (I see this as one of the biggest hurdles, knowing that it's worth spending on our health and ourselves. This isn't just an issue for people with diabetes; it's a global issue, and a challenge for all of us.)

"Tanisia, you know that the gene for diabetes is in your family," I told her. "Would it be worth it to change your habits so you can be a role model for them? Wouldn't it be easier for you now if you had learned a healthier way of eating and exercising when you were little?" *That* hit home. She nodded.

I wanted to touch on a few more topics so I asked, "Are you testing your blood sugars with your meter?"

She said what almost everyone does: "Oh, I know what my blood sugars are, I don't need to test them."

"Really? Tell me what you think your blood sugar is right now," as I pulled out a blood sugar meter.

"It's probably 200 or so," confident she knew her blood sugar level.

I set up the meter for her test, and she checked her blood sugar. The result was 438! (A blood sugar over 140 can lead to complications of

320

diabetes.) I pointed at the number and said, "I want you to remember this, because your internal health meter is off, and you cannot go by how you feel at this time. You need other means of checking your health than how you feel, as it isn't reliable." She admitted she was shocked at the result, and was willing to start testing more regularly so she knew what her blood sugar range was at various times of the day.

There was one last element I wanted to see if Tanisia would incorporate. I knew it was a stretch, but probably the best thing she could do for her health.

"You know that the easiest way to get your blood sugar under control is through exercise. You don't have to do much to start, but could you try increasing your activity throughout the day? You could walk after meals, take the stairs more, ride a bicycle—anything would be helpful."

Tanisia nodded. "Someone gave me a pedometer, and I could start wearing it again. I think you told me before that ultimately I needed 10,000 steps a day?" We spent a few more minutes discussing how she could incorporate more exercise and easy ways to change what she ate. She left happier and more hopeful, with a plan in place.

I wish I could report that Tanisia didn't lose her driver's license, but she did—for a few months. However, she was able to get it back because she chose to make her health a priority.

I recently read a report that we in the United States could spend up to $8 *trillion* each year on the complications of diabetes. Seeing my patients *experience* complications made me passionate about teaching prevention of them. Diabetes tricks your internal health meter to believe everything is just fine, when it isn't, paving the way for the complications of diabetes.

If you or a family member has diabetes, I want to give you three tips for improved health.

1. *Learn about carbohydrates, proteins and fats/oils.* When you eat, combine all three in the same meal as often as possible. Before adding carbohydrates ensure you have protein and healthy oil represented in your meal. For example, if you have a salad, add a protein such as meat, fish, egg, or tofu, and consider adding an avocado, or a salad dressing with a healthy oil (light olive oil). At lunch and dinner, one-

half of your plate should be vegetables, and the other half protein and carbohydrate. This could be multiple colored vegetables sautéed in olive or coconut oil, shrimp, chicken or another protein, and brown rice.

2. *Exercise* really is the fountain of youth, and improves all health measures. Make sure your doctor clears you first, and then slowly add exercise to your routine. Your goal is to work up to 30-60 minutes a day, most days of the week.

3. *Mindset* is most important, since it either will move you in the direction of health—or not. Start with the mindset that you deserve to have a healthy body. That is the beginning of changing an old operating system that no longer serves you. This should be your mindset from the minute you wake up until you go to bed at night. Determine your actions by evaluating if this is moving you toward or away from health.

Anyone who has diabetes or pre-diabetes can actually live a longer, healthier life. How is that possible? If you didn't know you had diabetes or pre-diabetes, you may have never made healthy lifestyle changes that can give you not just quantity, but quality of life. It's not easy, but as they say…it's worth it. To your best health!

NOTE: As is general medical common sense, always check with your Health Care Provider (HCP) to see if the recommendations will be right for you. The information provided above does not replace medical advice that is specific for you, only your HCP can determine that for you.

About Mary

Mary Costa, a Registered Nurse and Certified Diabetes Educator has worked for one of the largest HMO's in the country for nearly 30 years. She works exclusively with Adults who have diabetes: consulting, teaching, advising, and adjusting medications by protocol to help her patients reach healthy blood sugar levels. Mary is also the president and CEO of "Transform Your Diabetes Health" an online organization which offers education and coaching for people with diabetes, and that includes Holistic and Integrative health practices.

Mary has worked with diverse populations, across all walks of life, and loves the challenge of making complex information easy to understand, with clear, and "do-able" action steps. Mary has seen what works, and what doesn't, and recognizes that living with, and managing diabetes is not a sprint, but a marathon. While the end result may be the same, the journey for each of her patients to achieve their best Diabetes health, is individualized.

Mary and her work peers conducted a research project that evaluated the care of diabetics in groups, as opposed to one-on-one visits in the mid-1990s, and the results were published in Diabetes Care, December 1999. As a result of the research project, the program was implemented in all of the Northern California regions of the HMO she worked for. Mary is currently working in a program that focuses on promoting measures to prevent heart attack, stroke and the complications of diabetes. This program has won national awards. Mary has lectured in the US and Mexico about Diabetes and Cardiovascular health.

Mary received her Nursing degree in the 1980's. Mary has been a Certified Diabetes Educator since 1990's, and recently achieved her CDTC (Certified Diabetes Technology Clinician) designation in 2013. Mary belongs to the American Association of Diabetes Educators, the American Diabetes Association, American Holistic Nurses Association, and is a member of the Experts Industry Association.

CHAPTER 37

WEALTHY WOMEN HEALERS

BY SHAYLA KISER MIHALY

All of my life I have answered the call of Spirit. I was a pre-law College student, but answered the call to be a healer instead. At the age of 23, I moved to San Francisco, guided by Spirit, with $500 in my pocket and not knowing a single person there. A few years later I answered the call of Spirit again and spent a year traveling with a Native American Shaman, living on donations and faith.

Like many women healers, I had been programed to believe that money is evil, and that if I was a true spiritual practitioner and healer, I had to stay broke. For us spiritual women healers, if we think we have to choose between being spiritual and having money, between being good and causing harm, we will choose to be spiritual and do good every time. We can't help it. It's not "what we do," it's who we are. Because I had this belief, I worked really hard, and took care of many people, but never took care of myself financially, which meant that I went without a lot of the things that would support, nurture and feed me.

When I was 32, my 56-year old mother was diagnosed with a terminal illness and died seven months later. My mom was that special kind of West Virginia therapist called a hairdresser. She ran her own business, took great care of everyone around her, and didn't take great care of herself. She died broke and lonely, and this had a profound impact on me. My mother was and continues to be one of my greatest spiritual teachers. I saw that I was very much like her, and I realized that if I didn't make some major changes, and soon, that my life and death would look a lot like hers. Spirit called me to re-examine everything I believed to be true about spirituality and wealth, about receiving as well as giving. About my worth, and what God really wanted for me in this lifetime. I was called to make radical changes in my beliefs and in the world I was creating for myself. Just to make sure I really understood how deeply I needed to transform, the man I was in love with left me the same week my mother died. I had a lot to think about.

I realized that in order to have the life I wanted, I needed to create financial stability and abundance for myself – not wait for anyone else to give me permission or to help me do it, but to own it and claim it. I was now being called to heal the split between spirituality and money – to stay firmly rooted in Spirit, and to allow abundance into my own life. I decided to do keep doing good AND create wealth.

I quickly created a six-figure and then multi-six-figure holistic wellness business. I felt great about my work, had plenty of money, fell in love and got married to an amazing man. Things were going great.

By this point, having done over 20,000 hands-on healing sessions, I was getting burned out on seeing clients one-on-one, and was excited to move into more of a mentor role, to focus more on guiding my business and training my staff. It was time to expand my business. It took about a year to find the perfect location, negotiate the lease, get loans, and move in. We opened our doors at our new, expanded location September 8, 2008. Yep, right when the economy collapsed.

I was working over 80 hours per week, was exhausted and needed some help. We were still doing a multi-six-figure business, but I knew I needed to move out of the treatment room and into a different role. I just couldn't see how to do it, so I kept doing what I knew how to do, even though it was clearly time to move on. When we are resisting necessary change, the universe has a way of making it happen, one way or another.

A client approached me and said she and her husband were going to open the same business as mine very soon, and wondered if I would be interested in a partnership instead? Sounded great to me! I was very excited and welcomed them with open arms. We hired an attorney, had them talk with our CPA and financial advisor, and we all agreed that the deal looked good – on paper. The truth is, my husband and I had a bad feeling about it, but I was so exhausted, and we tried to tell ourselves it was old fear coming up, so we chose to ignore our intuition, which is always a big mistake.

I didn't have a mentor, and didn't know what else to do. I have been very blessed throughout my life to have had spiritual and personal growth mentors, but I had never had a business mentor. When I had decided to expand my business, I looked for a mentor, but was unsuccessful. I wanted a mentor who had walked in my shoes: who was a woman, a healer, a spiritual practitioner, and was also financially successful from her healing work —someone of the highest integrity, on the path, and very business savvy. I couldn't find her anywhere, so I stumbled along, doing the best with what I had and what I knew.

The agreement we made with our new partners was that they would do the business side of it, and I would still see some clients, train staff, create products and programs, and move into mentorship and guidance, as I had been wanting to do. We were excited by the possibilities. Within a few months, they locked me out of my office and did a hostile takeover of my business. I was shocked. "I mean, really, who does that to a woman healer?" I said. (Turns out, it's more common than you might think.) We sought legal counsel and were told that what they did was definitely unethical and unlawful, but that to fight it would cost us at least $50k with no guarantee of ever collecting.

So I moved on. Not knowing what else to do, I tried to keep going with my healing practice, but I could never recover financially and had to throw in the holistic, organic towel.

It was incredibly painful to lose my business, but the worst part was, I had no idea what to do. I didn't have a back up plan. It wasn't just a job; it was my life's work. It was painfully clear that Spirit was now calling me to do something else. But what was it?

I went through soul searching, surrendering, and letting go. I let the universe know that I was open to what I was being called to do next. I eventually relaxed into my deep abiding trust in the benevolence of existence, and trusted that the next step would be revealed to me. I started paying attention, accepting invitations, open to how my life was going to unfold next. One of those invitations led me to meeting and hiring my first business mentor.

I was so scared to invest, and it didn't make logical or financial sense. I had no income and was having a hard time paying rent, so it seemed like a really bad time to spend money. But I knew I was being called to do something different and I needed to find out what that was, how to do it, and how to make some money while I did it. I believed that this person could help me figure it out. So I took a deep breath and leapt, trusting my intuition over my rational mind this time. I said yes, invested in myself and in my vision. This was the first step towards understanding my deeper calling.

Since then, I have worked with amazing mentors, who have helped me and guided me along the path. I regrouped, and re-expanded my energy and vision. I got clear on what I most value, who I am here to serve and what I am here to do during my brief time on planet earth. I had a moment of clear thunderbolt awakening when I realized that

I was being called to become the mentor I had been searching for! …That I was to guide women healers, and teach them how to make money so that they would never have to suffer the way that I did. They would not have to stumble along, feeling unworthy, alone, exhausted, isolated and scared, and not knowing what to do. So that they would help more people and have a bigger impact in the healing of the planet and awakening of humanity… So that they would be empowered and free.

In my healing practice, I made plenty of mistakes, and it turns out I also did a lot of things right. While my healing practice was growing, I saw that my colleagues were struggling, because they still had the old belief, that you can't be a spiritual practitioner and a healer, and also make money. My call was to help heal this split. Now, my whole life makes sense. I am using all of my wisdom, strengths, training and experience to help other women healers help more people, make more money, and have a bigger impact in the world. My clients are going from burned out, exhausted and struggling, to creating thriving businesses while working less and doing only what they love to do. I recently gave a suggestion to one of my private clients, based on a mistake I made in the past, that is resulting in her adding an additional six figures to her business over the next few years, while doing very little to create it. This makes my heart sing with joy! I am also making more money than I ever have before, doing what I love doing most, while having plenty of time off for me. I am living what I'm teaching, and teaching what I'm living.

I trust that everything we go through is an opportunity to evolve, learn, and transform. And I now know that if I had had a mentor like me back then, I still would have become a business coach to women healers, but I would have done it with less trauma, more ease, and made more money along the way. I trust Spirit and I trust in my life, and I know that because of what I went through, I am even more dedicated to helping women healers than ever before.

The simple truth is, you want to fulfill your vision, and you need money to live the life you want and DESERVE!

We need you to show up with clear, strong energy. Your great sensitivity and incredible openness help make you a great healer, and you need to protect and renew yourself so that you can continue to be a channel of light, love, healing and awakening. The world does not need one more broke, exhausted, stressed-out healer. We need you to be strong. There is much work to do. It is not selfish to take great care of yourself. It is your duty and responsibility to take great care of yourself, and it is my duty and responsibility and honor and calling to support you to do that. You are an agent of change, a ray of light, and you need to be supported on every level, including financially, so that you can help even more people. We need you to shine.

I have a vision of a world that is run by wealthy women healers. Imagine how different this world will be when more wealthy women healers are leaders: the children are fed, the water is clean, the elders are cared for, the animals are protected... people are living in harmony with nature and each other, healing naturally, using technology for the good of all, connected to Spirit.

The world needs women healers to be empowered so that you can help more people, heal the planet and lead others on the path of transformation, awakening, love and freedom. The time for you to step up is now. The world is in trouble and can no longer wait. Are you ready to answer the call?

YOUR CALL TO ACTION!

Find Your Guide

> Someone that you trust, who is in alignment with your vision and values, and who has already been successful at what you want to do. She can help you move through all of the following action steps much faster, saving you years of wasted time, money and frustration.

Align Yourself

> Re-connect to your deepest values, biggest vision and true mission on this planet. Make sure everything in your business and your life is in alignment with your values and is moving you towards realizing your vision and expressing your mission. Staying connected to this will get you out of bed on those days when you want to stay there with the covers pulled over your head.

Understand Your Divine Unique Genius

> Learn how to say who you serve and what you do in one short sentence, so that your Divine Match Client™ can easily recognize you as the person she has been looking for to help her. For example, when people ask me what I do, I say, "I help women healers make money." You know right away if this is you and if you need my help. You have to be this clear when you say what you do in order to attract your Divine Match Clients™ to you.

Create Your Wealth

> Raise your prices. Do it today. This is an act of self-love and self-care. You and your services are more valuable than you think.

Break Free of Old Beliefs About Money

> Get over your money stuff. Don't let your unresolved money issues prevent you from being a force of good in the world. Do your work. Release your resistance to abundance, and play bigger in the world. Remember, the world needs you more than ever, and needs you to step up now.

About Shayla

Shayla Kiser Mihaly is a Holistic Business Coach to holistic women healers, teachers and coaches. She specializes in healing the split women healers have between being spiritual practitioners and creating material wealth. Shayla has been a Reiki Master, NLP Master Practitioner and holistic entrepreneur for over 20 years, has done over 20,000 hands-on healing sessions, and created her own multi-six-figure healing center using the same inner and outer tools and strategies that she now teaches her Divine Match Clients™.

Born an empath, Shayla began a formal meditation and spiritual practice at the age of 14, and has always been of service to spirit. Childhood illnesses and overwhelm led her to the world of holistic healing as a young adult, and set her on her path of bringing healing to herself, her clients and the planet.

Shayla Kiser Mihaly has spent a year traveling across the U.S. with a Native American Shaman, worked in development management with Georgetown University in Chiapas, Mexico, and lived quietly in a van in an apple orchard. She now resides near Golden Gate Park in San Francisco, CA with her amazing husband and magnificent cat.

Shayla Kiser Mihaly is in service to supporting women healers who are doing amazing transformational healing work and yet are struggling financially, because she knows having strong women healer-leaders who are fulfilling their missions and creating a bigger impact in the world is an essential key to the awakening of humanity and our planet.

You can reach Shayla:
Shayla@ShaylaMihaly.com
http://www.ShaylaMihaly.com
http://www.GetGreatClientsNow.com
http://www.WealthyWomenHealers.com

CHAPTER 38

THE ART OF CREATING A VIBRANT BUSINESS OR CAREER — ONE THAT LEADS TO FREEDOM, PROSPERITY AND PERSONAL FULFILLMENT

BY SUSANA VILMER

Purpose is defined as the reason for which anything is done, created, or exists. Things are created for a specific purpose and we humans also have a purpose. I believe that "answering the call" means to first understand and embrace our mission and purpose in this world and second to fully own and immerse into the process of growth and evolution – which requires us to have the motivation, willingness, courage, inner strength, commitment, time, and energy to make things happen. The number one reason why people feel unfulfilled in their jobs/businesses is because they don't feel joy. Think about your existence in this universe. How many people do you know that say, "I want to feel sad today." or "I want a business or career that makes me unhappy or miserable."? No one, right? Of course not! And the reason is because our true-life purpose is to feel joy and to learn to have fun. If you don't feel joy, you are no longer in alignment with your divine life purpose, with the totality of who you really are, which is joyous energy (otherwise we would try to feel the opposite, don't you think?). I invite you to reflect on this for a second because this is the foundation of what it really means to create a vibrant business/career that leads to freedom, prosperity and personal fulfillment.

Now, that you understand what it really means to live on purpose, I want to address the path that we all must take to fulfill our purpose and mission, and that is the path of growth and evolution. Here is where resistance surfaces, where we are tested over and over, where we can get paralyzed temporarily or indefinitely. We all experience this from time to time. Some more than others, but we all do. Steven Pressfield points this out in his book, *The War of Art*. His rule of thumb says, "The more important a call or action is to our soul's evolution, the more Resistance we will feel toward pursuing it." What I have learned throughout my journey is that the more we stay in the vibration of resistance, the more we delay our financial and personal fulfillment. When I understood the concept of vibration (emotion = energy in motion) and started to pay attention at my own fulfillment, miracles started to happen. The field of Quantum Physics has confirmed that all things have a vibration because everything in this world is made of energy, including us humans. I invite you to be open to this idea and consider that you are co-creating with this universe every day, all day.

The first thing I tell my students and clients is to see themselves as big magnets that have vibrations (emotions). The vibration is the signal that communicates with this universe and makes commands on your behalf. If you understand this concept, I promise that you will be empowered for life and even though you are tested in the future, which you will, this new awareness will give you the confidence, courage and strength to move forward no matter what. This philosophy is what has helped me navigate throughout the process of growth and evolution I discussed earlier. I am going to show you the little shifts in my awareness that transformed the quality of my life over a period of time and how I got to where I am today.

The isolation I felt after moving from Mexico to the US led to a transformational journey from loneliness, anxiety and depression to empowerment and joy. I successfully learned a new language, adapted to a complete different culture, created support systems to help me deal with the loneliness and I was able to achieve success in my career very fast. I live in the city of my dreams and I have a vibrant and fulfilling lifestyle. As good as this sounds, it was not easy at all. I used to feel so much frustration because it was very difficult to communicate and express myself the way I wanted. Sometimes people didn't take me seriously and I used to feel that I didn't belong.

I remember how shocking it was to attend school in the US without knowing the language. I was in a government class and we were learning how to pass a bill into law. The teacher selected the top three "bills" from the class and the chosen students were expected to advocate for their idea. Mine was one of the top three. When the teacher called my name, I could not believe it! I thought, "Oh no, why me? I don't even speak English!" I started to get really nervous and felt as if I was inside an oven because I was sweating so much. When it was my turn to speak, I fearfully said, "My bill should win because is good." The entire class laughed at me and I was very ashamed because I looked like a fool and I felt so impotent. Learning the language and being on my own in a foreign country was not easy. I had headaches and migraines regularly. As time passed, I started to feel homesick and lonely. I missed my family, friends, and lifestyle. My dad used to call me every Sunday. One of those Sundays, I was crying so much and was feeling miserable. My dad said to me, "If you feel so miserable, come home; you don't have to be there feeling alone and sad. You have your family here!" The fact that he gave me that option, made me feel a sense of relief, but I also realized that I was there for a purpose and all the frustration and challenges were in my life because I was stretching myself. I said to myself that I was not a quitter and that realization helped me get the strength I needed. Once I connected again to my dream and purpose, I asked for help and got involved in activities that helped me practice my English. The support helped me feel better, but I had to have that realization first. I understood that the easiest way to achieve my dreams was to connect with my passion and purpose.

After that experience, I continued my studies in Nevada, Texas, California and New York, and had to start from zero all over again. My passion has always been to help people, and most of my career I worked as an advocate for homeless students and their education. Committed to my passion, I moved up the latter rapidly and landed senior level management positions in government. However, as I continued to advance in my career in NYC, I felt so much stress, fear and self-doubt because I was feeling insecure about my ability to be an effective leader. And on top of that I was living in isolation. I was another single girl in NYC with a successful career, but with much need of family, love, connection and belonging, which degraded my emotional health and personal satisfaction. I was constantly feeling lonely, depressed and anxious. I remember one night I had to call my friend to help me get to the hospital because I felt I was going to have a heart attack. My friend told me, "Susana, it sounds that you are having a panic attack, not a heart attack." It was shocking for me. I visited my physician who prescribed me anti-anxiety pills, but this approach didn't feel right for me, so I started to do research on my own and I became an expert on finding self-empowerment tools that helped me overcome my negative feelings. This is how I discovered the power of our vibration and the Law of Attraction. These series of events inspired me to become a certified Law of Attraction Life Coach to empower myself and help other women to do the same.

So based on what I learned, here are seven steps to achieving freedom, prosperity and personal fulfillment:

Step 1. Value the life rules (as I like to call them). Why play the game of life without knowing its rules? The main life rule is the Law of Attraction, which says that you create and attract what you *think* about the most, and your vibration is the attractor factor. For example, if you feel anxiety or stress because you are having negative thoughts, you will continue to attract more situations/people that produce in you the same feeling. Every time you find yourself focusing on the negative aspects of your life or people, stop and say, "I know that I don't want that. So what do I want?" Focus on the solution instead.

Step 2. Ignite your joyous vision and clarify your career/business path. How well do you really know yourself? Go within and define your passions, unique gifts, talents and skills that you bring to this world, and ask yourself what gives you meaning and purpose. If you don't have a clear vision, it will take longer to realize your destiny. Don't worry about the "how" just make sure that you focus on "what" makes you feel joy. Also, because we are "growth-seeker" beings, I recommend that you revisit your vision twice a year.

Step 3. Be conscious of the unconscious. This is the number one reason why people stay stuck. Research shows that our unconscious mind controls our behavior, so it is crucial to be aware of our limiting beliefs. What are some beliefs that you are tolerating and need to let go of? When you become aware of any limiting beliefs, you can say, "Wait a minute, that is not helpful and it is disempowering." For a long time, I felt that I was not ready to move forward with my life's purpose, but as soon as I recognized that unconscious belief, I started part-time and no longer waited to be ready. *I learned that if you wait until you feel ready, you would never do it.*

Step 4. Reconnect with your vibrational support system (VSS). Each vibration (emotion) has a frequency. The better you feel, the higher your frequency. Fill in the blank: "When I have my ideal business/career I will feel _____." That is the vibration you must feel regularly to create your ideal business/career, because what you attract in life always matches your vibration. Also, in this step you learn to surrender, work with your intuition and let go of resistance (feeling bad).

Step 5. Attain new levels of self-acceptance and self-responsibility. The experiences I shared with you led to feelings of unworthiness, but I learned that just because the fact that we emerged into this physical body/world, this makes us worthy of anything we want. Yes, just because you were born, you are entitled to achieve your dream or whatever brings you joy. However, we need to take full ownership of that, which requires us to take responsibility of our value and stop blaming others or feeling like victims. Gay Hendricks addresses this in his book, *The Big Leap*, which says, "If there is any part of ourselves or our lives that we're not fully willing to accept, we will experience stress and friction in that area. The stress will disappear the moment we accept that part and claim ownership of it. At that moment, the disowned part of us is embraced into the wholeness of ourselves, and from that place of wholeness, miracles are born."

Step 6. Nurture your relationship with your future self. When you observe your future self as you reach forward into time, it is easier to stay committed to your life purpose because the positive things you will see when you have your ideal career/business will keep you motivated. Imagine right now that you are in front of your future self and listen to the messages she/he has for you.

Step 7. Thrive fast with an action/success plan that includes measurable and feasible goals that create systems. The more you pay attention to your plan, the faster you will create results – one, because you will uplift your vibration when you make progress, and two, because what you put your attention on expands. Always keep an open mind during this process because sometimes things may not go as planned, but will be better than expected.

About Susana

Susana Vilmer is the Founder and CEO of Uplift Your Vibration, a company that is devoted to teaching women professionals and business owners around the world how to use their vibration to create a more meaningful, fulfilling and financially rewarding life. Her motto is: "Uplifting the World One Vibration at a Time."

With her coaching programs, Susana empowers and guides women who are committed to their spiritual and personal evolution, and teaches them how to remove the mental blocks that are preventing them from living on purpose and have the vibrant lifestyle they desire. With her programs and Susana's coaching as their guide, they achieve big results faster and more easily than they ever could on their own.

Women professionals and business owners who are serious about creating a vibrant lifestyle of meaning and purpose and want to make a real difference in the world find Susana's step-by-step programs to be the support they need to accomplish their goals.

Susana's Career Path:

Susana was born in Mexico and came to the United States in 1997 to learn English and study. Her studies took her to various places of the country like Nevada, Texas, California and New York. From an early age, she discovered her passion for helping people and worked with homeless students and their families most of her career. Upon finishing her degree in Texas, she moved to New York City to continue her studies and held senior leadership positions in government. Susana became the leader of the homeless education program in NYC, the largest school district in the nation. She created new systems, policies and procedures to increase awareness in schools, which helped homeless students access more support services than ever before. In 2012, Susana earned her certification as a Life Coach specializing in Law of Attraction coaching to help her with her own personal and spiritual evolution.

The Law of Attraction Coaching Expert:

Clients consider Susana to be their go-to expert to learn the Law of Attraction and other Universal Laws to be successful with both professional and personal transformation. She's also the go-to resource for professionals and business owners who are looking for a deeper sense of purpose and meaning, and to accomplish worthwhile goals in life.

Education/Training:

Susana is a certified Law of Attraction Life Coach, Fit4Love Coach and Angel Card Reader. She received training from the Quantum Success Coaching Academy and Intentional Relationships. She holds a B.A. in Social Work from the University of Texas at El Paso and an M.A. in Public Administration from the City University of New York.

You can connect with Susana at:
www.upliftyourvibration.com
www.susanavilmer.com
support@susanavilmer.com
www.twitter.com/SusanaVilmer
www.facebook.com/SusanaVilmer

CHAPTER 39

EXIT LEFT

BY TANA DAWN

I haven't always been honest in my life. Not that I had been a 'liar' but just that I had needed to 'hide' some of the truth some of the time. Toxic shame can and does affect many of us in different ways and at different times in our lives. How we handle that shame and how we hide or present our truth can have long-lasting effects on us, our family and our surroundings.

As far as my surroundings were concerned, I guess you could say I wasn't exactly born with a silver spoon in my mouth. My mum and dad shared lodgings with another family when I came into the world and my first cot was a wooden drawer. I was definitely an open and shut case! Humble beginnings maybe, but it became apparent as the years rolled by, that my parents did the very best they could for me with what little they had. I was born in Burton upon Trent in Staffordshire, England, famous for its beer, Marmite and for being the farthest place from the sea.

I grew up alongside some adoring pets; Buster, my first collie sheepdog (accused of stealing washing off a neighbour's line), Tickles June, the cat, who was really a boy (but that's another story), Timmy the cankered-eared mouse and Whisky the budgie, aptly named after mum's favourite tipple. Then there was Hoppidy, the orphaned hare who loved to ride on the vacuum cleaner (and hopped into the toilet one day), Donald and Quackers, two ducks who hated water, a whole squad of bantam hens who refused to lay eggs, Samantha the brown hen who regularly invited herself indoors to eat the cat food and, Gobbles, our handsome turkey who sadly went off his legs one Christmas. Hmmm…or did he? So 'turkey patrol' for us children turned out to be fruitless that year and none of us could eat our Christmas dinner.

Although compassion was shown to the animals around us, it seemed somewhat different for me. Dad was a pretty volatile man and would easily throw in his job out of temper…and boy, did he have one. You always knew by the way he drove his car home if he had a job to go to the next day. The eldest of three girls, I got to be on the receiving end of his anger so I very soon learned not to make eye contact with him and, more poignantly, I learned not to use my voice. To be quiet. To be invisible.

Due to mum's ill health and dad's absence at the time, I quickly became an eleven year old 'little mum' to my six and four-year-old sisters. The stark reality of seeing mum with pneumonia for the third time, refusing to go into hospital, lying downstairs on a camp bed and almost permanently hooked up to an oxygen cylinder, put me in constant fear of losing her. I can clearly see now that my limiting beliefs around self-esteem, self-worth, lack of confidence and 'speaking out' were all established around my childhood years. I remember visiting a neighbour with mum one day for a cup of tea. If I was offered a biscuit, I may take one, but if offered another, I must say 'No thank you'. Admirably, manners were instilled in us from a very early age, but for me at the age of five the message was, 'You may have *this* much but *don't* ever ask for anything more.' So I never did. That maxim stayed with me well into adulthood and, just when I'm least expecting it, still comes and bites me on the bottom.

Paradoxically, for a girl with no voice but, thanks to mum's encouragement, I made my stage debut at my local drama school when I was eleven. Dad came along to watch. I was *astonished*. I don't know what felt worse. The sheer terror of knowing he was in the audience, or the ridicule I experienced from school friends the previous day when I had revealed, from underneath a woolly hat, the attempts of my mum's 'home perm'. I made my way to meet my parents at the end of my debut performance. There was no sign of Dad. He had gone home during the interval. I never questioned why. I didn't dare. Later that night I overheard him say that I had been 'rubbish'. He was probably right. I dare say my home perm performed better than I did. Dad's remark however stayed with me for many, *many* years. I gave up acting after that until I was in my late twenties. By the time I reached my mid-thirties, I had won many awards and accolades for 'Best Actress', received standing ovations and been told I should be on television and acting in the West End. Not bad for a little girl with no voice.

The needs and truths that were not met or acknowledged in this young 'unhealed child' became the beginning of my journey into self-discovery and self-development, gave me an inquisitive mind into what made people 'tick' and a great empathy for others. As a young teenager, I was acquiring my tools and skills in my quest to serve others. I became a source of consolation and advice for many.

However, I couldn't always walk my talk. Whilst in a long-term relationship during my adult years, I wore a mask to the outside world by not speaking my truth. To others, I had the perfect relationship but inside I was slowly dying. This had a detrimental effect on my health - I lost some of my hair (like most women, it was my crowning glory), suffered severe panic attacks, ground my teeth, developed crimson blotches the size of oven gloves all over my body, all of which ultimately led to episodes of depression. I travelled to Dorset to see a therapist who said I was tipping on the edge of developing ME. My body certainly was in dis-ease. I felt totally debilitated and emotionally and physically exhausted. I shut myself off from the outside world and, at times, it was a challenge to pick up the phone and talk to someone, anyone. I felt like a rag doll; once pretty with a painted smile, big blue eyes, rosy cheeks and a crisp cotton dress, I now peered out from a prison, through the dense glass of a washing machine into the big wide world. I had been washed hundreds of thousands of times, tumbled, drained and wrung out of every conceivable emotion. The painted face had all but disappeared, the smile gone, the dress faded and tattered. But still I clung on, clung on to empty promises, and was spun around and around like a top. I'd go again into that big dark drum, bashed from side to side, thrown and spun around until I was truly dizzy with desolation.

It wasn't until a good friend said one day, "Tana, I want what you've got" that I knew I finally had to speak my truth. I owed it to my friend but, more importantly, I owed it to myself. Twenty-seven years of loneliness, rejection and absolute pain came pouring from my lips. Years of toxic pus came oozing out from beneath my giant Band-Aid. I had played the victim, the martyr and the wounded healer, the most difficult roles I had ever played and all for far too long. It was time to exit the stage.

It's not until we look back that we realise just how far we've come through all our adversities and experiences. New beliefs, new thoughts, new behaviours and a new mindset can help us find the core strength to carry on and live the life we were *born* to live. So, if you're holding on to that cliff edge for dear life, too scared to make a move or speak your mind to the detriment of yourself and those around you, I would love to share with you my top ten tips to help you find your voice and speak your truth:

1. Use the beautiful gift of your voice. If your life doesn't currently bring you joy and fulfilment, ask yourself what is the cost to your emotional, physical, mental and spiritual health and wellbeing for not being happy, fulfilled and leading a purposeful life?

2. Ask yourself what are the consequences and implications on your lifestyle, work, values and beliefs and, ultimately, your soul by not using your voice and 'speaking your truth'? Make a list. Digest the words then regurgitate them. Say them out loud and listen. Say them in the mirror. Words have a power so great they can expand or contract a person without one point of physical contact. Words have the power to degrade, belittle, praise or elevate a person. Honour the gift of your voice. Use your words wisely as they create your reality. So…to change your reality, change your language!

3. Dig deep into your heart and into your soul. Breathe deeply. Breathe from your diaphragm not your chest. Three deep breaths, exhale completely on each outbreath. Be still. Ask your question and listen for the answer. When you allow your vulnerability to surface, through being open and truthful, you will find it brings with it a great inner strength.

4. Explore deeply any feelings of 'unworthiness.' Where have they come from? Are they true? The things that shape us are derived from our upbringing, our culture, our religion, our thoughts and our experiences and the thoughts and experiences of others – they don't belong to you - so be mindful of which ones are *actually* true. Beliefs that you have held for a very long time may need challenging.

5. Don't let silence pervade your relationship, whatever that relationship is. Don't be afraid to really voice your true feelings or emotions for fear of rocking the boat or losing the security of a partner, friend, family member or work colleague. You deserve and are entitled to be heard. Listen to and speak from your heart. The longer you deny yourself the right to open up and be heard, the more out of alignment you will become and the more energetically you will shut down.

6. Rid yourself of the old stories and the drama. They serve no purpose other than lessons to be learned, so don't let them define your life and don't allow yourself to be held hostage by your history. Say 'Yes' to yourself by giving yourself permission to step up and step out into a future you so richly deserve.

7. Forgive all those who have hurt you; they may not all deserve your forgiveness but by forgiving them you are setting yourself, your heart and your soul free.

8. Let go of people and situations that no longer serve you. Cut the shackles, for until you do, you will never receive what you truly deserve if you are welded to people and things that don't deserve you.

9. Be present. Shine a light on yourself. Step into your power, into your glory NOW, and live in the present moment. That's all we have…tomorrow is promised to no-one.

10. Talk to God, to Source, to the Universe…whichever one is right for you. ASK! Ask for help and for guidance. Ask God/Source what you are meant to be doing, what is your life's purpose? Ask for what you want.

Someone once said, "Do not regret growing older. It's a privilege denied to many." I respectfully add, "Do not regret not speaking your truth during your lifetime, it's not a privilege, it's your right to do so." So what are you waiting for? Give yourself radical permission to show up in the world as the true, authentic you.

Celebrate you and your beautiful new-found voice. It's not until we've been in the deepest valley do we know what it's like on the highest mountain, so go and shout, bellow, sing, holler! Let the world know you've arrived!

And me? I am now in the coveted role of the wise woman and this is one role that I'm happy to play for a very long time...

Postscript: Dad is in his eighth decade now. He's mellowed, yes, but underneath the thinning grey hair and cloud of cigarette smoke, he's still a bad boy racer. If you saw his car, you'd know exactly what I'm talking about. Thanks Dad. x

About Tana

The tools and skills that Tana Dawn has acquired throughout her real life experiences have equipped her in her role as a women's transformational coach. She follows her passion to help women elegantly glide through the decades by empowering, supporting and mentoring them from a place of love and respect. She uses her intuition, perception and inner knowing to move women forward and give them the tools to help themselves to become more visible.

Tana holds a space for women where they are heard and not judged, where they are given the opportunity to express themselves, explore their options and encouraged to take responsibility and hold themselves accountable as they access their power. She makes a difference in the lives of women who have had no voice, who have put themselves on the bottom of the pile, women who have always served others before themselves and women with low self-esteem and self-worth. Tana listens in order to learn more. She has been described as truly inspirational, has ferocious willpower and a spine of steel. People say 'She fizzes'. Although she shoots from the hip, she works in complete integrity always with love and always from the heart, and fun is always part of the deal!

Tana is a graduate of the University of Derby and is the CEO and founder of TanaDawn. com. She is an EFT (Emotional Freedom Technique) Practitioner, uses NLP in her coaching, has studied Emotional Intelligence at post-graduate level, has a Diploma in Performance Coaching and is a member of the National Council of Psychotherapists. She has undertaken many coaching programs and holds Counseling certificates with Relate. Tana is part of Gina DeVee's Divine Living Coaching Certification Academy and proudly claims of her love of working with the awesome Lisa Sasevich!

You can connect with Tana at:
www.tanadawn.com
tana@tanadawn.com
https://twitter.com/TanaDawn1

CHAPTER 40

ZELATIOUS LIVING, THE BALANCED LIFE FORMULA

BY SUSAN DELANO SWIM

We thought we had the perfectly packed life. My husband worked round the clock and pushed himself to the brink daily. I worked while raising our four daughters and kept the house and family running like clockwork. Like so many moms and wives, I thought I could do it all; I pushed myself hard every day and only ever said "no" to myself. I would get up early and go to bed late, barely breathing, while trying to balance it all; I was superwoman! I thought living that way was normal. I did not realize how crazy it was. We both thought we were invincible. Then reality hit, my husband became ill and could barely work.

I wanted to do something that would help lighten our financial load and thought, "What can I do to contribute?" In the past, I had held many jobs, but what did I really want to do now? What was the one thing that was truly calling me? Despite all the things that I had done, I realized that I had built nothing of my own. I desperately wanted to do something that answered my calling and at which I could make a living.

I have always supported women with their daily struggles of managing everything from being exhausted, frustrated, overwhelmed, anxious and stressed out. Friends directed me towards the path of career and life coaching, an area of which I had never heard of in 1999. After becoming a Certified Life Coach and continuing my education in relationship coaching, I built my coaching business. It didn't take long before I realized my business was naturally attracting woman. During this time, I was working with my husband in his business and before I knew it, my life became increasingly unbalanced again. Just like in the movie, "I Don't Know How She Does It," with Sarah Jessica Parker, I never slowed down and paid precious little attention to my body and my own health. When the shocking news came that my own health was in jeopardy all I could think was, "holy crap, what have I done?" It was at that moment I realized, yet again, my unbalanced life would ultimately lead to my demise if I did not give myself a kick in the butt, throw myself into a new life game plan, and stop sabotaging all my efforts.

All too often we pay attention to everything and everyone but ourselves. Women especially miss the subtle signals of increasing stress levels until the ultimate happens – their own health is in jeopardy. They are either too busy to pay attention, somehow believe that they can "will away" their problems, or think tomorrow will always be better.

My last 15 years of personal soul-searching, training, and coaching women to a more balanced and fulfilling life resulted in a multi-faceted program called *The Zelatious Living Program*. Zelatious Living refers to a life filled with more passion, greater joy, improved balance, improved mental and physical health, and a sense of overall excitement for life! Designed to help women de-stress, create balance and find peace – every step is a gift you give yourself. These steps work equally well for CEOs and stay at home moms. Everyone deserves to feel the Zelatious Life throughout their body, flowing naturally without any barriers and operating consistently from the heart, embracing their real, passionate, empowered selves.

As a rule, women want less stress, less self-doubt, to stop procrastinating, and to gain clarity and a plan for their future. We need to rediscover our self-worth and to have more personal fulfillment. The answers are inside each of us, but for many, uncovering these answers requires assistance. The benefits of my coaching include: guiding you in developing an organic plan and strategy to pursue your dreams, improve your personal awareness, connect your thoughts with what you are experiencing, learn to live in the moment, accelerate your journey to clarity, gain confidence and create a power plan to move forward that fits your schedule, life style and dreams.

I have a client who is now entering her 70's and happily owns her power to make better decisions for herself and is thriving. When she came to me ten years ago, she was in the abyss. She was unfulfilled at work and in her marriage. She was on the brink of divorce, blaming her unhappiness on her husband. Yet, my client had no idea what would make her happy. Together with my coaching utilizing my Zelatious Living Program, she gained direction, learned to like herself, and started to pay attention to herself. She stopped blaming others, and ceased looking to her husband to make her feel happy. She learned internally what makes her happy, and became decisive and more secure in her own skin. Today, she has more control of what she seeks. Her marriage has benefited greatly as she is happier with herself. Without a combination of my coaching and learning new life strategies, along with her determination to succeed, her personal life would have continued to struggle at best.

Consider this. Do you ever wake up exhausted, wondering how you will get through the day? Are you tired of being tired? Was this the life you created for yourself or is it the life you fell into? Do your habits hurt you or help you? Do you sometimes suspect that at least a hint of self-sabotage is at play? Do you have the habits you want to have or do they need an adjustment so you can re-design them to have the life that you want? Do you stare at your office or your home wondering if this is it for you? Or, do you wonder if it is possible to somehow change what you are doing so life feels easier and you will still get it all done.

Do you begin sentences with "How am I going to…" more than once each day? Through the *Zelatious Living Program*, you can gain clarity to understand what makes you happy, gives you a stronger sense of direction, more control over your health, the ability to trust your own judgment, improve your self-worth, how to have fun and have a plan so you know you are on a path you've designed. You can achieve this by cleaning out your life closets, setting and attaining goals, noticing and paying attention to red flags, and following through.

Are you living your highest and best life? We usually do not talk in those terms, but when you really ask yourself that question, nine times out of ten the answer is, "No, I am not." Is this the life you dreamed of as a child? If not, why? Be your own best friend so you can live your highest and best life and know how to treat yourself. Have the courage to create a life and path you are deeply in love with and be committed to knowing and getting what you want. You are the only one that can do this for you.

When was the last time you felt your inner sparkle shine? Do you even know what your inner sparkle is? It is your energy, charisma and confidence and it is what attracts other people to you. Your sparkle, or mojo, influences how you feel in your own skin and how you show up in everything that you do. Do you show up or are you too tired to show up? In my program we look at all of you: how you feel about yourself, how you honor yourself and what your inner dialogue is. When your inner sparkle is shining in your life, you will make the best of any situation and people will want to be around you.

Do you dream? What do you do with your dreams? Do you believe you will have what you dream of, or do you think your dreams will never come true? Learn how to dream again. Create your vision and then implement a plan that will walk you step-by-step toward making your dream a reality. If you do not have goals and dreams, years will pass and nothing will change except you getting older. So many people are so busy that they cannot even think about anything beyond wanting to get through this day. If you cannot plan to make it different then it won't be. When you want big things to happen or you deeply desire change you must be willing to do the work to make it happen. We go through life unconsciously about 90% of the time, wishing for something to be different. To do what it takes to create and live your dream, you must live consciously and create the space for this work. Clearing the space to allow yourself to feel inspired and empowered by your dreams, you will give them the space to take root.

You can clear a little space and start living zelatiously today by giving yourself a few simple gifts:

1. Give yourself the gift of...a Relaxed Body and Mind

Give yourself the gift of learning to relax your mind and body in any given moment. Imagine if you acquired the toolset to be able to train your mind to release negative thoughts and to replace those thoughts with productive, here and now thoughts. How much more could you accomplish in a day without the clutter you normally store in your brain?

2. *Give yourself the gift of...Connecting to Your Inner Strength*

Finding the force of calmness, stability and strength requires that you look no further than inside yourself. Connect to your unshakable inner strength, power and wisdom and you will feel more confident.

Connecting to your inner strength enables you to return to the well every time you feel depleted. Instead of looking for outside reinforcement and stabilizers, seek your inner strength instead to make decisions and to train your mind away from the old habits and beliefs that feed your negative thinking. Your well of inner strength goes with you everywhere you go, silently waiting to be tapped, regardless of who else surrounds you or which activities you must tackle today.

3. *Give yourself the gift of...Positive Thinking*

Thinking positive is transforming. There are advocates of positive thinking everywhere. The ability to shift your thoughts from worry, anger and negativity to a place of positivity and gratitude changes you on a cellular level.

Instead of allowing yourself to sink into habitually negative thoughts, you can consciously redirect your thoughts, and your emotions will follow. You can shift your feelings from anxiety, stress or worry to feeling relaxed and happy, any time you choose.

My clients have benefited from coaching by creating a shift to positive thinking. Through a series of exercises, you can channel your thoughts into a different and more beneficial direction. How different would your life be if you woke up each morning with feelings of exuberation, not feelings of dread? Could you accomplish more and feel more successful without the black ball of doom and gloom yoking you? I know you will. Believe that you can and will achieve more through positive thinking and seek help to achieve the outcomes you are looking for to get results faster.

4. *Give yourself the gift of...Choice*

Have you ever woken up angry and not had a clue as to why? Sure, you have. We all have. Setting our daily intentions provides footing when negative feelings or self-doubt might allow us to slip into the abyss. Decide who and how you want to be every day. Choose to be happy. Choose to be successful. It is all within your control, when you decide to take control.

Think of this as setting the table for a gathering. The dishes, flowers, tablecloth and time of day all set the tone for those who will attend. So too, does setting your day dictate how you and others will treat you that day. Remember, we often treat ourselves far worse than any enemy would treat us. Make the choice to treat yourself with kindness and respect, and others will follow your example.

There are always more tasks than there are hours in the day, so selecting the ones important for that specific day is paramount. Your choices will include business items, personal items and family tasks. No two days are alike and the list keeps growing. Moving an entire list of unaccomplished tasks from one day to the next is a set-up for failure. Why go there mentally? Better use of your day planner and your time will occur when you select and accomplish the priority items on your list.

5. *Give yourself a gift of…Understanding your Life Purpose*

Why wait until your life becomes extremely difficult or you receive a catastrophic health diagnosis to re-evaluate your life? I am sure you have heard or read many times about having a **life purpose**. Over the years of coaching, I realized that most of my clients came to me without a **life purpose** and did not know what their life purpose is or how to figure it out. When you know your **life purpose**, your life flows easier, you are excited, you feel good and you are inspired daily because you are refilling your tank everyday. When you are living your **life purpose,** you are taking action steps based on living your life on purpose following your dreams. We can all do this no matter what our circumstances are. When you are living and honouring your **life's purpose,** your natural special gifts and talents emerge and you gain a sense of personal fulfillment and heartfelt joy – knowing you are doing exactly what you are destined to do. No one else can do what you do the way that you do it; you are unique and special in every way.

One of the first steps to knowing your **life purpose** is to pay attention to your intuition, your knowing! This is your inner voice that tells you when something is right and when something is wrong. Too often, we ignore this voice because our brain has taken over and we think that if we think harder or better our brain has the right answer for us. As we do this, we bury or lose track of our hearts over time; we selectively turn off our natural barometer. At this point, we are not living our **life purpose; we are self-sabotaging our dreams.** We exist, doing what we feel is necessary to survive. Our heart, our intuition is never wrong. All we need to do is pay attention to the important nudges and know that our heart always has the best intentions for us.

If you have tried everything else and you are still not getting the results that you want, try *The Zelatious Living Program!* If you are stressed, overwhelmed, frustrated and /or anxious, *The Zelatious Living Program* will show you the steps you can start today that will lead you to developing a blue print for your future. Imagine embracing your life with excitement and passion with a plan in your back pocket that energizes you daily, because you know you are working towards your personalized life-success plan. Change your limiting beliefs, change your outcome, change your story and turn life on fully to having more of the things that you dream about.

About Susan

Susan Delano Swim, the balance lifestyle expert, founded The Zelatious Living Program after retiring from a successful sales and marketing career for some of the leading Fortune 100 companies.

After applying the strategies and principles she now teaches, Susan found the courage to leave the safety net of working in the corporate grind to step out into the realm of retail sales where she owned and operated a high-end children's retail clothing store in Canada. Soon Susan found herself working her own grind as the "lone ranger", running two successful family businesses and raising her four daughters, in addition to volunteering and running Dress For Success workshops across Canada. Susan started to see she was enslaving herself to a life of imbalance that ultimately took its toll on her own well-being as well as that of her family's. Something had to change and she quickly learned it had to start with herself.

Susan quickly pivoted, extracting her strong interpersonal skills she had honed as a top sales and marketing director to launching a career in coaching and advising women as a Balanced Life Strategist. Susan teaches from first-hand knowledge. She helps women to find their voice, rise up and avoid the pitfalls she has experienced herself and knows all too well. She advises a broad list of clients both at home and internationally – teaching real, practical applications so women can begin to think, speak and live more authentic, fulfilling and productive lives.

Because Susan is able to laugh and learn from her own self, she is able to guide women to take a heartfelt look at themselves in such a way that cultivates honest self-awareness and positive long-lasting change.

For more information and to connect with Susan go to:
www.zelatious.com
Susan@SusanDelanoSwim.com
www.twitter.com/SusanDSwim
www.facebook.com/SusanDelanoSwim
http://ca.linkedin.com/in/susandswim/

CHAPTER 41

YOUR GENES, YOUR DIET, AND YOU: EAT YOUR WAY TO WELLNESS

BY DR. ROSANE OLIVEIRA

"Like flipping a light switch on and off, we could control cancer promotion merely by changing levels of protein...but the cancer-promoting factor in this case was cow's milk protein." When I first read those words by Dr. T. Colin Campbell, I had no idea that they would completely change my life.

Giving dairy up was the last thing on my mind, having spent the past decade focused on preventive medicine and infectious diseases in dairy cattle (completing both my Masters and PhD degrees performing research to improve milk production). But, The China Study discoveries made me question everything I thought I knew about food and sparked my curiosity to discover the relationship between genetics, diseases, and diet in humans.

At the time, I had already been vegetarian for 20 years and dairy was my favorite food. Thick slices of cave-aged Gruyère cheese on a warm, crisp, freshly baked baguette was the best meal a girl could ask for. And Belgian dark chocolate ice cream was the proof that God not only existed, but loved me!

I hated the idea that both my life's work and favorite foods were linked to the onset and progression of chronic diseases. I wanted to ignore that information, label it as nonsense, and move on with my life. But my mother-in-law was battling breast cancer and I could not disregard legitimate findings that linked increased dairy consumption to cancers; which also includes cancers of the prostate and colon. The evidence was overpowering and caused me to think about my own health, and given the history of breast cancer in my family, I decided to take action.

I knew that I could not convince anyone to stop eating dairy if I did not eliminate it from my diet first. I thought of making the commitment for a year, but I was not sure that I could make it that long. I battled with the idea of giving up my favorite foods for a disease I did not even have. After some "internal negotiating," I decided to live without dairy for 6 months and so it started.

After just three months dairy free, without increasing exercise, I lost almost 20 lbs. My total cholesterol went from 176 (normal range) down to 139. My high-density lipoprotein (HDL) or good cholesterol remained the same at 68, while my low-density lipoprotein (LDL) or bad cholesterol went from 94 (upper normal range) to 55. I did not miss or want dairy anymore and much to my surprise, if I ate dairy by accident, my body would no longer tolerate it. Most of all, I felt amazing, looked younger and my skin was glowing. My food cravings completely disappeared and for the first time in my life, I was eating, not dieting.

All along, I was Research Assistant Professor at the University of Illinois and part of a team of researchers who examined the interrelationships between nutritional health of a cow and the high-energy demand for milk production right after giving birth (calving). The present practice has been to increase the amount of fat in the cow's diet before calving, which gives the cow more calories to produce milk. However, cows moderately overfed (40% above their daily requirements) before calving, even without becoming obese, are at greater risk of developing health complications, such as fatty liver, ketosis and other metabolic disorders.

Our study showed that the expression of 85 genes was affected by level of fat intake before calving. More importantly, through genotyping the *DGAT1* (diglyceride acyltransferase 1) gene, which initiates the formation of triglycerides, we further discovered that the greater risk of metabolic diseases was linked to cows with a specific *DGAT1* gene variant and the consumption of a high fat diet. Our research confirmed the importance of understanding the relationship between genetics and diet in the onset and promotion of disease.

These results validated the idea that genes alone do not cause the development of common diseases, and that nutrition plays a critical role in determining which genes, good or bad, are activated or expressed. Given the results of our research, the scientific evidence from similar studies in humans, and the transformation of my own health, I walked away from over a decade of research in dairy cattle to focus on how genetics and nutrition impact health and wellness in humans.

I changed my career orientation and moved to California to oversee the development of the integrative medicine program at the University of California, Davis. We focus on lifestyle medicine and behavioral interventions for the prevention and treatment of chronic health conditions such as obesity, hypertension, type 2 diabetes, and cardiovascular disease. We will research how food choices change the expression of genes in different populations and how that relates to the onset and progression of common diseases.

In my family life, evidence for the interaction between genes and diet had been there for almost two decades without me even noticing it. I was born an identical twin and for the first half of our lives, Renata and I were truly identical in the physical sense. That changed in 1995, when I moved to Germany to learn molecular biology and she graduated from Law School. That was when we stopped living under the same roof and started to eat differently.

As surprising as it may sound, even with identical genes, we lived most of the past two decades 40 to 60 pounds apart! My sister's struggle to lose weight burdened my heart and made me want to find answers to why our bodies became so different.

As you can imagine, like anyone needing to lose 40+ pounds, Renata tried everything she could – counting calories, cutting carbs, weight watchers, shakes, 21-day fasting. You name it, she tried it.

In the past 10 years, she had two major weight loss experiences, one monitoring calories and the other following a low-carb, low-fat diet. When Renata lost weight through calorie-counting, her total cholesterol, LDL, and triglycerides significantly increased. She lost 20 lbs., but her cholesterol went from 195 up to 219. Even though she appeared healthier, her biomarkers got worse since she was just eating less of the same types of food. Just like most people discover, moderation does not work. She was left hungry, exhausted, and eventually gave up on dieting, quickly gaining all the weight back.

She finally decided to make a big change in 2012 when she came to live with me and adopted my lifestyle. That included following a low-fat, whole food, plant-based diet. This made our blood markers almost identical for the very first time in a decade – her cholesterol dropped all the way down to 131, while her LDL cholesterol and triglycerides went from 115 to 60 and 184 to 60, respectively. The results were nothing short of remarkable; in a three month period she lost 25 lbs. and for the first time, has kept it off for over a year! These results reinforce the notion that, even for genetically identical twins, your diet determines your fate!

People often blame their genes for their health issues or being overweight. These genetic excuses like "diabetes runs in my family" or "every man in my family died of heart disease" prevent people from taking control of their own health and wellbeing.

Coming from a Brazilian family with a rich culture centered on food, making the decision to be different was difficult. But I chose to follow the healthier plant-based path and eat to nurture my genes and my body. Every woman in my family struggles with their weight, except me. What people seem to forget is that bad habits and unhealthy lifestyles are learned from our family.

Genetic variants alone do not directly cause common chronic diseases, and are believed to explain only ~5% of all cancers. The risk of disease depends on multiple factors that include your genetics, lifestyle choices such as smoking, exercise, and diet, and other environmental factors. It is estimated that 20%-60% of cancers in the United States are related to nutritional and dietary factors. In other words, genetics loads the gun, but a bad diet can pull the trigger.

For example, variations in a gene called *ACE* (angiotensin I converting enzyme) influence the effect of sodium on blood pressure. Individuals with gene variants in *ACE* have a 230% increased risk of high blood pressure when consuming more than 3/4 teaspoon or 1,500 mg of sodium per day.

Seven in ten people present at least one of the *ACE* risk variants, but 90% of Americans consume a staggering 3,000 to 5,000 mg of salt every single day! This overindulgence is one of the reasons why one in every three American adults has high blood pressure. If individuals with *ACE* risk variants eat less than 3/4 teaspoon of salt per day, they may control hypertension without medication.

The *APOA5* (apolipoprotein A5) gene influences the relationship between host genetics, diet, and obesity. People with genetic variants in the *APOA5* gene have a higher risk of obesity and increased Body Mass Index (BMI) when eating a high fat diet (i.e. consuming more than 30% of calories from fat).

Advocates of low carb, high fat diets ignore both this key genetic association and the fact that Americans on a "low fat" diet consume 33-35% of their calories from fats; while a true low fat diet consists of less than 10% of calories from fat. Given that nine in ten people present the *APOA5* high-risk variants, most of us must eat less than 30% of our daily calories from fat in order to promote weight loss or prevent weight gain.

How can you start eating your way to wellness? Programs work differently for every person, which is why I suggest personalized dietary plans based on your own genetic makeup and food sensitivity profile. Through programs like these I am able to help clients lower their cholesterol and blood pressure, lose weight, rejuvenate, and feel fabulous without taking prescription medications.

Even without being my client, you can start losing weight and improving your health today by following three simple rules. These rules are the foundation of the *W.O.W. Plan* that I teach my clients and will give you the results you want no matter what genes you were born with.

Water In

Water matters. Our bodies are 75% water. Water intake controls skin elasticity, digestion, toxin and fat elimination and pH maintenance.

Choosing water as a beverage and eating water–rich foods will increase your metabolism, accelerate your weight loss, and dramatically improve your health.

Oil Out

Why oil? Oil is the most caloric food available with 4,000 calories per pound and the most concentrated form of fat. Fat contributes to the genetic risk for obesity and damages the endothelial cells, which line the interior walls of blood vessels. They are also, for the most part, empty calories. You can cook without oils by using water, vegetable broth, tomato sauce or wine, without compromising flavor.

White Out

White foods such as sugar, salt, refined flours, and dairy, lower blood pH, raise blood sugar, make us hungry faster, increase cravings and can be high in saturated fat. Dairy products promote mucus in the body and exacerbate intolerances to lactose or casein. Giving preference to whole grains, eating whole fruits as snack or dessert, and using low-fat non-dairy milk substitutes will help eliminate "white" foods.

The *W.O.W. Plan* is designed to give you results independent of your genetic makeup. However, you can further empower yourself by both understanding your genotype and individual responses to food, and following a personalized dietary plan, which will guarantee that you maximize your health and weight loss results.

I believe you can be healthy, fit and vibrant no matter how old you are or what genes you were born with. Your genes are not your destiny. Your daily choices are. If you are ready to take control of your health and your destiny, I can show you how.

About Rosane

Dr. Rosane Oliveira helps clients lose weight and be healthy by eating according to their personal DNA. Her passion for food and nutrition ignited at an early age while learning to cook delicious dishes with her Portuguese grandparents. A breakthrough in her genetics research in 2008 sparked her to change her career to focus on lifestyle medicine.

She promotes the idea that food and lifestyle choices affect gene expression and are the catalysts that determine the onset of many of the common chronic diseases. Through harnessing the knowledge hidden in their genes, her clients learn to eat their way to wellness and get back into their skinny jeans in the process.

Dr. Oliveira is the owner-manager of *A Taste of Green* and the Director of Integrative Medicine at the University of California, Davis. She has over 18 years of experience as a molecular geneticist. Applying her background in genetics, she creates personalized nutrition plans for her clients so they can maximize the effectiveness of their diet based on their genetic profiles. Her expertise has helped clients lose stubborn body fat, attain better results from their workout, and lower their cholesterol without taking prescription medications.

Dr. Oliveira has earned a masters and a PhD in Preventive Medicine, Epidemiology, and Public Health from the State University of São Paulo, Brazil, and is also a Doctor of Veterinary Medicine. She conducted post-doctoral research at the University of Illinois at Urbana-Champaign, focusing on the onset and progression of cancer and how food, especially fat, affects gene expression that eventually leads to chronic diseases.

Dr. Oliveira is a national speaker and has shared the stage with the leading health and wellness experts in the world, such as Dr. Michael Roizen, Dr. Caldwell Esselstyn, Jr., Dr. T. Colin Campbell and many others. She is involved in the Quantified Self international collaboration and is conducting a groundbreaking study comparing her nutrition and lifestyle choices to those of her identical twin sister. Dr. Oliveira speaks five languages including English, Spanish, German, Italian and her native Portuguese.

You can connect with Dr. Oliveira at:
doctor@rosaneoliveira.com
www.rosaneoliveira.com
www.twitter.com/atasteofgreen
www.facebook.com/rosaneoliveirafan